The Rape of Lucrece, Titus Andronicus, Julius Caesar, Antony and Cleopatra, and *Coriolanus*

An Annotated Bibliography of Shakespeare Studies
1910–2000

PEGASUS SHAKESPEARE BIBLIOGRAPHIES
General Editor
RICHARD L. NOCHIMSON
Yeshiva University

The Rape of Lucrece, Titus Andronicus, Julius Caesar, Antony and Cleopatra, and *Coriolanus*

An Annotated Bibliography of Shakespeare Studies
1910–2000

Edited by
CLIFFORD CHALMERS HUFFMAN
and
JOHN W. VELZ

Pegasus Press
FAIRVIEW, NC
2002

© Copyright 2002

Pegasus Press

PO BOX 2265
FAIRVIEW, NORTH CAROLINA 28730

www.pegpress.org

Library of Congress Cataloguing-in-Publication Data

The rape of Lucrece, Titus Andronicus, Julius Caesar, Antony and Cleopatra, and Coriolanus : an annotated bibliography of Shakespeare studies / edited by Clifford Chalmers Huffman and John W. Velz.
    p. cm. — (Pegasus Shakespeare bibliographies)
  Includes index.
ISBN 1-889818-30-5
  1. Shakespeare, William, 1564-1616. Rape of Lucrece--Bibliography.
2. Shakespeare, William, 1564-1616. Titus Andronicus--Bibliography.
3. Shakespeare, William, 1564-1616. Julius Caesar--Bibliography.
4. Shakespeare, William, 1564-1616. Antony and Cleopatra--Bibliography.
I. Huffman, Clifford Chalmers, 1940- II. Velz, John W. III. Series.

Z8812.R37 R37 2002
[PR2846]
016.8223'3--dc21

2002013554
Rev.

Cover illustration & center-spread: From *Topographia Romae*, 1627. Used by permission of the Folger Shakespeare Library.

This book has been typeset in Garamond
at Pegasus Press and has been made to last.
It is printed on acid-free paper
to library specifications.

Printed in the United States of America.

CONTENTS

Preface	vii
List of Abbreviations	x
I. Editions of Shakespeare's Plays and Basic Reference Works	
A. Single-Volume Editions of Shakespeare's Plays	1
B. Multi-Volume Editions of Shakespeare's Plays	4
C. Basic Reference Works for Shakespeare Studies	8
II. *Romanitas*: General Works on the Roman Works of Shakespeare	17
III. *The Rape of Lucrece*	
A. Editions	28
B. Influences; Sources; Historical and Intellectual Backgrounds; Topicality	30
C. Language and Linguistics	34
D. Criticism	36
E. Bibliography	38
IV. *Titus Andronicus*	
A. Editions	39
B. Authorship, Dating, and Textual Studies	40
C. Influences; Sources; Historical and Intellectual Backgrounds; Topicality	41
D. Language and Linguistics	44
E. Criticism	45
F. Stage History and Performance Criticism; Film Version	52
G. Teaching and Collection of Essays	53
H. Bibliographies	53
V. *Julius Caesar*	
A. Editions	55
B. Authorship, Dating, and Textual Studies	56
C. Influences; Sources; Historical and Intellectual Backgrounds; Topicality	58

D. Language and Linguistics	64
E. Criticism	65
F. Stage History and Performance Criticism; Adaptations	73
G. Afterlife	77
H. Teaching and Collections of Essays	78
I. Bibliographies	80

VI. *Antony and Cleopatra*

A. Editions	82
B. Authorship, Dating, and Textual Studies	84
C. Influences; Sources; Historical and Intellectual Backgrounds; Topicality	85
D. Language and Linguistics	89
E. Criticism	90
F. Stage History and Performance Criticism; Adaptations	103
G. Teaching and Collections of Essays	106
H. Bibliographies	107

VII. *Coriolanus*

A. Editions	109
B. Authorship, Dating, and Textual Studies	111
C. Influences; Sources; Historical and Intellectual Backgrounds; Topicality	111
D. Language and Linguistics	115
E. Criticism	117
F. Stage History and Performance Criticism	125
G. Adaptations	127
H. Teaching and Collections of Essays	127
I. Bibliographies	129

Index I: Authors and Editors (Sections II–VII)	131
Index II: Subjects (Sections II–VII)	135

PREFACE

The twelve volumes of this series, of which this is the sixth, are designed to provide a guide to secondary materials on Shakespeare not only for scholars but also for graduate and undergraduate students and for college and high school teachers. In nine of the twelve volumes, entries will refer to materials that focus on individual works by Shakespeare; a total of twenty-five plays, plus *The Rape of Lucrece*, will be covered in these volumes. The remaining three volumes will present materials that treat Shakespeare in more general ways. These are highly selective bibliographies. While making every effort to represent a variety of approaches to the study of Shakespeare, the editors include only work that is either of high quality or of great influence.

In this volume, entries for the works included are numbered consecutively throughout the volume. Within each subsection, entries are organized alphabetically by author.

Each entry contains the basic factual information and a brief annotation. Though inclusion of a given entry implies a positive evaluation, in some cases, especially in some of the entries written by John W. Velz on *The Rape of Lucrece* and *Julius Caesar*, merits and faults of the work are pointed out at the end of the descriptive annotation.

The organization of this volume is as follows.

Section I, which will be essentially the same in all twelve volumes, contains those editions and general reference works that in the collective opinion of the editors are most basic to the study of Shakespeare. The annotations in this section have been written by the following series editors: Jean E. Howard, Clifford C. Huffman, John S. Mebane (who has undertaken the updating as well as the composing of the annotations in subsections A and B), Richard L. Nochimson, Hugh M. Richmond, Barbara H. Traister, and John W. Velz.

Section II results from the fact that the five works of Shakespeare treated in this volume all have a common setting, Ancient Rome. Books and articles that provide significant treatments of all or most of these five works are listed and annotated in this section. The second half of the 20th century has seen increasing scholarly recognition of the ways in which these five works form a group. (*Cymbeline* is a sixth work in which Roman characters and a Roman setting figure; but the major thrust of that play is in another direction, and it properly belongs in the volume that also treats *The Winter's Tale* and *The Tempest*.) The two compiling editors, Clifford C. Huffman and John W. Velz, divided the annotating of Section II equally between them. The common setting, of course, implies a common culture in the worlds of these art objects. In the annotations, the editors have devoted some attention to *Romanitas* (Roman values, lifestyle, and cultural assumptions); where it is discussed in these books and articles, it will be found mentioned in the corresponding entries.

Section III treats *Lucrece*, taking the poem before the other four works as its narrative mode makes it an art object of a different kind. Sections IV–VII take the four plays covered in this book chronologically, as most experts place them in the Shakespeare canon. Each of these five sections is divided into subsections, usually eight or nine subsections in a section (there is of course no "Stage History" subsection for *Lucrece*, and no "Adaptations" subsection for that work—though some entries in *Lucrece* subsections trace the influence of the Lucretia legend in the centuries after Shakespeare's version). The table of contents describes the kinds of works to be found in the various subsections of each of these five sections.

Clifford C. Huffman is responsible for the sections on *Titus Andronicus, Antony and Cleopatra*, and *Coriolanus*; as mentioned above, John W. Velz is responsible for the sections on *The Rape of Lucrece* and *Julius Caesar*. Within each section, the editor has placed items of relevance to two or more subsections in the most appropriate subsection and then cross-referenced them at the end of one or more other subsections. So A. S. Weber's article on *Antony and Cleopatra* appears under "Criticism" and is cross-referenced at the end of the section on "Influences; Sources; Historical and Intellectual Backgrounds; Topicality." To see the full range of material relevant to a particular area or topic, readers should consult the occasional references to additional works appearing at the end of an annotation (see, e.g., no. 74), the cross-references after various subsections, and the subject index. Since all of the items in this bibliography could be considered forms of "criticism," only in special cases are cross-references listed after the Criticism subsections.

The subsections headed "Teaching and Collections of Essays" in several sections (see table of contents) include collections of both previously published and original materials. Selected materials in most of these collections are annotated elsewhere in the volume; in such cases, individual entries include a cross-reference to the pertinent collection. Works (plays, films, and in one case a poem) that diverge enough from a recognizably Shakespearean text that the work may be considered an independent artifact appear, for *Julius Caesar* and *Antony and Cleopatra*, in subsection F, which includes "Adaptations," and, for *Coriolanus*, separately in subsection G, "Adaptations." Additionally, *Julius Caesar* has a subsection which, because of the special nature of its two entries, is labeled "Afterlife." *The Rape of Lucrece* and *Titus Andronicus* lack such subsections altogether.

Within the entries, numbers prefaced by "no." indicate cross-references; numbers in parentheses indicate either the page numbers in the book or article where a specific topic is discussed or quoted, or the act, scene, and line numbers of the passage discussed, divided by periods (e.g., 2.3.1–5). Unless specified otherwise, the act, scene, and line designations are taken from *The Riverside Shakespeare* (no. 2).

Abbreviations used are listed on the next page.

The editors wish to thank their families as well as all those colleagues and friends who helped with the compiling of this bibliography.

Clifford C. Huffman
State University of New York, Stony Brook

John W. Velz
University of Texas

Richard L. Nochimson
Yeshiva University

March 2000

Abbreviations

Ant.	*Antony and Cleopatra*
app.	appendix
BCE	Before Common Era (= BC)
c.	about
CE	Common Era (= AD)
cf.	compare
chap., chaps.	chapter(s)
Cor.	*Coriolanus*
ed., eds.	edited by/editor(s)
e.g.	for example
esp.	especially
et al.	and others
etc.	and so forth
F1	first folio
ff.	and following
f.n.	footnote
ibid.	the same
i.e.	that is
JC	*Julius Caesar*
Luc.	*The Rape of Lucrece*
ms.	manuscript
no., nos.	number(s)
n.p.	no place
n.s.	new series
p., pp.	page(s)
pub.	published
Q	quarto
repr.	reprint/reprinted
rev.	revised
SQ	*Shakespeare Quarterly*
Tit.	*Titus Andronicus*
trans.	translated by
Univ.	University
vol., vols.	volume(s)
vs.	versus

*The Rape of Lucrece, Titus Andronicus,
Julius Caesar, Antony and Cleopatra,*
and *Coriolanus*

An Annotated Bibliography of Shakespeare Studies
1910–2000

I. EDITIONS AND REFERENCE WORKS

A. Single-Volume Editions.

1. Bevington, David, ed. *The Complete Works of Shakespeare.* Updated 4th edition. New York: Addison Wesley Longman, 1997.

Bevington's *Complete Works* includes 38 plays and the nondramatic poems. Introductions, aimed at a broad audience, focus upon questions of interpretation. The general introduction discusses social, intellectual, and theatrical history; Shakespeare's biography and his career as a dramatist; his language and versification; editions and editors of Shakespeare; and the history of Shakespearean criticism. Appendices include discussions of canon, dates, and early texts; brief summaries of sources; and performance history. There are genealogical charts, maps, and a selected bibliography. Emendations of the copy text are recorded only in an appendix; they are not bracketed in the texts of the plays. Spelling is modernized unless an exception is necessary for scansion, to indicate a pun, or for other reasons discussed in the preface. Notes appear at the bottom of the column. Speech prefixes are expanded. Illustrations include photographs from recent performances. Features ranging from the clarity and high quality of the introductions to the readability of the typeface combine to make the texts in this edition admirably accessible to students and general readers. Available with this edition are the BBC's CD-ROM programs on *Macbeth* and *A Midsummer Night's Dream.* These multimedia resources provide the full text and complete audio recordings; footnotes; word and image searches; sources; comments and audio-visual aids on plot, themes, language, performance history, historical background, and characterization; print capability; and clips from film and video performances. A *Teacher's Guide* to the CD provides suggestions for assignments and classroom use.

2. Evans, G. Blakemore, et al., eds. *The Riverside Shakespeare.* 2nd edition. Boston: Houghton Mifflin, 1997.

This edition includes 39 plays, the nondramatic poems, and segments of *Sir Thomas More.* Introductions by Herschel Baker (histories), Frank Kermode (tragedies), Hallett Smith (romances and nondramatic poems), Anne Barton (comedies), and J. J. M. Tobin ("A Funeral Elegy" by W. S.

and *Edward III*) discuss dates, sources, and major interpretive issues. Harry Levin's general introduction discusses Shakespeare's biography, artistic development, and reputation; intellectual backgrounds; Renaissance playhouses and theatrical conventions; Elizabethan English; and stylistic techniques. Heather Dubrow provides an analytical survey of twentieth-century Shakespeare criticism. Evans provides an introduction to textual criticism. Appendices include a history of Shakespearean performance by Charles H. Shattuck and William T. Liston; substantial excerpts from historical documents related to Shakespeare's life and works, including some early responses to the plays; "Annals, 1552–1616," a listing in four parallel columns of events in political history, Shakespeare's biography, theater history, and nondramatic literature; a selected bibliography; indexes; and a glossary. Emendations of the copy text are enclosed in square brackets, and each play is followed by a summary discussion of editorial problems and by textual notes listing the sources of all emendations. Spelling is modernized except for "a selection of Elizabethan spelling forms that reflect ... contemporary pronunciation" (67). Notes appear at the bottom of the column. The volume includes numerous illustrations, including color plates. While the *Riverside* has many features aimed at general readers, the impressive textual apparatus, Evans's fine discussion of textual criticism, and the collection of documents make this edition of special interest to advanced graduate students and to scholars.

3. Greenblatt, Stephen, Walter Cohen, Jean E. Howard, and Katharine Eisaman Maus, eds. *The Norton Shakespeare, Based on the Oxford Edition.* New York: Norton, 1997.

This edition includes 38 plays (including quarto, folio, and conflated texts of *King Lear*) and the nondramatic poems, including works of uncertain authorship not included in other single-volume editions. The texts (except for "A Funeral Elegy," ed. Donald Foster) are updated versions of those in the modern-spelling, single-volume *Oxford Shakespeare* (1988) produced by general editors Stanley Wells and Gary Taylor with John Jowett and William Montgomery. The *Oxford* edition is based on revisionary editorial principles, including the belief that some texts previously regarded as having limited authority are in reality records (at times highly imperfect) of early authorial versions later revised in the theater. The revised versions are usually chosen as control texts. In the *Oxford*, passages from earlier versions are often reprinted in appendices; the *Norton* prints these passages from earlier versions, indented, within the texts. *The Norton Shakespeare* provides marginal glosses and numerous explanatory notes; the latter are numbered in the text and appear at the bottom of each page. Textual variants are listed after each work. Stage directions added after the 1623 Folio appear in brackets. Greenblatt's general introduction discusses Renaissance economic, social, religious, and political life; Shakespeare's biography; textual criticism; and aspects of Shakespeare's art, including "The Paradoxes of Identity" in characterization and analysis of the "overpowering exuberance and generosity" (63) of Shakespeare's language. Introductions to individual works discuss a range of historical and aesthetic issues. Appendices include Andrew Gurr's "The Shakespearean Stage"; a collection of documents; a chronicle of events in political and literary history; a bibliography; and a glossary. This edition combines traditional scholarship with a focus on such recent concerns as the status of women and "The English and Otherness." Also available is *The Norton Shakespeare Workshop*, ed. Mark Rose, a set of interactive multimedia programs on CD-ROM that can be purchased either separately or in a package with *The Norton Shakespeare*. The *Workshop* provides searchable texts of *A Midsummer Night's Dream*; *The Merchant of Venice*; *Henry IV, Part Two*; *Othello*; *Hamlet*; *The Tempest*; and Sonnets 55 and 138. Students can find analyses of selected passages, sources, essays that illustrate the play's critical and performance history, clips from classic and from specially commissioned performances, selections of music inspired by the plays, and tools for developing paper topics.

4. Hinman, Charlton, ed. *The Norton Facsimile: The First Folio of Shakespeare*. 2nd edition. Introduction by Peter Blayney. New York: W. W. Norton, 1996.

The First Folio of 1623 is a collection of 36 plays made by Shakespeare's fellow actors, Heminge and Condell. *Pericles, The Two Noble Kinsmen*, and the nondramatic poems are not included. Heminge and Condell claim to have provided "perfect" texts, distinguishing them from what they describe as "stolne, and surreptitious copies, maimed, and deformed by the frauds and stealthes of injurious impostors" (A3). While some of the previously published quartos are regarded today as superior versions, the First Folio indeed provides the most authoritative texts for the majority of Shakespeare's plays. It also includes commendatory poems by four authors, including Ben Jonson, and the Droeshout portrait of Shakespeare. During the two years that the 1623 edition was in press, corrections were made continually, and the uncorrected pages became mingled with corrected ones. In addition, imperfections of various sorts render portions of numerous pages difficult or impossible to read. Hinman has examined the 80 copies of the First Folio in the Folger Shakespeare Library and selected the clearest versions of what appear to be the finally corrected pages. In the left and right margins, he provides for reference his system of "through line numbering," by which he numbers each typographical line throughout the text of a play (the verse and prose of the play as well as all other material such as scene headings and stage directions). In a page from *King John*, for example, which includes what might otherwise be referred to as 3.1.324 through 3.3.74 (this form of reference appears in the bottom margin), the through line numbers run from 1257 to 1380. Appendix A presents some variant states of the Folio text, and Appendix B lists the Folger copies used in compiling this edition. Hinman's introduction discusses the nature and authority of the Folio, the printing and proofreading process, and the procedures followed in editing the facsimile, explaining, among other points, the advantages of through line numbering. Blayney's introduction updates Hinman's discussions of such matters as the status of quarto texts, the types of play-manuscripts available to printers, and the printing and proofreading processes. Blayney also discusses the theory that, since different versions of a given play may represent authorial or collaborative revisions, in such cases there is no "ideal text." No interpretive introductions or glosses are provided. While some valuable facsimiles of quarto versions are available, the Hinman First Folio is clearly an excellent place to begin one's encounter with early printed texts that are not mediated by centuries of editorial tradition.

B. Multi–Volume Editions.

5. Barnet, Sylvan, general ed. *The Signet Classic Shakespeare*. New York: Penguin.

   Originally edited in the 1960s, the Signet series was updated in the 1980s; newly revised volumes began to appear in 1998. The 35-volume series includes 38 plays and the nondramatic poems. Collections entitled *Four Great Comedies, Four Great Tragedies*, and *The Sonnets and Nondramatic Poems* are available. Each volume in the newly revised series includes a general introduction with discussions of Shakespeare's biography, including the "anti-Stratfordian" authorship phenomenon; Shakespeare's English; Elizabethan theaters; "Shakespeare's Dramatic Language: Costumes, Gestures and Silences; Prose and Poetry"; editorial principles; and the staging of Shakespeare's plays, including consideration of the concept of the play as a collaboration among the playwright, theatrical ensemble, and audience. Spelling is generally modernized, and speech prefixes are expanded. Explanatory notes appear at the bottom of each page. Appendices contain textual notes, discussion of (and often excerpts from) sources, several critical essays, a survey of each play's performance history, and a bibliography. Although introductions in this series are written for beginning students, the substantial selection of distinguished critical essays is useful for more advanced students, as well.

6. **Bevington, David,** ed. David Scott Kastan, James Hammersmith, and Robert Kean Turner, associate eds. *The Bantam Shakespeare.* New York: Bantam, 1988.

In 1988, 37 plays and the nondramatic poems were published in the 29 volumes of *The Bantam Shakespeare.* Collections entitled *Four Comedies* and *Four Tragedies* are available. Texts, explanatory notes (at the bottom of each page), and interpretive introductions are similar to those of Bevington's *Complete Works of Shakespeare* (see no. 1). Included in the Bantam series are brief performance histories of individual plays and Joseph Papp's forewords on Shakespeare's enduring appeal. Each volume includes a one-page biography of Shakespeare and an introduction to Elizabethan playhouses. Appendices include concise discussions of dates and early texts, textual notes, substantial excerpts from sources, and a brief annotated bibliography. While this series necessarily excludes some of the historical information found in the *Complete Works*, the forewords by an eminent producer/director and the well-written performance histories are engaging features, especially appropriate for students and general readers.

7. **Brockbank, Philip,** founding general ed. Brian Gibbons, general ed. A. R. Braunmuller and R. C. Hood, associate general eds. *The New Cambridge Shakespeare.* Cambridge: Cambridge Univ. Press, 1982—.

The New Cambridge series will eventually include 40 plays definitely or possibly by Shakespeare (including *The Reign of Edward III*), Shakespeare's nondramatic poems, and the anonymous play *The Taming of a Shrew*. So far, 38 volumes have appeared; among these are two separate editions (one based on an early quarto) of *King Lear*, of *Hamlet*, and of *Richard III*. Introductions discuss date, sources, critical history and interpretive issues, staging, and performance history (with numerous illustrations). Discussion of the text precedes each play, and more detailed textual analysis sometimes appears in an appendix. All volumes include a selected bibliography. Spelling is generally modernized; speech prefixes are expanded. Textual notes signaling departures from the copy text and extensive explanatory notes appear at the bottom of each page. Designed for students and scholars, *The New Cambridge Shakespeare* provides more detailed attention to stagecraft and performance history than most other editions. This series succeeds *The New Shakespeare*, edited by Arthur Quiller-Couch and John Dover Wilson.

8. Knowles, Richard, and Paul Werstine, general eds. Robert K. Turner, senior consulting editor. *A New Variorum Edition of Shakespeare.* New York: Modern Language Association.

From 1871 to 1928 H. H. Furness, Sr., and H. H. Furness, Jr., published 19 works of the Variorum Shakespeare. Since 1933, nine new editions have appeared in the MLA series. The completed 40-volume variorum will contain 38 plays and the nondramatic poems. Each volume provides an old-spelling text and a collation of significant emendations from previous editions. Explanatory notes (printed below the textual notes at the bottom of each page) try to record all important previous annotation. Appendices include discussions of a play's text and date. Recent volumes survey the history of criticism and performance and refer to a substantial bibliography; early volumes include excerpts from previous criticism. Sources and analogues are discussed and reprinted. As compilations of scholarship, criticism, and textual analysis, these volumes represent a significant resource for scholars and teachers.

9. Mowat, Barbara A., and Paul Werstine, eds. *The New Folger Library Shakespeare.* New York: Pocket Books, Washington Square Press, 1992—.

Twenty-four volumes of the New Folger series, which replaces *The Folger Library General Reader's Shakespeare*, appeared between 1992 and 1999. Several new titles will come out each year until the series of 38 plays and the nondramatic poems is complete. Each volume provides a brief initial comment on the play followed by basic introductions to Shakespeare's language and style, his biography, Elizabethan theaters, early editions, and the editorial principles of the series. Half brackets enclose emendations of the copy text; in some volumes square or pointed brackets indicate the sources of passages that appear (for example) only in the folio or an earlier quarto. Explanatory notes appear on pages facing the text, textual notes in an appendix. Spelling is selectively modernized, and speech prefixes are expanded. For each play a different critic offers the "Modern Perspective" that follows the text. A brief annotated bibliography focuses mostly on recent approaches to the play; standard works on language, biography, theatrical setting, and early texts also appear. While this series aims at the broadest possible audience, the clarity and helpfulness of its introductions and explanatory notes make it especially well suited for beginning students.

10. Proudfoot, Richard, Ann Thompson, and David Scott Kastan, general eds. *The Arden Shakespeare.* Walton-on-Thames, Surrey: Nelson House.

The 40-volume *Arden Shakespeare* includes 38 plays and 2 volumes of the nondramatic poems. The edition is continually updated; although some current volumes are from the 1950s, thirteen plays and the Sonnets have appeared in revised third editions in recent years. Introductions provide extensive discussion of dates, texts, editorial principles, sources, and a wide range of interpretive issues. Extensive textual and explanatory notes appear at the bottom of each page. Appendices typically include additional textual analysis, excerpts from sources, and (sometimes) settings for songs. The Arden series often includes scholarship and criticism that are essential for advanced students and scholars. The complete second edition of the Arden series is available on CD-ROM from Primary Source Media. The CD-ROMs enable one to view the edited texts simultaneously with materials from the following: early quarto and folio editions; Bullough's *Narrative and Dramatic Sources* (no. 15); Abbott's *Shakespearian Grammar*; Onions's *Shakespeare Glossary* (no. 22); Partridge's *Shakespeare's Bawdy*; and a 4,600-item bibliography. The complete Arden set is also available on-line, with additional materials for those works that have appeared in the third edition.

11. Spencer, T. J. B., general ed. Stanley Wells, associate ed. *The New Penguin Shakespeare*. London: Penguin Books.

The 39-volume New Penguin series now includes 36 plays and the nondramatic poems; *Titus Andronicus* and *Cymbeline* are planned. Dates range from the 1960s through the 1980s. Introductions discuss a range of interpretive issues and are followed by brief bibliographical essays. Explanatory notes follow the text, succeeded by textual analysis, selective textual notes, and (as appropriate) settings for songs. Spelling is modernized, and speech prefixes are expanded. Emendations of the copy text are not bracketed. The New Penguin will appeal especially to those who wish the pages of the text to be free of annotation.

12. Wells, Stanley, general ed. Advisory eds. S. Schoenbaum, G. R. Proudfoot, and F. W. Sternfeld. *The Oxford Shakespeare*. Oxford: Oxford Univ. Press.

Between 1982 and 1999, 25 plays (plus collections entitled *Comedies, Histories,* and *Tragedies*) were published in the multi-volume *Oxford Shakespeare*. The completed series will include 38 plays and the nondramatic poems. Introductions provide detailed discussion of dates, sources, textual criticism, questions of interpretation, and performance history. Textual notes and extensive commentary appear at the bottom of each page. The commentary and introduction are indexed. Spelling is modernized, and speech prefixes are expanded. The Oxford series is based on revisionary editorial principles, including the belief that some texts previously regarded as of little value are in reality records (at times highly imperfect) of early authorial versions later revised in the theater. The revised versions are usually chosen as copy texts, and appendices sometimes include passages from earlier printed versions. Some appendices include musical settings for songs. Partly because of its editorial principles, this series is of special interest to scholars and advanced students.

C. Basic Reference Works for Shakespeare Studies.

13. Beckerman, Bernard. *Shakespeare at the Globe: 1599-1609.* New York: Macmillan, 1962.

This study of the 29 extant plays (including 15 by Shakespeare) produced at the Globe in its first decade yields information about the playhouse and how Shakespeare's company performed in it. The first chapter, on the repertory system, is based on analysis of Henslowe's diary. Subsequent chapters about the stage itself, acting styles, the dramatic form of plays and of scenes within plays, and the staging derive from study of the Globe repertory. Detailed appendices provide statistics on which Beckerman's analysis partly depends. Beckerman concludes that the style in which these plays were presented was neither symbolic nor what modern audiences would call realistic. Rather, he suggests, passion by the actors was presented within a framework of staging and scenic conventions in various styles according to the needs of particular plays.

14. Bentley, G. E. *The Jacobean and Caroline Stage.* 7 vols. Oxford: Clarendon Press, 1941-68.

Bentley designed his survey of British drama to carry on that of Chambers (see no. 16) and cover the years 1616-42. The 11 chapters in vol. 1 provide detailed information about 11 adult and children's acting companies (1-342); vol. 2 surveys information about actors, listed alphabetically (343-629), with relevant documents reprinted and annotated (630-96), with an index (697-748). Vols. 3, 4, 5 are an alphabetical list, by author, with bibliographical material and commentary, of "all plays, masques, shows, and dramatic entertainments which were written or first performed in England between 1616 ... and ... 1642" (3.v), from "M.A." to Richard Zouche, with a final section (5. 1281-1456) on anonymous and untitled plays. Vol. 6 considers theater buildings (private, 3-117; public, 121-252; court, 255-88; and two that were only projected, 291-309). Vol. 7 gathers together, as appendices to vol. 6, "scattered material concerning Lenten performances and Sunday performances" and arranges chronologically "a large number of dramatic and semi-dramatic events" of interest to

EDITIONS AND REFERENCE WORKS   9

students of dramatic literature and theater history (6.v); it includes a
general index for vols. 1-7 (129-390) which has numerous references
(344-45) to Shakespeare and his plays.

15. Bullough, Geoffrey. *Narrative and Dramatic Sources of Shakespeare.*
8 vols. London and New York: Routledge & Kegan Paul and Columbia
Univ. Press, 1957-75.

This work is a comprehensive compendium of the texts of Shakespeare's sources for 37 plays and several poems. Bullough includes analogues as well as sources and "possible sources" as well as "probable sources." All texts are in English, old-spelling Elizabethan when extant, and in some other cases in the compiler's translation. Bullough includes a separate introduction for each play. In the early volumes, interpretation is largely left to the reader; introductions in the later volumes include more interpretation and tend to be longer. There have been complaints of occasional errors in transcription. The major caveat, however, about using this learned, thorough, and imaginative work concerns what Bullough could not conceivably print: the passages in his sources that Shakespeare presumably read but either chose to omit or neglected to include.

16. Chambers, E. K. *The Elizabethan Stage.* 4 vols. Oxford: Clarendon
Press, 1923. Revised 1945; with corrections 1967.

In vol. 1, Chambers provides detailed information about the court (1-234): the monarchs, their households, the Revels Office, pageantry, the mask, and the court play. In the section entitled "The Control of the Stage" (236-388), he covers the struggles between the city of London and the court and between Humanism and Puritanism, and treats the status of actors and the socio-economic realities of actors' lives. In vol. 2, Chambers focuses on the history of 38 different acting companies (children, adult, and foreign) (1-294), gives details, such as are known, about an alphabetical list of actors (295-350), and treats the playhouses (16 public and 2 private theaters), including discussion of their structure and management (351-557). In vol. 3, Chambers surveys the conditions of staging in the court and theaters (1-154), the printing of plays (157-200), and then offers a bibliographical survey, including brief biographies, of playwrights alphabetically arranged, from William Alabaster through Christopher Yelverton (201-518). In vol. 4, Chambers concludes that bibliography with anonymous work (1-74) and presents 13 appendices that reprint or summarize relevant historical documents. Chambers concludes this work with four indices (to plays, persons, places, and subjects) to the four volumes (409-67). In these four volumes, Chambers presents an encyclopedia of all aspects of English drama during the reigns of Elizabeth I and

James I up to the date of Shakespeare's death in 1616. A subsequent and detailed index to this entire work was compiled by Beatrice White, *An Index to "The Elizabethan Stage" and "William Shakespeare" by Sir Edmund Chambers*. Oxford: Oxford Univ. Press, 1934.

17. **Chambers, E. K.** *William Shakespeare: A Study of Facts and Problems.* 2 vols. Oxford: Clarendon Press, 1930. Repr., 1931.

This work is an encyclopedia of information relating to Shakespeare. The principal topics of the first volume are the dramatist's family origins, his relations to the theater and its professionals, the nature of the texts of his plays—including their preparation for performance and publication, and also questions of authenticity and chronology (relevant tables about the quartos and metrics are in the second volume). The data available (and plausible conjectures) concerning all texts attributed to Shakespeare, including poems and uncertain attributions, are then laid out title by title. The second volume cites the significant Shakespeare records then available, including contemporary allusions, performance data, legends, and even forgeries (the last two items are more fully covered in Schoenbaum's *Shakespeare's Lives*). There are comprehensive indices and a substantial bibliography. While it is sometimes necessary to update this book by correlation with Schoenbaum's *Documentary Life* (see no. 24) and other, more recent, texts, Chambers's scholarship has been supplemented rather than invalidated by more recent research, and his work remains a convenient starting point for pursuit of background data on Shakespeare's life and works.

18. **Doran, Madeleine.** *Endeavors of Art: A Study of Form in Elizabethan Drama.* Madison: Univ. of Wisconsin Press, 1954.

Doran reconstructs the Elizabethan assumptions about many aspects of dramatic form, defined broadly enough to include genre, eloquence and copiousness, character, and "moral aim." A detailed exploration of classical, medieval, and Renaissance backgrounds makes this a study in historical criticism; however, the cultural context laid out is aesthetic, not ideational. Doran examines the problems of form faced by Shakespeare and his contemporaries—problems of genre, of character, of plot construction—in an attempt to explain the success (or, sometimes, lack of success) of the major dramatists in "achieving form adequate to meaning" (23). Doran's unpretentious, readable study is justly famous as the first book on the aesthetics of Renaissance drama to understand the entire context, to perceive the Renaissance assumptions about dramatic art as a fusion of classical and medieval influences.

19. **Gurr, Andrew.** *Playgoing in Shakespeare's London.* 2nd edition. Cambridge: Cambridge Univ. Press, 1996.

Gurr focuses on the identity, class, and changing tastes of London playgoers from the opening of the Red Lion in 1567 to the closing of the theaters in 1642. He examines the locations, physical features, price scales, and repertories of the various playhouses, distinguishing particularly between "halls" and "amphitheatres" and rejecting the more common labels "private" and "public." Turning from the theaters, Gurr examines the playgoers, asking such questions as whether they ventured to the playhouses primarily to "hear" a text or to "see" a spectacle. In a final chapter, entitled "The evolution of tastes," he discusses assorted playgoing fashions: from the craze for Tarlton's clowning to the taste for pastoral and romance in the last years of Charles I. Two appendices list identifiable playgoers and references to playgoing during the time period.

20. **Gurr, Andrew.** *The Shakespearean Stage 1574–1642.* 3rd edition. Cambridge: Cambridge Univ. Press, 1992.

Gurr summarizes a vast amount of scholarship concerning the material conditions of Elizabethan, Jacobean, and Caroline theatrical production. Each of his six chapters provides a wealth of detailed information on theatrical life. The first gives an overview of the place of the theater in urban London from the 1570s until 1642, including an examination of the social status of playwrights, the differences and similarities between the repertories at the open-air amphitheaters (public) and at the indoor playhouses (private), and the changing role of court patronage of theater. Chapter two describes the typical composition of London theater companies and their regulation by the Crown. It also gives an historical account of the theatrical companies that at various times dominated the London theatrical scene. In his third chapter, Gurr looks at actors, discussing the famous clowns of the Elizabethan era, prominent tragic actors such as Burbage and Alleyn, and the repertory system within which they worked. The fourth chapter summarizes what is known about the playhouses, including information gleaned from the recent excavation of the remains of the Rose Theater, as well as accounts of the Globe Theater, The Fortune, the hall playhouses, and the Banqueting Hall. Chapter five discusses staging conventions and the differences between public and private theaters, and among the various particular theaters, in their use of song, music, clowning, and jigging. Also examined are stage properties and costumes. The final chapter analyzes information about audiences: who went to which kinds of playhouse and how they behaved. Gurr argues that women and all social classes were represented in theatrical audiences, with an increasing tendency in the seventeenth century for the private theaters to cater to a wealthier clientele who demanded a more sophisticated repertory with more new plays. This valuable book concludes with an appendix indicating at which playhouses and by which companies various plays were staged.

21. Kastan, David Scott, ed. *A Companion to Shakespeare*. Oxford: Blackwell Publishers, 1999.

This collection of 28 essays, most with notes and references for further reading, aims to locate Shakespeare in relation to the historical matrix in which he wrote his plays and poems. Following the editor's introduction, the volume is framed by two essays dealing with Shakespeare the man. The first, by David Bevington, deals with what is known, factually, about his life; the last, by Michael Bristol, deals with various myths surrounding the figure of Shakespeare. In between, the book is divided into five sections. The first contains six essays, mainly by historians, dealing with Shakespeare's England, the city of London, religious identities of the period, the family and household structures, Shakespeare and political thought, and the political culture of the Tudor-Stuart period. The second section contains five essays, mostly by literary critics, and discusses readers and reading practices in the early modern period. It includes a general essay on literacy, illiteracy, and reading practices, and four essays focusing on reading, respectively, the Bible, the classics, historical writings, and vernacular literature. The third part of the book deals with writing and writing practices and contains five essays by literary scholars on writing plays, on the state of the English language in Shakespeare's day, on technical aspects of Shakespeare's dramatic verse, on the rhetorical culture of the times, and on genre. These essays are followed by a section on playing and performance. It contains five essays, mostly by theater historians, on the economics of playing, on The Chamberlain's-King's Men, on Shakespeare's repertory, on playhouses of the day, and on licensing and censorship. The final section, consisting of five essays by literary critics, deals with aspects of printing and print culture, including Shakespeare's works in print between 1593 and 1640, manuscript playbooks, the craft of printing, the London book trade, and press censorship. Mixing traditional and newer topics and concerns, *A Companion to Shakespeare* is an up-to-date guide to the historical conditions and the literary and theatrical resources enabling Shakespeare's art.

22. Onions, C. T. *A Shakespeare Glossary*. Oxford: Clarendon Press, 1911. 2nd edition revised, 1919. Repr., with corrections, 1946; with enlarged Addenda, 1958. Enlarged and revised by Robert D. Eagleson, 1986; corrected, 1988.

EDITIONS AND REFERENCE WORKS   13

Onions's dictionary of Elizabethan vocabulary as it applies to Shakespeare was an offshoot of his work on the *Oxford English Dictionary*. Eagleson updates the third edition with new entries, using modern research (now aided by citations from the Riverside edition [see no. 2], keyed by the Spevack *Concordance* [see no. 25]), while conserving much from Onions's adaptation of *OED* entries to distinguish Shakespearean uses from those of his contemporaries and from modern standard meanings. The glossary covers only expressions that differ from modern usage, as with "cousin" or "noise." It includes some proper names with distinctive associations, such as "Machiavel," and explains unfamiliar stage directions: "sennet" (a trumpet signal). Many allusions are more fully elucidated, as with the origin of "hobby-horse" in morris dances, or the bearing of "wayward" on *Macbeth*'s "weird sisters." This text, which demonstrates the importance of historical awareness of language for accuracy in the close reading of Shakespeare, now has a brief bibliography of relevant texts. It still needs to be supplemented in two areas: information about definite and possible sexual significance of many common and obscure words appears in Gordon Williams's 3-volume *A Dictionary of Sexual Language and Imagery in Shakespearean and Stuart Literature* (1994); often contradictory guidance about the likely pronunciation of Shakespeare's language is provided by Helge Kökeritz's *Shakespeare's Pronunciation* (1953) and by Fausto Cercignani's *Shakespeare's Works and Elizabethan Pronunciation* (1981).

23. Rothwell, Kenneth S., and Annabelle Henkin Melzer. *Shakespeare on Screen: An International Filmography and Videography.* New York: Neal-Schuman, 1990.

This list of film and video versions of Shakespeare seeks to be comprehensive, covering the years 1899–1989, except that it excludes most silent films, referring the reader to Robert Hamilton Ball's *Shakespeare on Silent Film* (1968). It does include "modernizations, spinoffs, musical and dance versions, abridgements, travesties and excerpts" (x). The introduction, by Rothwell, offers an overview of screen versions of Shakespeare (1–17). The body of the work, with over 675 entries (21–316), is organized by play, listed alphabetically, and within each play chronologically. Represented are 37 plays and the *Sonnets*. *Pericles* and *Timon of Athens* appear only in the BBC versions in "The Shakespeare Plays" series. For *Hamlet* we have 87 entries. Included also are another 74 entries (317–35) for documentaries and other "unclassifiable" films and videos that present Shakespeare in some form, such as John Barton's "Playing Shakespeare" series and James Ivory's film, "Shakespeare Wallah." The sometimes quite extensive entries include information about and evaluation of the production, and an attempt to provide information about distribution and availability. The work concludes with a useful selected bibliography with brief annotations (337–45), a series of helpful indices (349–98), and a list of the names and addresses of distributors, dealers, and archives (399–404).

24. Schoenbaum, S. *William Shakespeare: A Compact Documentary Life.* Oxford: Oxford Univ. Press, 1977. Repr., with corrections, 1978.

An abridged version of Schoenbaum's massive documentary study of Shakespeare published by Oxford in 1975, the *Compact Documentary Life* traces all textual evidence about Shakespeare chronologically from his grandfather's generation up to the deaths of Shakespeare's surviving family members. Legends for which there is no specific documentation—such as the deer-poaching incident—are examined for probability on the basis of surviving materials. Where appropriate, Schoenbaum juxtaposes biographical details with specific passages in Shakespeare's works. Amply illustrated and annotated, this work, unlike Schoenbaum's earlier, larger version and his later (1981) *William Shakespeare: Records and Images*, refers to documents but generally does not reprint them.

25. Spevack, Marvin. *The Harvard Concordance to Shakespeare.* Cambridge: Belknap Press of Harvard Univ. Press, 1973.

This text covers the total of 29,066 words (including proper names) used by Shakespeare in his plays and poems, in the modern-spelling text of *The Riverside Shakespeare* (see no. 2). Stage directions appear in another volume. Contexts are omitted for the first 43 words in order of frequency, mostly pronouns, prepositions, conjunctions, auxiliary verbs, and articles. Individual entries distinguish between prose and verse, and between total and relative frequencies. The modern spelling is not enforced with proper names or significant Elizabethan divergencies: "embassador-ambassador." While the cited context of each use is normally the line of text in which it appears, other limits occur when the sense requires further wording. This concordance helps to locate specific passages and also invites subtler research uses, such as study of the recurrence of words in each play: thus the continuity of *Henry VIII* from *Richard III* appears in their shared distinctive use of certain religious terms. Similarly, accumulated references show the divergence or consistency of meaning or associations for particular terms (Shakespeare's references to dogs are unfavorable). In using this text, one must remember that variant spellings or forms of speech may conceal recurrences of words with the same root or meaning (guilt, gilt, guilts, guilty, guiltily, guiltless), while similar spellings of the same word may have contrasting senses (your grace [the Duke] of York, the grace of God, external grace). The provided contexts reveal the complications, but often are too brief to ensure exact interpretation of a word. The magnitude of the effort involved in this concordance indicates the research gain from electronic procedures, which also permit many permutations of its data, as seen in the nine volumes of Spevack's *A Complete and Systematic Concordance to the Works of Shakespeare* (1968–80).

26. **Styan, J. L.** *Shakespeare's Stagecraft.* Cambridge: Cambridge Univ. Press, 1967. Repr., with corrections, 1971.

Styan's book explores how Shakespeare's plays would have worked, theatrically, on the Elizabethan stage. Beginning with a discussion of the kind of stage for which Shakespeare wrote and of the conventions of performance that obtained on that stage, Styan then devotes the bulk of his attention to Shakespeare's handling of the visual and aural dimensions of performance. He argues that the scripts guide actors in communicating aurally, visually, and kinetically with an audience. Topics considered include gesture, entrances and exits, the use of downstage and upstage playing areas, eavesdropping encounters, the visual orchestration of scenes involving one or several or many characters, the manipulation of rhythm and tempo, and variations among stage voices. The final chapter, "Total Theater," discusses the inseparability of all the elements of Shakespeare's stagecraft in the shaping of a theatrical event aimed at provoking and engaging the audience's fullest response. The book makes a strong case for studying Shakespeare's plays as flexible blueprints for performance that skillfully utilize and transform the stagecraft conventions of the Elizabethan theater.

27. **Wells, Stanley,** ed. *The Cambridge Companion to Shakespeare Studies.* Cambridge: Cambridge Univ. Press, 1986. Repr., 1991.

Wells has assembled 19 other scholars to write on different aspects of Shakespeare studies; most of the essays include endnotes and a reading list. S. Schoenbaum writes about Shakespeare's life (chap. 1), W. R. Elton places him in the context of the thought of his age (chap. 2), Peter Thomson discusses contemporaneous playhouses and actors (chap. 5), and Alan C. Dessen places Shakespeare in the context of his age's theater conventions (chap. 6). Essays more on Shakespeare's writing are Robert Ellrodt's on the nondramatic poetry (chap. 3), Inga-Stina Ewbank's on his use of the arts of language (chap. 4), and the pairing of David Daniell's on the traditions of comedy (chap. 7) and G. K. Hunter's on the traditions of tragedy (chap. 8). R. L. Smallwood focuses on the ten plays about English history (chap. 9). MacD. P. Jackson discusses canonical and textual questions (chap. 10). The last chapters cover stage history and the history of literary criticism. Russell Jackson reviews stage history from 1660 to 1900 (chap. 11), Roger Warren carries this review into the twentieth century (chap. 14), and Robert Hapgood extends the coverage to film and television (chap. 15). Harry Levin surveys the dominant critical approaches from 1660 to 1904 (chap. 12), and in chap. 13 three scholars discuss twentieth-century trends in the study of the comedies (Lawrence Danson), tragedies (Kenneth Muir), and histories (Edward Berry). Terence Hawkes defines some of the newer critical approaches (chap. 16), and Dieter Mehl concludes the volume with a discursive list of important Shakespearean reference books (chap. 17). This book replaces the earlier *A New Companion to Shakespeare Studies*, edited by K. Muir and S. Schoenbaum in 1971.

Note on Bibliographies

In addition to the above works, readers should be aware of the various bibliographies of Shakespeare studies. Among the most valuable are Stanley Wells, *Shakespeare: A Bibliographical Guide*, Oxford: Clarendon Press, 1990; David M. Bergeron and Geraldo U. De Sousa, *Shakespeare: A Study and Research Guide*, 3rd edition, Lawrence: Univ. Press of Kansas, 1995; Larry S. Champion, *The Essential Shakespeare: An Annotated Bibliography of Major Modern Studies*, 2nd edition, New York: Hall, 1993. Thorough bibliographies for each of a gradually increasing number of plays have been appearing since 1980 in the Garland Shakespeare Bibliographies, general editor William L. Godshalk. An important specialized bibliography is John W. Velz, *Shakespeare and the Classical Tradition: A Critical Guide to Commentary, 1660–1960*, Minneapolis: Univ. of Minnesota Press, 1968 (available on-line). In the special area of Shakespearean pedagogy, a useful (although brief) bibliography appears in Peggy O'Brien, "'And Gladly Teach': Books, Articles, and a Bibliography on the Teaching of Shakespeare," *Shakespeare Quarterly* 46 (1995): 165–72. For information on new materials on the study of Shakespeare, readers should consult the annual bibliographies published by *Shakespeare Quarterly* (*World Shakespeare Bibliography*, also available on line), *PMLA* (*The MLA International Bibliography*, also available on-line and on CD ROM), the Modern Humanities Research Association (*Annual Bibliography of English Language and Literature*, available on-line), and the English Association (*The Year's Work in English Studies*). Ph.D. theses on Shakespeare are listed in *Dissertation Abstracts International*, which is also available on-line.

II. *ROMANITAS:* GENERAL WORKS ON THE ROMAN WORKS OF SHAKESPEARE

28. Barroll, J. Leeds. "Shakespeare and Roman History." *Modern Language Review* 53 (1958): 327-43.

In a study of "Roman history as it was viewed in the Elizabethan period" (327), and with special focus on *JC* and *Ant.*, Barroll presents authors and titles (with brief summaries) that formed Elizabethan attitudes and assumptions regarding the Classical past. Barroll studies the sources in the Classical writings, Christian writings on Rome, and publications on this subject by Elizabethans. Barroll highlights, in the first group, biographies by Suetonius and Plutarch; histories by Dio Cassius and Appian; summaries of lost material; and occasional commentary by a large number of writers including Cicero, Virgil, Horace, and Ovid. Barroll discusses these works with regard to their presentation of the Civil wars (especially relevant to *JC*, 328-29); he also studies Christian writings, especially by St. Augustine and Orosius (329-33), focusing on the succession of four monarchies, which he relates to *Ant.* (330-38). Barroll documents all this material in extensive footnotes. For Elizabethans, the author reminds us, history illustrated God's purpose in the world (338), a philosophical outlook which earlier critics had not, in his view, properly applied to dramatic works set in pagan times.

29. Doran, Madeleine. *Shakespeare's Dramatic Language: Essays.* Madison: Univ. of Wisconsin Press, 1976.

This book, which posits that each of Shakespeare's best plays has a feature of language that is suited "especially to the fable as a whole" (4) in that play, deals with *JC*, "What should be in that 'Caesar' ? Proper Names in *Julius Caesar*" 120-53; "High events as these: The Language of Hyperbole in *Antony and Cleopatra*" 154-81; and "All's in anger : The Language of Contention in *Coriolanus*" 182-217. The insistent repetition of Caesar's name, often paired with Brutus's, sometimes invoked when he is not present, calls attention to the values of Rome epitomized in his name, and to the role of Brutus as his chief antagonist. The "stretch and ripeness" (183) of the nascent Empire and the lavishness of the love are conveyed by hyperbole in *Ant.*, while the many hostile confrontations of *Cor.* are given focus by a variety of forms of equally hyperbolic stylistic contrariety and contradiction. For Doran, *Cor.* uses rhetorical figures "of contrariety and contradiction: antithesis, paradox, and dilemma" (184), qualities that she defines and illustrates in many passages (esp. 188-203). Doran points out that the expected conflict within the hero takes the form not of inner questioning but of "a brief resistance or a reluctant yielding to pressure" (185-86). She studies the issue of Coriolanus's integrity and its expression in language and shows that rhetoric helps to express it, especially in the scenes with Volumnia (211-15) and in Corioli (216-17).

30. **Gregson, J. M.** *Public and Private Man in Shakespeare.* London: Croom Helm; Totowa, N.J.: Barnes & Noble, 1983. Chap. 8, pp. 205-43.

All of the major persons in *JC*, *Ant.*, and *Cor.* are analyzed in light of the private-public conflict, which suffuses the Shakespeare canon. Gregson is shrewd in his comments about the characters: Brutus's mistake is in thinking the Plebeians are influenced by his logic, when it is his oratorical rhetoric that carries them away (213); in *JC*, "Antony, for all his political qualities, retains the individual responses of a man who has more in his life than politics" (216); in *Ant.*, "Shakespeare shows what might have happened if Aeneas had stayed with Dido" (219); Coriolanus "cannot dissimulate his private feelings about the Plebeians long enough to secure office ... and [in 5.3] he turns aside from public triumph to his death precisely because he responds to the call of the ancient private bond between mother and son" (232). In the *Cor.* section there are some astute contrasts with aspects of *Ant.* and *JC*. It is never made quite clear how the Roman plays differ in kind in the treatment of this theme from the other tragedies in the canon which also treat it; there is little of Plutarch in this chapter and nearly nothing of ancient Roman concepts of citizenship.

31. **Kahn, Coppélia.** *Roman Shakespeare: Warriors, Wounds, and Women.* Feminist Readings of Shakespeare. London and NY: Routledge, 1997.

Kahn argues that "Shakespeare's Roman works articulate a critique of the ideology of gender on which Renaissance understanding of Rome was based" (1). Kahn reviews the sources of Shakespeare's knowledge of Rome in English chronicle history, in earlier plays with Roman settings, and in Elizabethan political arguments (2-7). She reviews recent criticism to focus an analysis on the "representations of Roman virtue" (6) on the stage; Rome "is the testing ground rather than the backdrop" of the characters' virtues (14). In the discussions of specific plays that highlight patriarchy and gender identification from a feminist perspective, Kahn argues that *virtus* is divided within itself, and that its contradictions generate complexity and energy. In Chap. 3 (46-76), Kahn studies "the politics of sexuality" (47) in *Tit.* by focusing successively on Titus's strengths and failures as patriarchal figure and the implications of his patriarchal role on the female characters (48-57), the role of Lavinia (relating it to the mythic patterns associated with Philomela, Hecuba, and Lucrece [62-67]), and the revenge plot (67-72). For Kahn, Lucius's political "over-plot" (71) of marching on Rome parallels and is interwoven with the Titus-Tamora revenge plot. In *Ant.* (which, rather than *Cor.*, may be Shakespeare's last Roman play [110]), Kahn argues that Rome is "drawn to, repelled by, and finally fused with what is Other to it," (110) a change from the sources in Virgil, Ovid, and Horace, all of whom polarized an opposition between Egypt (embodied by Cleopatra) and Rome (embodied by the uneasy, fragile bonding of Antony and Caesar). Kahn analyzes the issues involved in Antony's attempt at suicide (121-23), which she also relates to sexual violation, and which is ultimately a "performance ... intended to effect an ideological transformation whereby he can regain the Roman virtue he lost in being defeated by Caesar" (132). By contrast, Kahn argues, Cleopatra's death ends the "jouissance" (pleasure) associated with her, which holds a threat of emasculation. Opening her *Cor.* chapter with a discussion of "the interaction between mothering and warmaking" (145), Kahn discusses the relationship between Coriolanus and Volumnia and the latter's role not only as mother but "as metaphor for her more powerful part in 'framing' her son's temperament and value system" (148), which ultimately functions to cancel masculinity. In Kahn's view, the play ends ironically: although Volumnia is "the life of Rome" who prevails over the male Coriolanus and the patricians, she also turns him into an enemy of Rome who is destroyed so that the state may live (157-58). (See also Linda Bamber, *Comic Women, Tragic Men: A Study of Gender and Genre in Shakespeare* [Stanford: Stanford Univ. Press, 1982], esp. chap. 6, 91-107.)

32. Knight, G. Wilson. *The Imperial Theme: Further Interpretations of Shakespeare's Tragedies Including the Roman Plays.* Oxford: Oxford Univ. Press, 1931. 3rd edition, revised, London: Methuen, 1951.

In the first chapter (1-31) Knight outlines his approach, which lies in the tradition of A.C. Bradley, but which is also open to the "mystical" (v). The critic then studies *JC* (chap. 2, 32-62; chap. 3, 63-95), *Cor.* (chap. 6, 154-98), and *Ant.* (chap. 7, 199-262; chap. 8, 263-326; chap. 9, 327-42; and chap. 10, 343-50). Knight's notion of interpretation focuses on images and symbols, from a perspective immersed in the work's theme, speaking from its "creative center" (vi); and his discussions link images and symbols to the play's action. Knight surveys "values," including war, love, honor, soldiership, and ceremony, which Shakespeare presents as ideas and "symbolic images" (19), re-grouping them as needed, to make new plays. Knight emphasizes that for Shakespeare the play is "imaginative" rather than psychological or didactic, and too much emphasis on character is, in his view, misguided effort. Among the many symbols Knight identifies are "sun," "moon," "stars," "nature's productiveness," "feasting," "jewel," "iron," "fire," "music," and "tempests." See also Knight, nos. 131, 132, and 190.

33. Kujawinska-Courtney, Krystyna. *"Th' Interpretation of the Time": The Dramaturgy of Shakespeare's Roman Plays* (ELS Monograph Series, no. 57) Victoria: English Literary Studies, 1993.

This close reading interprets the dramaturgy of the three Plutarch plays as a function of tension between direct representation (*mimesis*) and narrated and/or interpreted action (*diegesis*). A preliminary chapter shows that, from the time of Plato, criticism has regarded narration in drama as an intrusion requiring justification, and that Plutarch offered Shakespeare a rhetorical model for his own practice in the "dramatic" interplay in the *Lives* between the dominant mode of *diegesis* and frequently juxtaposed *mimesis* (quoted or invented speeches for historical persons). Chapter 2 shows that Shakespeare saw from the beginnings in *JC* that the interplay between *mimesis* and *diegesis* could problematize the action and the characters (especially the moral image of Caesar); conflicting *diegeses* are played off limited *mimesis*. In *Ant.*, Shakespeare is shown to complicate this paradigm by focusing it on issues of gender and ethnicity (male vs. female; Rome vs. Egypt). Chapter 4 interprets the ambiguities of *Cor.* as the result of Shakespeare's deliberate decentering of the audience by mutual subversion of *diegesis* and *mimesis*; the author regards the artistic product as one of Shakespeare's most problematic plays, an anticipation of postmodern drama. An afterword touches on the critical perspective as applied to the last plays, an implied invitation to broader application of the methodology to the Shakespeare canon. This is a major study of style in the Roman plays which has broad implications for other groups of Shakespearean plays.

34. Leggatt, Alexander. *Shakespeare's Political Drama: The History Plays and the Roman Plays*. London and NY: Routledge, 1988.

In a book concentrating on the "political" in Shakespeare, "the ordering and enforcing, the gaining and losing, of public power in the state" (ix), Leggatt analyzes eight English history plays (*1-2-3 Henry VI, Richard III, 1-2 Henry IV, Henry V,* and *Henry VIII* (chaps. 1-5, 1-138, and chap. 9, 214-37), which show that history is not "a straight line moving through time" but, rather, one that "turns back on itself and forms a circle, an image not of perfection but of futility" (138); yet Leggatt is not nihilistic, for in his view the audience recognizes that the hero and "the art that creates him" fuse to "protect human achievement from the erosion of time" (138). Leggatt discusses *JC* (chap. 6, 139-60), *Ant.* (chap. 7, 161-88), and *Cor.* (chap. 8, 189-213).

35. MacCallum, M[ungo] W. *Shakespeare's Roman Plays and Their Background.* London: Macmillan, 1910.

This large and learned book was the first book-length study of Shakespeare's Plutarch plays as a group. It surveys attempts at Roman dramatic themes before Shakespeare, provides an excellent account of Plutarch and of his Renaissance translators, including the best biography of Sir Thomas North, and gives a full analysis of *JC*, *Ant.*, and *Cor.* in light of North, Shakespeare's source. The criticism is excellent yet it is limited: sensitive analysis of characters and genres receives the bulk of MacCallum's attention; other aesthetic considerations are somewhat neglected. Another limitation, given the book's title, is the lack of attention to Virgil, Ovid, Livy, Seneca, Caesar (*Commentaries*), and other Roman authors. Other reservations can be found in T.J.B. Spencer's "Foreword" in his reprint (1967) of MacCallum. The book on balance is an excellent place to begin study of the Plutarch plays of Shakespeare and how they got to be the way they are. See also MacCallum, nos. 168, 232.

36. Martindale, Charles and Michelle. *Shakespeare and the Uses of Antiquity: An Introductory Essay.* London and NY: Routledge, 1990.

Charles and Michelle Martindale concentrate on the usefulness, to reader and audience, of a knowledge of Shakespeare's Classical sources. In chapter 1, 1-44, the authors survey Shakespeare's knowledge of the Classics, the meaning of rhetorical "imitation," and the influence of Seneca; in chap. 2, 45-90, they survey Ovid and Classical mythology (with reference to *Tit.*, 47-55; *Venus and Adonis* and *Luc.*, 56-64); in chap. 3, 91-120, they survey the Troy story largely from Virgil. In chap. 4, the Martindales concentrate less on earlier writers than on Shakespeare and those of his age, discussing anachronism (121-25), other treatments of Rome on the stage (125-41), and, finally, the "secular and detached ... historical vision" (146), new at the time, that distinguished clearly between Rome and later England, as well as different periods within Rome (141-54). In chapter 5, 165-89, the authors present the doctrines of stoicism, especially "constancy," both in Classical philosophy and in Shakespeare's poems and plays (in *Cor.*, 179-81; in *Ant.*, 181-89).

37. McGrail, Mary Ann, ed. *Shakespeare's Plutarch* (*Poetica* 48, 1997). Tokyo: Shubun, 1997.

Of the eleven new essays that constitute this book, six are relevant to the Roman plays of Shakespeare; McGrail's Introduction surveys commentary on Plutarch and Shakespeare and concludes that important questions about that subject remain to be dealt with. Christopher Pelling considers Shakespeare's *Cor.* in relation to Plutarch and Plutarch in relation to his source, Dionysius of Halicarnassus. Susanne L. Wofford looks at Antony's desire for heroism and for Bacchic apotheosis in *Ant.* Paul A. Cantor explores a possible process by which *Ant.* and *Cor.* were written—as a pair of portraits in the Plutarchan manner, emblematizing the lifestyles of the Empire and the Republic, respectively. Albert Cook focuses on what Shakespeare learned from Plutarch about characterization, including *inter alia* comparison with other characters, and significant anecdote. John W. Velz traces some of Shakespeare's concepts of love and friendship in *Ant.* and other plays to Plutarch (*Moralia* and *Lives*). Yasunari Takada looks for sources for the "agnostic" Cicero who appears in 1.3 of *JC.* The essays are learned and provocatively original, reaching beyond conventional commentaries on Shakespeare's use of North's Plutarch to new insights and new approaches.

38. Miles, Gary B. "How Roman Are Shakespeare's 'Romans'?" *SQ* 40 (1989): 257–83.

The first part of this scholarly article discusses several of the historical Romans that Shakespeare portrays or alludes to (Octavius, Julius Caesar, Marcus Brutus, Marcus Antonius, Pompeius Magnus). Miles points out that the tradition came down to Shakespeare through Plutarch, a Greek who wrote a century and a half after the lives and events he records, and through the humanist translators, Jacques Amyot and Thomas North. Shakespeare is said to have had little or no direct access to Latin writings about Roman character and political lifestyle. Part I also draws on the evidence of *elogia* (posthumous lists of a man's public achievements), and of Roman and Greek statuary in which character is revealed: Cicero's solemnity under the burden of civic life; Alexander's looking up to the realm of the gods; Pompeius Magnus's attempt to seem another Alexander, etc. In Part II, Miles distinguishes between post-Classical honor as conscience and Classical honor as *dignitas*. (The two definitions of honor, as moral integrity and as reputation, make the distinction.) The Romans did not live by conscience but for reputation, extending to family lineage, to supervised portraiture, and even to official deification in the Caesars' cases. Miles points out that the Western tradition beginning with Augustine shaped the modern view that a person's character is an internal integrity. He sees Shakespeare as adding post-Classical personal virtue to some of his Romans, as not properly understanding that political *dignitas* is the essence of a Roman aristocrat's life. Miles indicates some of the frequent ambiguities in Shakespeare's Marcus Brutus: does Brutus choose a course of action to protect his reputation or to satisfy his philosophical sense of "what is right"? Unless Brutus chooses the former, Shakespeare is adding to what the historical Brutus would have seen as the more important criterion in choice. We can question Miles's assertion that Shakespeare did not know Latin accounts of *Romanitas*; he knew Cicero's *Offices*, Caesar's *Commentaries*, Sallust, Tacitus, Livy, and possibly also Florus's epitome of Livy, with other Roman historians. We also might question Miles about the role of philosophy in the formation of character and the making of choices. Plutarch begins his "Brutus," for instance, with a brief account of Brutus as a student at the Academy in Athens, and Cassius identifies himself as an Epicurean (5.1); there has been much talk in the late twentieth century of the role of Stoicism in the moral world of Shakespeare's Roman Plays. These caveats aside, the article is highly perceptive, a classicist's perspective on Shakespeare's art and its origins.

39. Miles, Geoffrey. *Shakespeare and the Constant Romans.* Oxford: Clarendon Press, 1996.

Miles aims to provide "a closer analysis of [Roman] 'constancy' that acknowledges the complexities of its meanings and the tangled roots from which it springs" (vii) as this virtue is presented in *JC* (chap. 7, 123-48), *Cor.* (chap. 8, 149-68), and *Ant.* (chap. 9, 169-88), excluding *Tit.* and *Cymbeline*. Miles traces constancy in philosophical and literary treatments from Plato, the Greek Stoics, Cicero (chap. 2, 18-37), and Seneca (chap. 3, 38-62) though it is Shakespeare's originality to emphasize the complexities inherent in the different meanings of the word. In Miles's view, aspects of constancy were debated anew by Renaissance readers and writers (Erasmus, Calvin, Justus Lipsius, and such English writers as Sir William Cornwallis and Joseph Hall), especially its rivalry with the idea of "opinion" (chap. 4, 63-82), and were further developed by Montaigne (chap. 5, 83-109), several of whose essays Miles analyzes. In chap. 6, 110-22, Miles studies Sir Thomas North's translation of Plutarch's *Lives* for its presentation of Brutus, Antony, and Coriolanus as a "kind of triptych on the theme of constancy" (110). See also Miles, nos. 169, 233.

40. Miola, Robert S. *Shakespeare's Rome.* Cambridge: Cambridge Univ. Press, 1983.

This study offers a more complex view of Shakespeare's Roman world than any book that preceded it. The first chapter lays out the multiple paths Shakespeare took to ancient Rome: translations, commonplaces, Elizabethan reference books, and school texts including learned commentaries. All can be seen to have made contributions to his sense of *Romanitas*. Rome is austere and demanding and sometimes dehumanizing as Miola sees it, and he finds that Shakespeare came to criticize or even to reject this severe Roman lifestyle late in his career. Each of Shakespeare's six works that have Roman settings (*Cymbeline* is included) is accorded a chapter of close reading and probing analysis. A major thrust of the book taken as a whole is the uncovering of Virgil as a background to each of Shakespeare's Roman works. (Virgil had been only sporadically looked at as an influence on Shakespeare to Miola's time.) The book is accessible despite its impressive learning. It is the best comprehensive survey of Shakespeare's response to the Roman world. See also Miola, nos. 74, 114–16, 170, 234.

41. Ronan, Clifford J. *"Antike Roman": Power Symbology and the Roman Play in Early Modern England 1585–1635.* Athens: Univ. of Georgia Press, 1995.

This ambitious book takes on the 43 extant plays in English with Roman settings that were written in the fifty years from 1585, before Shakespeare's career began, to more than twenty years after his career ended. There actually were nearly twice the number of such plays written, as appendices show. *Luc.* is discussed here at several points though it is technically (not a play) irrelevant. The plays in this Pegasus volume are all repeatedly called up, and *Cymbeline* is as well. The structure of the book is topical, neither chronological nor canonical, and therefore the nominal index is a necessity for those interested in Shakespeare or any other dramatist. After an introduction, the topics are anachronism in Renaissance drama; the Renaissance sense of Rome as a place of political power; *nobilitas* and *majestas*, virtues with an edge to them; suicide and its dependence on Stoic *constantia*; and the vices of *superbia* (overweening pride) and above all *saevitia* (cruelty). The book turns in part on a pun "antike" = "antique" (= "antic"); *Romanitas* evokes the solemnity of an old and high culture, and at the same time *Romanitas* is ambivalent, its moral postures wildly alien to early modern English sensibilities, even a threat to sanity itself. The learning is impressive, both about Renaissance plays and about their Classical backgrounds.

42. *Shakespeare Survey: An Annual Survey of Shakespearean Study & Production* 10. Ed. Allardyce Nicoll. Cambridge: Cambridge Univ. Press, 1957.

Almost half of this 170-page vol. is devoted to important studies of the Roman plays. J.C. Maxwell surveys trends in scholarship and criticism of the Roman plays, 1900–56. J. Dover Wilson surveys opinion on Shakespeare's Latinity from Shakespeare's own time to the 1950s. T.J.B.

Spencer shows that the Elizabethans saw Rome as a morally significant world of tumults ("garboyles") like those in *Tit.*, and that the statuesque dignity in Shakespeare's Plutarch plays runs counter to contemporary literary fashion, especially in *Cor.*, an unprecedented and very "Roman" play (repr. in no. 152). Eugene Waith identifies the juxtaposition of hyperbolic emotion and distancing rhetoric in Ovid's *Metamorphoses* as operative in the strange aesthetics of *Tit.* R. F. Hill argues for Shakespeare's authorship of *Tit.* on stylistic grounds. Hermann Heuer considers what Amyot, North, and Shakespeare successively did to Plutarch's account of Coriolanus, especially Volumnia's dissuasion of her son from sacking Rome. W. M. Merchant writes an illustrated brief history of Classical costume in Shakespearean productions. Most of these essays have aged well: Hill's methodology in some sense anticipates the "stylometry" of the 1980s as a criterion for authorship; Spencer's and Waith's essays are frequently cited today. Few scholars, however, would now agree that Shakespeare's Latin was as small as Wilson concludes it was.

43. Simmons, J.L. *Shakespeare's Pagan World: The Roman Tragedies.* Charlottesville: Univ. Press of Virginia, 1973.

In the introduction (chap. 1, 1–17) to Simmons' three chapters on the Roman plays (*Cor.*, chap. 2, 18–64; *JC*, chap. 3, 65–108; and *Ant.*, chap. 4, 109–63), Simmons separates the plays from A.C. Bradley's "Great Four" (*Hamlet, Macbeth, King Lear*, and *Othello*, 3) and finds them characterized by their "integral relationship" to their pre-Christian environment; in them, the conflict does not "involve the struggle between characters associated with the clarifying absolutes of good and evil" (3), and there is no clear moral perspective for the audience. Simmons argues that from a Christian perspective on history, pagan Rome is "doomed" (9) and was usually seen as the fourth and last world empire, before Christ's eternal fifth (9), and that the plays accordingly have an ironic treatment of history and character (the insights and understanding of Brutus, Antony, and Caesar, for instance, are severely limited). In the conclusion (chap. 5, 164–67), Simmons comments very briefly on *Cymbeline*. See also Simmons, no. 171.

44. Simmons, J. L. "Shakespeare's Treatment of Roman History." In *William Shakespeare: His World, His Work, His Influence*, ed. John F. Andrews. 3 vols. 2: 473-88. NY: Charles Scribner's Sons, 1985.

The thrust of Simmons' essay is to broaden the cultural context of *Romanitas* in Shakespeare beyond Plutarch, Ovid, and Seneca to embrace Virgil, rhetoricians, and philosophers, and even Christianity. For Simmons, a major question for the Roman works is "Can Rome endure?"

Cor. suggests a positive answer, but *Tit.* had already offered evidence of the collapse of *Romanitas.* In both plays, the first and the last of Shakespeare's tragedies, *Romanitas* is seen as dehumanization. The essay is full of gems: the irony of *virtus* in *Cor.* is pointed out; there is an excellent contrast between the philosophies of Brutus and Cassius and between their attitudes toward assassination; Shakespeare's Cleopatra is said to be enigmatic like his Caesar; she is the only major character in the Roman works who is not limited by a Roman point of view; the origin of the histrionic mode in *JC* is perceptively discussed; Antony is seen as an actor in his oration. Simmons assumes a reader well versed in the four plays (*Cymbeline* and *Luc.* are discussed briefly as well). See also no. 171.

45. Thomas, Vivian. *Shakespeare's Roman Worlds.* London and NY: Routledge, 1989.

Before devoting individual chapters to *JC, Ant.,* and *Cor.*, Thomas discusses Shakespeare's "Roman worlds" (chap. 1, 1–39), arguing that "a clear understanding of Shakespeare's exploration and articulation of Roman values provides an invaluable means of gaining fresh critical insights" (1); the "central" Roman values are service to the state, constancy, fortitude, valor, friendship, love of family, and respect for the gods (1), and the catalyst of conflict is collision among these values or the divergence between personal goals and obligations to Roman society. In this chapter, Thomas summarizes the issues dramatized in the three focal plays, tracing them to Plutarch's treatment of history, and reviews earlier critical discussions of the Roman plays; in the "Conclusion," (chap. 5, 220–23), Thomas restates and summarizes his findings. See also Thomas, nos. 79, 172, 235.

46. Traversi, Derek. *Shakespeare: The Roman Plays.* Stanford: Stanford Univ. Press, 1963.

In the introduction (chap. 1, 9–18), Traversi studies style (the plays unite "colloquial ease with the heights of emotional expression," 10), action (derived from Plutarch), and politics (Shakespeare refused to simplify issues). Although in his discussions of specific plays Traversi generally comments scene-by-scene, he argues that in *Ant.* and *Cor.* there is a growth of tragic vision, and wider relevance to human experience than had existed in *JC,* and he distinguishes the concerns of these three plays from the political concerns of the English history plays (15–17); although in both groups of plays the notion of order is important, Traversi finds that in the Roman plays Shakespeare brings together political and personal elements "in a new and distinctively Roman vision for which Plutarch provided the foundation" (17). For this critic, Coriolanus is divided within and must confront a politically divided Rome; like the other Roman heroes, he must choose between loyalty to a political ideal that will achieve harmony (at whatever personal cost) and loyalty to a personal ideal that will achieve integrity (at whatever political cost).

47. Velz, John W. "The Ancient World in Shakespeare: Authenticity or Anachronism? A Retrospect." *Shakespeare Survey* 31 (1978): 1–12.

After a 3+-page account of scholarly opinion on the authenticity question from the time of Nahum Tate to the 1950s and a 3-page account of Shakespeare's access to Greek culture, this bibliographical essay proceeds to a review of opinion on several aspects of *Romanitas* in Shakespeare: Roman style (especially), including oratory and *illeism* (referring to oneself in the third person, as Julius Caesar does in his *Commentaries* and in Shakespeare's *JC*), Roman character and lifestyle, Roman institutions, the *Urbs Romae*, and the notion that Shakespeare's Rome is "a world apart" (8). The essay advances some new ideas, e.g., that Shakespeare got his conception of Greeks as harsh from a misreading of St. Paul, and that the Roman wall is the great symbol of cultural apartness in the Roman works of Shakespeare. This bibliographical account is more than twenty years out of date and should be supplemented from other, later, works compiled in this Pegasus volume (see especially Miles, no. 38, Ronan, no. 41, Parker, no. 117).

III. THE RAPE OF LUCRECE

A. Editions.

48. Prince, F. T., ed. *The Poems.* The Arden Edition of the Works of William Shakespeare. London: Methuen; Cambridge, Mass.: Harvard Univ. Press, 1960.

More than one half of this volume is devoted to *Venus and Adonis* and Shakespeare's minor poems (excluding the sonnets), and therefore is technically relevant here. A major part (xi–xx) of the Introduction is devoted to texts and publication history. There is frequent comparison to *Venus and Adonis* in the account of *Luc.* in the Introduction. Also helpful are the foot-of-page lexical and explanatory notes on difficult passages. Appendices for *Luc.* are the account of the Lucretia story from Chaucer's *Legend of Good Women*; an extract from Painter's *Palace of Pleasure* translating Livy's account of the rape of Lucretia, Collatinus' wife; and the passage of Ovid's *Fasti* in both Latin and English in which Lucretia's story is told (essentially what Bullough offers, see no. 52). Although Prince is responsive at times to the stylistic brilliance of parts of the poem, on the whole he regards *Luc.* as aesthetically unsatisfactory. He neglects Shakespeare's rhetorical tropes, except to condemn them in general terms as prolixity, labelling the poem "a failure" (xxxiii–xxxiv). Prince represents a tradition that regarded the poem less favorably than do some more recent commentators, such as Maus (no. 61) and Scholz (no. 64). His edition is a standard text used by most of the commentators on *Luc.* included in this bibliography, although Roe's edition (no. 49) now supersedes it.

49. Roe, John, ed. *The Poems: "Venus and Adonis," "The Rape of Lucrece," "The Phoenix and the Turtle," "The Passionate Pilgrim," "A Lover's Complaint."* The New Cambridge Shakespeare. Cambridge: Cambridge Univ. Press, 1992.

The introduction to *Luc.* (22–41) includes sections on "The Poem and Interpretation," "The Southampton Connection," and "Sources." It contains criticism of *Luc.*, some of it in relation to criticism of its companion piece *Venus and Adonis*, and some of it in relation to the Shakespeare canon more generally. The foot-of-page annotation of the text of the poem is full, offering occasional aesthetic criticism as well as lexical, usage, and explicatory notes; some notes point out unusual rhetorical tropes. The notes aim at scholars as well as students. Four longer "Supplementary Notes" on *Luc.* (283-85) deal with The Argument, the night weasels at line 307, Lucrece's bedclothes, and the *ekphrasis* on Troy. The extent of the scholarship in this edition is partly conveyed by the list of abbreviations of scholarly works consulted (viii-xiv). The text is based on Q1 (1594). The "Note on the Text" (74-76) treats *Luc.* with *Venus and Adonis*, since they appeared from the same printer (Richard Field) within two years of one another. The appendix of "Textual Analysis" appears for *Luc.* on pp. 289-92. Two black-and-white photographs of paintings of Lucretia by Titian (the rape scene) and Cranach (the suicide) illustrate the poem in this edition. Roe's is the best general purpose edition of *Luc.*

50. Rollins, Hyder Edward. *A New Variorum Edition of Shakespeare: The Poems*. Philadelphia: Lippincott, 1938.

The text of *Luc.* and its local apparatus—textual notes, and lexical, interpretive, and historically arranged commentary notes—appear on pp. 109-263. The collations of the eight quartos after Q1 1594, Rollins' copy text, and of some 43 post-quarto editions are accompanied by exhaustive notes that can be regarded as comprehensive for materials up to its date. There are other appendices on text (406-13), and on date (413-15), a topic which was sufficiently disputed in early scholarship to make for more than two pages of excerpts. Much of the criticism of *Luc.* and *Venus and Adonis* summarized or excerpted in an appendix (476-523) also makes this volume the place to start for work on responses to the poem up to 1936. A supplement to the Criticism appendix is "The Vogue of *Venus and Adonis* and *Lucrece.*" (447-75), extensive notes on the popularity of the two poems. The *Luc.* Sources appendix (416-46) treats Livy, Ovid, Chaucer, and Painter; it includes excerpts from commentary on the sources as well. John Quarles's *Tarquin Banished* is reprinted in this section, although it was not published until 1655.

51. Wilbur, Richard, and Alfred Harbage, eds. *The Narrative Poems.* The Pelican Shakespeare. Baltimore: Penguin Books (1966), 1974.

This edition is modestly annotated; most notes are lexical and aimed at college students. The principal value of the edition lies in the criticism of the poem (closely associated with *Venus and Adonis*) in Wilbur's Introduction (17-20). Wilbur brings a poet's sensitive ear to a number of passages, and he chafes at perceived failures of economy and decorum. His comments on the *ekphrasis* about Troy and on Shakespeare's preference for poetry over action are cogent, although most writers on *Luc.* since Wilbur's time have thought better of the poem than he. Wilbur is very perceptive on the stance and on the historical and cultural occasions of the poem.

B. Influences; Sources; Historical and Intellectual Backgrounds; Topicality.

52. Bullough, Geoffrey. *"The Rape of Lucrece."* In no. 15. Vol. 1: 177-99.

This small gathering of sources and analogues of *Luc.* reprints the relevant passage in Ovid's *Fasti* in both Latin and a late (1640) English translation; Livy appears here only in William Painter's fairly close rendering into English (1566); Chaucer's account of Lucretia from *The Legend of Good Women* is the only other text given. The "Introduction" (179-83) follows tradition in recognizing that *Luc.* and *Venus and Adonis* are in Shakespeare's intention a pair of poems: "[H]aving described desire unaccomplished against reluctance [in *Venus and Adonis*], Shakespeare now [in *Luc.*] gives desire accomplished by force" (179). Bullough sees Ovid's "terse" story in the *Fasti* as the primary source. There are precedents for parts of the poem in Ovid's *Metamorphoses* that neither Bullough nor other commentators on sources of *Luc.* have noticed. For one of them, see Velz, "The Ovidian Soliloquy in Shakespeare," *Shakespeare Studies* 18 (1986): 1-24. For discussion of other materials relevant to the story, see nos. 53, 55, and 58.

53. Donaldson, Ian. *The Rapes of Lucretia: A Myth and its Transformation.* Oxford: Oxford Univ. Press, 1982.

Chapter 3 (40-56) deals with Shakespeare's poem in light of the tradition, which is carefully laid out in seven earlier and later chapters. Donaldson sees the rhetorical speeches, especially of Lucrece, as evidence of a mind deeply injured by intense emotion. The author reasons that Christian allusions, however fleeting, make the question of suicide as an option for Lucrece a difficult one; she never really works it out until the end, where she chooses the pagan tradition. Another major theme is seen as possession (who "owns" Lucrece's valued chastity?). See also 115-17 on the political dimension of the poem, including the theme of government (of the state and of the self), and Shakespeare's skillful avoidance of seeming (dangerously) anti-monarchical. The chapter of which Shakespeare's political coloring in the story is a part shows that Lucius Junius Brutus was an ambiguous, even a controversial, figure both before and after Shakespeare. The book is very learned, yet entirely accessible through a lucid prose style. Of special interest are the reproductions of 20 paintings, mainly of the rape or suicide of Lucretia, with full analytical commentary. Donaldson concludes by labeling *Luc.* "a poem of remarkable yet sporadic brilliance" (55). A virtue of the review of Donaldson's book by Harriett Hawkins (*Essays in Criticism* 34 [1984]: 79–87) is its comparison between the rape and crimes against men, including suicides of public figures for political reasons (e.g., Cato).

53a. Enterline, Lynn. "'Poor Instruments' and Unspeakable Events in *The Rape of Lucrece.*" In *The Rhetoric of the Body from Ovid to Shakespeare.* Cambridge Studies in Literature and Culture 35. 152–97, 253–57. Cambridge: Cambridge Univ. Press, 2000.

This scholarly study of the background of the pattern of references to voicelessness or to interruptions of voice in *Luc.* finds important connections to the Petrarchan tradition and to Ovid (who is also the source of the Petrarchan trope of the voiceless beloved). Shakespeare is seen to give a voice to Ovid's voiceless Lucretia (in the *Fasti*). The voices heard and unheard in Shakespeare's poem also lead Enterline to concepts of subjectivity and will. There is also a section on musical allusions in the poem with ties to Orpheus. The chapter is arguably the best study of the relation between rape and silence yet to appear; it makes aesthetic virtues of some of the discourse in the poem that critics have found irritating. The full notes make this a good place to begin study of the motif in *Luc.*

54. Hulse, Clark. "*A Skilful Painting of Lucrece.*" In *Metamorphic Verse: The Elizabethan Minor Epic*, 175–94. Princeton: Princeton Univ. Press, 1981.

This section of a chapter entitled "Shakespeare Poet and Painter" is a detailed account of the *ekphrasis* (pictorial set piece) of Troy which is pictured in the tapestry that Lucrece stands before after her rape by Tarquin. The approach to the poem is through technique and theory of art from the ancient world to the Renaissance, especially the former. This is unquestionably the best account of this dimension of the Troy digression in *Luc.*; but more can and should be said about the suitability of the Troy story to Lucrece's situation (see no. 64).

54a. Koppenfels, Werner von. "Dis-covering the Female Body: Erotic Exploration in Elizabethan Poetry." *Shakespeare Survey* 47 (1994): 127–37. A "free translation" and expansion of Chapter 2 of the author's *Bild und Metamorphose*, Darmstadt, 1991.

This intertextual study analyzes the final scene of Marlowe's *Hero and Leander* as a primary intertext for analogous scenes of erotic disrobement and copulation in Elizabethan narrative verse and prose. It shows that Marlowe added erotic details borrowed from Ovid's *Amores* to his sources, Musaeus and Ovid's *Heroides*, and likewise added an ominous note of predation and warfare with tragedy to follow; this second dimension of the scene is traced to the Philomela story in *Metamorphoses* 6. The rape scene in *Luc.* is clearly indebted to the scene in *Hero and Leander*, as Koppenfels shows, for these two manifestations of Ovidianism, the erotic and the horrific.

55. MacDonald, Joyce Green. "Speech, Silence, and History in *The Rape of Lucrece*." *Shakespeare Studies* 22 (1994): 77–103.

This scholarly study constructs an elaborate set of backdrops against which to see *Luc.* The Lucretia tradition, which MacDonald sees as being rather different (more political, less personal) from what Donaldson observed (see no. 53) is one of them. Another is Renaissance English social mores in which women's chastity was made analogous to their silence and reclusiveness. A third is the backdrop Shakespeare himself creates in the *ekphrasis* on Troy, where voiceless Hecuba and unchaste Helen are emblems for Lucrece's situation and her psychological state. The learning is impressive: 61 footnotes, many of them citing primary texts, lend support to the author's thesis that Lucrece exemplifies the use of women as tools in male-constructed history. The thesis is persuasive, although other readings of Lucrece's character and situation are possible.

56. Majors, G. W. "Shakespeare's First Brutus: His Role in *Lucrece*." *Modern Language Quarterly* 35 (1974): 339–51.

Majors points out that the last seven stanzas of the poem, a kind of epilogue, focus on Lucius Junius Brutus, especially his ambivalent character. According to one perspective, he is, like Prince Hal, Fortinbras, and Octavius, biding his time for power. On the other hand, Majors says, he may be a culture hero, a leader of a revolution. Or yet again, he may be a twister of truth, exploiting the rape and suicide for ulterior purposes. Majors recognizes that the ambiguity is in the tradition stemming from Machiavelli's commentary on Livy and from Paulus Marsus' commentary on Ovid's *Fasti*. Majors says that, while following his sources (Ovid and Livy), Shakespeare departs from them significantly "by insisting on the equivocality that was always there" (346). Majors opines that, unlike naïve Lucrece, Lucius Junius Brutus has depths that are "unsounded." He sees *Luc.* as a "sentimental moral tale" (351) whose characters he himself examines "on a basis unsentimental and unmoral" (351).

57. Miola, Robert S. "*The Rape of Lucrece*: Rome and Romans." In *Shakespeare's Rome*, 18–41. Cambridge: Cambridge Univ. Press, 1983.

Miola sees the poem as offering a portrait of Rome as a city and as a set of political and social relationships in the narrative of a personal crime against a Roman matron. The political context (tyranny) and consequence (civil war) of the crime are seen as conveyed by images of predation and siege. The similarities and differences between *Luc.* and its sources are made to throw light on Shakespeare's intentions. The disruption by the rape of order in the family of Collatine is seen (25) to be represented by Lucrece's distrust of her servant after the crime. Included is an important revisionist interpretation of Virgil's account of the fall of Troy. The implication is clear that Shakespeare modeled his view of the fall of Collatine's household as a metaphor for the collapse of Roman society, echoing Virgil's similar hint that Priam's violated palace stands for the whole City of falling Troy. Yet this interpretation insists that Lucrece kills herself not to bring down the House of Tarquin but to vindicate her own integrity as a person and a Roman, to preserve her name and her memory. Miola does not use the term *dignitas* for Lucrece's motivation, but that is the concept Shakespeare has in mind according to this important interpretation of the poem. (On *dignitas*, see no. 38.) Miola's close reading is notably alert, and thus revealing of faults in the poem as well as its aesthetic merits (among the faults, too much *copia* and insistent imagery). Miola also recognizes in *Luc.* a germ for Shakespeare's later portrayal of Roman characters in crisis.

57a. Newman, Jane O. "'And Let Mild Women to Him Lose Their Mildness': Philomela, Female Violence, and Shakespeare's *The Rape of Lucrece.*" *SQ* 45 (1994): 304–26.

This scholarly feminist *cum* classicist study uses a quasi-archaeological approach to the text of *Luc.* to uncover in its "margins" a scenario of female violence that Shakespeare suppresses in the narrative itself, but which is inherent in the Philomela myth twice referred to in the poem, in which women take violent revenge for a rape. One of these "margins" is in the title of this article (l. 979). Newman sees "phallocratic" political implications in the suppression of female vengeful power in *Luc.*

57b. Williams, Carolyn D. "'Silence, like a Lucrece knife': Shakespeare and the Meanings of Rape." *Yearbook of English Studies* 23 (1993): 93–110.

A full exploration of rape as presented in Ovid's *Fasti* and Livy's *Ab urbe condita*, in Ovid's *Metamorphoses* (including the Callisto story as well as Io and Philomela) and in literature and law in the 16th and 17th centuries shows that the emphasis falls on a rape victim's silence. "*Lucrece* explores the heroine's disastrous relationship with language. The poem is organized by the things people say, or might say, about Lucrece, and the things Tarquin tries to stop her saying." (109) Suicide, Williams concludes, is the conventional way in the literature for a rape victim to communicate her shame and keep it from being thought guilt.

58. Young, Arthur M. *Echoes of Two Cultures.* Pittsburgh: Univ. of Pittsburgh Press, 1964.

The two cultures echoed in this unusual book are the Hellenic and the Roman, each of which is represented by cultural response to a semilegendary figure, respectively Cyrus the Great and Lucretia. The Lucretian tradition occupies pages 59–125 and 130–36. The sources, analogues, and allusions are not excerpted but discussed in ways that frequently throw light on the poem. The commentary on texts relevant to Lucretia's story is more inclusive than in nos. 52 and 53; nine Classical authorities are discussed, as well as more than three dozen authors of the Middle Ages and the Renaissance. One short section of special interest (63–64) places Lucretia in the Antigone tradition. The commentary on Shakespeare is only three pages long (103–06), but it offers the information that Shakespeare could have found details from Dionysius of Halicarnassus and from Livy (both of them discussed here) in the Paulus Marsus *commentarium* on Ovid's *Fasti*. Young's book should be consulted as a supplement to other treatments of the Lucretian tradition.

C. Language and Linguistics.

59. Dubrow, Heather. "'Full of forged lies': *The Rape of Lucrece*." In *Captive Victors: Shakespeare's Narrative Poems and Sonnets*, 80–168. Ithaca: Cornell Univ. Press, 1987.

In an essay that makes sense of the rhetorical complexities of *Luc.*, Dubrow singles out *syneciosis* (the appealing juxtaposition of incompatibles, e.g., "captive victors") to apply to the characterization of Lucrece, Tarquin, and Brutus. *Syneciosis* also is applied here to *Romanitas* in the poem, where Romans are not so much a community as a set of divisive, contentious rivalries. Dubrow reasons that the description of Lucrece is more complex than her view of reality, which is single and simple. She is seen in military and political terms perhaps more than in personal terms. To Dubrow, she is not a mere symbol or a toy, but a person—the beginnings of real success for Shakespeare in the art of characterization. Tarquin, too, is more complex than a rhetoric-less version of the poem might imply. He is a "captive victor," and he also has a divided nature, reflected in equivocal paradoxes in his speeches to Lucrece. The essay is complex, like its subject. Slander is seen as a vice with dangerous consequences. The responses of the poem to the complaint tradition and to the Renaissance debate about historiography are discussed at length. Speechlessness, a kind of anti-rhetoric, is seen to convey the powerlessness of those who suffer. Heraldry, anthropology ("shame" vs. "guilt" societies), the psychology of rape victims (Lucrece responds to her violation as modern women do to theirs), and several rhetorical devices subordinate to *syneciosis (anadiplosis, synecdoche, oxymoron, copia*, and predication, especially) are all assets of the commentary. For another profound approach to history in the poem, see Dubrow's earlier essay, "The Rape of Clio: Attitudes to History in *The Rape of Lucrece," English Literary Renaissance* (1986): 425–41.

60. **Lanham, Richard A.** *The Motives of Eloquence: Literary Rhetoric in the Renaissance.* New Haven and London: Yale Univ. Press, 1976.

Chapter 4, "The Ovidian Shakespeare: *Venus and Adonis* and *Lucrece*" (82–110, *Luc.* 94–110), offers a somewhat negative view of the poem and its two principal characters. Tarquin is seen to be in love not with Lucrece but with the Medieval-flavored rhetoric that he and the narrator attach to her; Lucrece's outbursts after the rape are seen as "sentimental" (i.e., excessive) and motivated by theatrical display. It is this putative failure to locate the poem in psychological motives, preferring rhetoric to inner feeling, that, as Lanham sees it, distresses modern critics. Lanham is among the best of the negative critics of the poem, fully analytical in his reservations about the poem and keenly aware of literary as well as rhetorical modes. The essay might well be read in its entirety, as *Luc.* is compared several times with *Venus and Adonis*, but the *Luc.* section also can stand alone. Four years later, Lanham published a more positive critical view of the poem, "The Politics of *Lucrece*," *Hebrew University Studies in Literature* 8 (1980): 66–76.

61. **Maus, Katharine Eisaman.** "Taking Tropes Seriously: Language and Violence in Shakespeare's *Rape of Lucrece.*" *SQ* 37 (1986): 66–82.

In this article, the two principal characters in *Luc.* are seen through the implications of the tropes and figures they use or that are used about them by the narrator. Maus points out that they take metaphors literally, with profound implications for their characters and for the tone of the poem. Tarquin uses military metaphors for his lawless act, wishfully implying an order, a discipline, he cannot attain; Lucrece reminds him of his political responsibilities (calls his majesty "exiled" at line 640). In Maus's view, Lucrece uses *prosopopoeia* and *metalepsis* (in the latter of which Night, Opportunity, and Time are blamed instead of Tarquin to enable Lucrece to face her self, divided into innocent mind and tainted body). Maus also sees that the rape of Lucrece's body results in a rape of her mind; her value system is seriously injured. Maus perceives that language fails Lucrece (and her husband) at times, but that at others she pours out discourse. Shakespeare gives her ambiguities in her speech (e.g., "my reproach," line 816), to suggest that there is ground for her suicide. Many other tropes are discussed, including the battered mansion/fortress image that the narrator uses for her violated body.

D. Criticism.

62. Girard, René. "Envy of So Rich a Thing: *The Rape of Lucrece*." In *The Scope of Words: In Honor of Albert S. Cook*, edited by Peter Baker, Sarah Webster Goodwin, and Gary Handwerk, 135–44. NY: Peter Lang, 1991.

This essay compares *Two Gentlemen of Verona*, in which the attempted rape of Sylvia is "mimetic" ("suggested" by Valentine's praise of her), with *Luc.*, in which the actual rape of Lucrece is provoked by Collatine's praise of Lucrece's chastity and beauty. Girard sees that the notion of the "mimetic" in crime is carried over into Lucrece's argument that if Tarquin rapes her he will set a precedent for other rapes (lines 615–21). Girard also reasons that Shakespeare deliberately departed from his source in Livy, where Tarquinius sees Lucretia before he conceives his lust for her, as Shakespeare's Tarquin does not; the departure was intended to focus attention on envious emulation in Shakespeare's version. It is noteworthy, he points out, that both *Luc.* and *Two Gentlemen of Verona* are (probably) 1594. Girard proposes that the comedic version of a rape attempt came before the tragic version of an analogous rape attempt. The argument is focused on a close analysis of lines 15–42 of the poem. In Girard's view, Tarquin and Collatine are "co-responsible authors of a crime for which they swiftly punish one another" (137). The essay comments on the generic difference between the narrative and the drama; our assumption that a copy is inferior to an original has, wrongly in his view, caused criticism to take a negative view of *Luc.*

63. Kahn, Coppélia. "The Rape in Shakespeare's *Lucrece*." *Shakespeare Studies* 9 (1976): 45–72.

This article was first to reason, as many now do, that the violation of Lucrece is actually a violation of the patriarchal Roman social system. Kahn sees that both Tarquin and Lucrece regard Tarquin's rape of her as an offense against Collatine, her husband. Lucrece's suicide in this formulation is the enactment of her "selflessly patriarchal conception of the role of woman in [Roman] marriage" (66). The rape also has large political implications, as Kahn perceives that "Tarquin's private conduct in seizing his friend's wife is parallel to his [Tarquin's] father's public conduct in seizing the throne" (55). There is an acute discussion of the metaphorical virginity of Lucrece and of the imagery that makes her a property capable of being carried off by a thief. Here the double meaning of the Latin *raptus* (carried off; raped) is relevant, though Kahn does not say so. The article is informed about *Romanitas,* and it still rightly holds pride of place among studies of Shakespeare's *Romanitas* in the poem. For an unrelated (more directly feminist and more symbolic) approach, see Kahn's chapter on the poem (no. 31). The later essay was first published in Lyn Higgins and Brenda Silver, eds., *Rape and Representation* (NY: Columbia Univ. Press, 1991).

64. Scholz, Susanne. "Textualizing the Body Politic: National Identity and the Female Body in *The Rape of Lucrece." Shakespeare-Jahrbuch* 132 (1996): 103-13.

Four pages of theory about female bodies as symbolic of national states introduce an analysis of Lucrece in these terms. A nation's identity is said to be impenetrable, like a chaste woman, e.g., Lucrece before the rape; and national identity is also said to be a narrative that must be reaffirmed in the telling. In the *Luc.* pages, the focus falls on Lucrece and what happens to her body—seen in images of cities, fortresses, besieged islands, etc.—not on the political consequences of Tarquin's invasion of her body. Lucrece the impermeable is contrasted with Helen of Troy, who was all too permeable, effectively killing a nation when she accepted a foreign man into her body.

65. Wilson, R. Rawdon. "Shakespeare and Narrative: *The Rape of Lucrece* Reconsidered." *Studies in English Literature 1500-1900* 28 (1988): 39-59.

Wilson's essay discusses narrative strategies in the plays as well as in *Luc.* The account of the poem points out that Shakespeare uses narrative to "intensify" and to "defer" the *telos* of the action in a story that is very much a traditional tale. Shakespeare is seen to rely on *copia* (variations on a theme or an image), interior monologue, the divided self, narrative reflexivity, retold narratives, and culminative manipulation of detail—all of which are diegetic dimensions which make the poem (14 times the length of Ovid's simple narrative) good art as well as a good story; Wilson sees the poem as "a superbly compelling work [whose] intricate narrativity foreshadows the manner in which the narratives of the plays are written" (42). Wilson discusses the c. 200-line *ekphrasis* on Troy as a focal point of the poem. The author also treats, sometimes briefly, Shakespeare's use of narrative techniques (some of which, in fact, are not found in *Luc.)* in *1 Henry IV, A Midsummer Night's Dream, Cor., Ant.,* and *Ham-*

let. The tendency to reach beyond the poem makes this article an entry-point for study of narrative in Shakespeare generally (cf. Kujawinska-Courtney [no. 33]). Thirty-seven footnotes offer a good bibliography of narrativity studies and of *Luc.* commentary.

E. Bibliography.

66. Lever, J. W. "The Poems." In "Twentieth-century Studies in Shakespeare's Songs, Sonnets, and Poems." *Shakespeare Survey* 15 (1962): 18–30.

Lever's portion of this discursive bibliography also embraces *Venus and Adonis* and *The Phoenix and the Turtle*. On *Luc.*, Lever comments *passim* on important trends in scholarship and criticism (1900–1960) of several dimensions of the poem, including the place of the poem in the Shakespeare canon and Prince's observations about the poem as tragedy (see no. 48). The trends have changed significantly since 1960, and for those trends one should consult footnotes in nos. 49, 53, 59, 63, and 65.

IV. TITUS ANDRONICUS

A. Editions.

67. Bate, Jonathan, ed. *Titus Andronicus*. Arden Shakespeare, 3rd series. London and NY: Routledge, 1995.

Bate's introduction (1–121) is divided into four parts: "dramatic achievement" (4–37), covering the areas of plot, Roman political institutions, Goths, revenge and the law, and language; "theatrical life" (37–69), discussing the Peacham drawing, a 1620 German version, and selected productions; "origins" (69–95), arguing that *Tit.* is Shakespearean, was not based on the prose chapbook, and was first performed in early 1594; and "establishing the text" (95–121), analyzing the four earliest editions, Bate's editorial procedures, and the textual transmission. For this editor, Q1 is the copy-text, with the addition of the Folio "Fly-killing scene" (3.2), which is discussed in detail (14–21). There are notes to the text and on the text at the foot of each page, providing glosses on difficult words, background information, and critical commentary. The Appendix provides source texts from Ovid and Livy and a selection of Elizabethan "dramatic precedents" (279–89). "Abbreviations and references" (291–302), in effect a bibliography, is followed by an index to the introduction and commentary (303–08). Bate's Arden replaces that edited by J.C. Maxwell (1953).

68. Hughes, Alan, ed. *Titus Andronicus*. New Cambridge Shakespeare. Cambridge: Cambridge Univ. Press, 1994.

Hughes' introduction (1–47) discusses probable date of first performance and early references to the play, conjecturing that a first draft may have existed in 1588 (1–6); sources, including the chapbook (6–10); earlier critical disputes over Shakespeare's authorship (10–13); stage history from 1594 to 1641; the Peacham drawing and its possible relation to a stage performance (15–22); performance history from the Restoration to the 19th century (23–29); and a combination of performance history and literary criticism of *Tit.* in the 20th century (31–47). The editor discusses the four early texts (48–50 and 145–53) and offers the text of *Tit.* (53–143), based on Q1, with discussion of how the play might have been acted by a small group of players at the Rose Theater (Appendix I, 154–

61) and a scheme of "doubling" for 14 players (Appendix II, 162–63). Hughes concludes the volume with a bibliography for further reading (164–66), which supplements similar material given in the earlier "Abbreviations and Conventions" section (xiii–xvi). The New Cambridge Shakespeare succeeds "The New Shakespeare," in which John Dover Wilson's edition first appeared in 1948.

69. Waith, Eugene M., ed. *Titus Andronicus*. The Oxford Shakespeare. Oxford: Clarendon Press, 1984. Repr. Oxford World Classics Paperback. Oxford and NY: Oxford Univ. Press, 1994.

Waith's introduction (1–69) discusses what is known of *Tit.* up to 1623 (2–4), its date of first performance (before 23 January 1594), the arguments for and against Shakespeare's authorship (11–20), the Peacham drawing (20–27), which he tentatively dates 1595, sources and earlier analyses of them (27–38), and the early printed texts (39–43), to support his use of Q1 as the copy text. Waith also presents a history of the play in performance from 1594 to 1967 (43–58), surveys the history of critical response (58–69), and outlines his editorial procedures (71–77) with bibliographical references. Following the text of the play (83–194), he offers a series of appendices: in A (195–203) the text of the chapbook (a discussion of whether or not it is a source for the play follows, Appendix F, 213–15); in B the 1620 ballad (204–07); in C a summary of the "crimes against the Andronici" from play, chapbook, and ballad (208–09); in D an engagement with an earlier critic (210); in E the textual issue of a "false start" in 4.3.97–109 (211–12) which in this edition involves Waith's omission of a few lines of text; in G a way of "doubling" for performance by 27 actors (216–17); these are followed by an index to the introduction and commentary (219–26).

B. Authorship, Dating, and Textual Studies.

70. Wells, Stanley. "The Integration of Violent Action in *Titus Andronicus*." In *Shakespearean Continuities: Essays in Honour of E.A.J. Honigmann*, ed. John Batchelor, Tom Cain, and Claire Lamont, 206–20. London: Macmillan; NY: St. Martin's, 1997.

After reviewing the "critical rehabilitation" of *Tit.* as authentically Shakespearean (a process marked by key productions in 1955 by Peter Brook and in 1987 by Deborah Warner [see Dessen, no. 100], and by criticism in 1994 by Alan Hughes [no. 68] and in 1995 by Jonathan Bate [no. 67]), Wells attributes the earlier negative reactions to a lack in *Tit.* of sufficient integration of the violent action into the surrounding dialogue, and a concomitant failure to build into the play hints as to how audience and reader are to respond to the discrepancy. (For an example of this earlier reaction, see Jane S. Carducci, "Shakespeare's *Titus Andronicus*: An Experiment in Expression," *Cahiers Elisabéthains* 31 [1987]: 1-9.) Wells concludes with the suggestion that this manner of handling violent action helps in establishing the chronology of Shakespeare's early plays: he places *Tit.* before *1-2-3 Henry VI*, and dates it in 1590 or before.

See also nos. 67, 68, 69, 92, and 93.

C. Influences; Sources; Historical and Intellectual Backgrounds; Topicality.

71. Bowers, F.T. *Elizabethan Revenge Tragedy, 1587-1642.* Princeton: Princeton Univ. Press, 1940. In chap. 4, 110-18.

In a discussion of revenge tragedy ranging over its background, origins, and later developments, Bowers argues that *Tit.* (based, he believes, on Kyd's *The Spanish Tragedy*, earlier Continental versions of the story in German and Dutch texts—today generally believed to be shortened traveling texts of Shakespeare's play—and a putative Kydian ur-*Hamlet*) follows the model provided by Kyd, especially in revenge by a male relative, a ghost, hesitation, madness, and "Machiavellian" villainy. However, for Bowers, *Tit.* is less successful than *The Spanish Tragedy* from the point of view of motivation for the revenge.

72. Haaker, Ann. "*Non sine causa*: The Use of Emblematic Method and Iconology in the Thematic Structure of *Titus Andronicus*." *Research Opportunities in Renaissance Drama* 13-14 (1972): 143-68.

Haaker draws attention to Shakespeare's deliberate use of Renaissance emblems, consisting of picture, motto, and interpretation, to enforce the play's thematic structure: the picture is represented by onstage character positioning; the motto is articulated by a leading character; and the interpretation is provided by dialogue. Haaker illustrates this approach in a discussion of act one and relates moments in the play to emblem books printed in the 16th century.

73. Kistner, A.L. and M.K. "The Senecan Background of Despair in *The Spanish Tragedy* and *Titus Andronicus*." *Shakespeare Studies* 7 (1974): 1-9.

The authors argue strongly that the influence of Seneca (without the non-Senecan background proposed by some other scholars) is sufficient to account for *Tit.*'s structure and treatment of character. The Kistners present a full list of Senecan elements, in character types (chorus, messenger, nurse, tyrant), language (for instance, *stychomythia*), dramatic structure (5 acts), tone (sensational violence), and language (rhetoric, reflection, philosophical ideas, and foreshadowing).

74. Miola, Robert S. *Shakespeare's Rome.* Cambridge: Cambridge Univ. Press, 1983. Chap. 5, 42–75. Repr. in Kolin (no. 101), 195–224.

In this book, which chronicles how Shakespeare's treatment of Rome changed both as he developed as a playwright and as he dramatized different historical periods of Roman history, Miola argues that in *Tit.* Shakespeare has combined details from different myths to arrange them for his own purposes. The dramatic time of action, in this view, is the Iron Age, an early wilderness settlement stage of social evolution described in Ovid's *Metamorphoses* and Virgil's *Aeneid* and *Georgics*, a time without truth or faith, when violence, greed, and civil discord are rampant; these qualities are all present in the play's depiction of Rome. For Miola, only Lucius is able to take constructive action: he allies himself with the Goths, and returns to the city a wise man capable of effective leadership. (For other studies stressing Ovid's influence, see Jonathan Bate, *Shakespeare and Ovid* [Oxford: Clarendon Press, 1993]; and Heather James, "Cultural Disintegration in *Titus Andronicus*: Mutilating Titus, Vergil and Rome," in *Violence in Drama*, ed. James Redmond, 123–40. Themes in Drama 15. [Cambridge: Cambridge Univ. Press, 1991], which is repr. in Kolin [no. 101] 285–303.)

75. Nevo, Ruth. "Tragic Form in *Titus Andronicus*." In *Further Studies in English Language and Literature*, ed. A.A. Mendilow, 1–18. Jerusalem: Magnes Press, 1973.

Nevo analyzes *Tit.* by dividing it into sections according to Classical rhetorical theory: an opening *protasis* presents the potentially tragic situation and the nature of the character of the protagonist who will be tried by it; an *epitasis* follows, a period of turbulence, and a reversal of the protagonist's initial situation; and the *catastrophe* concludes the play, in which, through the actions of Aaron, Tamora, and Titus, there is total destruction. Although in this view Lucius heals Rome, the note of tragic destruction is dominant: *Tit.* foreshadows *King Lear*.

76. Ray, Sid. "'Rape, I Fear, was Root of Thy Annoy': The Politics of Consent in *Titus Andronicus*." *SQ* 49 (1998): 22–39.

Beginning with recent studies that relate hand severing, amputation, and rape to "early modern ideologies of marriage and monarchy" (22), Ray argues that the play "associates the right of a woman to consent to marriage with the ancient right of the social body to consent to the ruling power of the monarch" (22). Citing Elizabethan public debates, published tracts on marriage, the wedding ceremony in *The Book of Common Prayer*, laws and customs of arranged marriage and the bride's rights, and publications touching on these issues by such authors as Erasmus, John Ponet, Sir John Fortescue, and Sir Thomas Smith, Ray concludes that *Tit.* expresses Shakespeare's progressive politics.

77. **Schlueter, June.** "Rereading the Peacham Drawing." *SQ* 50 (1999): 171–84.

Schlueter rereads the often-discussed Peacham pen-and-ink drawing, which appears on the Longleat manuscript, in the bottom portion of which are some 40 lines of text from *Tit.* and the signature or attribution, "Henricus Peacham." Schlueter proposes that the drawing does not illustrate a scene or scenes from *Tit.*, but, rather, a sequence from *A Very Lamentable Tragedy of Titus Andronicus and the Haughty Empress*, which was performed in Germany by English actors; it was printed, in German, in 1620. Schlueter also proposes that this German play may be a translation of the lost *tittus & vespacia* listed in *Henslowe's Diary*, itself a possible source for Shakespeare's play. In this essay, which reviews the many studies that attempt to correlate the drawing, the signature, and the lines from *Tit.*, Schlueter argues that the first two elements are unconnected to the third.

78. **Spivack, Bernard.** *Shakespeare and the Allegory of Evil.* NY: Columbia Univ. Press, 1958. In chap. 11, 379–86. Repr. Kolin (no. 101), 163–70.

Spivack's historical study chronicles the continued dramatic life of the Vice figure from the allegorical traditions of early-16th-century morality plays down to Shakespeare; such evil characters (Aaron, Richard III, Don John, and Iago) have readily identifiable traits, for they are physically and linguistically lively, they reveal their inner natures to the audience, they enjoy planning and carrying out evil actions, and they are humorous and entirely lacking in regret for their evil. In *Tit.*, Spivack points out, Aaron, chiefly because of his joy in his unmotivated evil and his refusal to repent, and the masque in which Tamora and her sons are named allegorically (5.2), recurs to this long-lived dramatic tradition. (See also later studies that place Aaron in the context of race issues, for example: Emily C. Bartels, "Making More of the Moor: Aaron, Othello, and Renaissance Refashionings of Race," *SQ* 41 [1990]: 433–54; Anthony Gerard Barthelemy, *Black Face Maligned Race* [Baton Rouge, La: Louisiana State Univ. Press, 1987]; and Virginia Mason Vaughan, "The Construction of Barbarism in *Titus Andronicus*," in *Race, Ethnicity, and Power in the Renaissance*, ed. Joyce Green MacDonald, 165–80 [Madison, N.J.: Fairleigh Dickinson Univ. Press, 1997].)

79. Thomas, Vivian. *Shakespeare's Roman Worlds*. London: Routledge: 1989. In chap. 1, 22–39.

According to Thomas, *Tit.* explores the conflict between warfare and civilized life; it carefully and fully evokes a sense of Rome (its common people, government officials, the Capitol as the symbolic center) and its limitations and fragility in the face of warfare. Thomas argues that, although later plays such as *JC, Ant.,* and *Cor.* present Rome with more detailed historical source material, in *Tit.* Shakespeare presents his early sense of the importance of Roman values for civilization. (For an earlier study questioning the proposition that Rome embodies strong positive qualities of law, justice, and political order, see Andrew V. Ettin, "Shakespeare's First Roman Tragedy," *ELH* 37 [1970]: 325–41.)

See also no. 92.

D. Language and Linguistics.

80. Braunmuller, A.R. "Characterization through Language in the Early Plays of Shakespeare and His Contemporaries." In *Shakespeare Man of the Theater,* ed. Kenneth Muir, Jay L. Halio, and D.J. Palmer, 128–47. Newark: Univ. of Delaware Press, 1983.

Braunmuller focuses on the relation between dramatic language and characterization in *Tit.*, and argues that the play differs from contemporaneous plays by other writers, which ignore truly individualistic speech patterns. In Shakespeare, he argues, the individual is given a particular imagery pattern and from this fact audiences infer a definite character who is speaking the words (Braunmuller gives many examples, notably Aaron, who is able to move from one speech pattern to another); however, this externalized use of language diminishes motivation for action, which originates within a character. Braunmuller argues that the play offers instead a structural pattern whereby action links to earlier and later action in an echo pattern.

81. Palmer, D.J. "The Unspeakable in Pursuit of the Uneatable: Language and Action in *Titus Andronicus*." *Critical Quarterly* 14 (1972): 320–39.

For Palmer, the atrocities in *Tit.* are a test of the limits of theater; for instance, Marcus's lament over the ravished Lavinia is a test not only of psychological reaction but of the ability of language to express this reaction. In a detailed reading of the play, Palmer draws attention to Shakespeare's selection of Saturninus as the name of the Emperor, for Saturn's influence is malignant in astrology, and Rome does, in fact, degenerate into barbarism. Palmer argues that language is only one way in which this play expresses its meaning, for groupings of figures, tableaux, movement, and gesture all contribute. Palmer concentrates on one symbol in particular, the "devouring mouth" (the Andronici's burial place; the pit that consumes several characters; Lavinia's mutilated mouth) that speaks and devours (335). In this critic's reading, *Tit.* is filled with references to dramatic art; it moves its audience not so much to compassion as to admiration (in the Elizabethan sense of "wonder" or "amazement").

82. Tricomi, Albert H. "The Aesthetics of Mutilation in *Titus Andronicus*." *Shakespeare Survey* 27 (1974): 11–19.

Tricomi argues that the highly rhetorical language of *Tit.* intensifies the horrors of the play; whereas metaphor typically extends the imaginative world beyond the confines of stage representation, in *Tit.* a contraction takes place. According to this critic's analysis of language, Shakespeare was exploring relations between poetry and event, the powers inherent in metaphor, and he deliberately placed himself, as a writer, in competition with Ovid and Seneca, whom he was attempting to surpass.

See also nos. 85, 86, 90, 95, and 96.

E. Criticism.

83. Broude, Ronald. "Four Forms of Vengeance in *Titus Andronicus*." *Journal of English and Germanic Philology* 78 (1979): 494–507.

Broude isolates four forms that vengeance takes in *Tit.*: the first two, individual actions of human sacrifice and of vendetta, are non-Christian and concern chiefly the sacrifice of Alarbus and Tamora's evil actions against the Andronici; the second two, state justice and divine vengeance, are in accord with Christian teachings and assume an overall condition of order which retribution can disrupt only temporarily. In Broude's view, Titus's appalling revenge is a divinely sanctioned action that provides support for Lucius's celebration of the principles of state justice. (See also Clifford Chalmers Huffman, "*Titus Andronicus*: Metamorphosis and Renewal,' *Modern Language Review* 67 [1972]: 730–41.)

84. Broude, Ronald. "Roman and Goth in *Titus Andronicus*." *Shakespeare Survey* 6 (1970): 27–34.

Broude argues that Elizabethans had positive views of the Goths, admiring particularly their valor, vitality, and integrity; although also admiring Roman qualities of civilization and order (but prey also to vices), they would not have approved of them fully due to 16th-century English antipathy to Roman Catholicism. The play's resolution, whereby the Goths and Romans are united under Lucius, is, in this view, entirely appropriate and aesthetically satisfying.

85. Brower, Reuben A. *Hero and Saint: Shakespeare and the Graeco-Roman Heroic Tradition*. NY: Oxford Univ. Press, 1971. Chap. 4, 173–203.

Brower sees *Tit.* as an interesting but flawed play: it attempts to merge tragedy, Roman history, revenge, horror, epic parody, and Ovidian lyricism. Given this wide variety of material, it is remarkable, he believes, that *Tit.* presents four such notable characters as Titus, Tamora, Aaron, and Lucius, as well as passages of Roman eloquence. For this critic, the play fails to make a dramatic unity of its stark opposites, innocence and evil, civilization and chaos, the disintegration of Rome and of Titus; Lucius, spokesperson for a renewed Rome, is in this view essentially unconnected with the tragic action of the play.

86. Charney, Maurice. *Titus Andronicus*, 104–28. Harvester New Critical Introductions to Shakespeare. Hemel Hempstead: Harvester Wheatsheaf, 1990. Repr. Kolin (no. 101), 261–64.

Following short initial sections on the history of performance from 1594 to 1987 (xiii–xvii) and on literary-critical reception chiefly from 1968 to 1984 (xix–xxii), Charney's introduction and the following six chapters present a sustained, scene-by-scene critical reading of the play. For Charney, *Tit.* is closely linked with *King Lear* "in its emphasis on suffering, madness and the violations of civilized discourse" (4), the last expressed particularly in the struggle between Roman values and barbarism (6), and in the characters Titus and Tamora. Charney consistently illuminates these and other issues by reference to other Shakespeare plays. In chapter 7 (104–21), Charney discusses style, stressing the importance of Ovid, and argues for understanding *Tit.*'s poetic imagery in its dramatic context, and against earlier critics who saw "a large element of undigested narrative poetry that is insufficiently dramatised" (109–10). He illustrates his argument by discussing "blood" in its scenic and verbal presences (111–15) and "sea" ("to indicate passion," 115–18), before concluding with a brief discussion of Lavinia and Renaissance attitudes toward rape (118–21). Charney provides a bibliography (122–26) and an index (127–28).

87. **Cohen, Derek.** *Shakespeare's Culture of Violence.* London: Macmillan; NY: St. Martin's, 1993. Chap. 6, 79–93.

In a book that studies "the cultural and political manifestations of violence in eight Shakespeare plays" (1), Cohen's discussion of *Tit.* focuses on the rape of Lavinia: "the mute and handless Lavinia seeking the means to express herself" (80) is the play's central, haunting image, against which the excesses of language and action stand. Cohen contrasts Lavinia and Tamora in detail (86–90), and understands the black male child of Tamora and Aaron to be a "symbol of great power in the play" (90). In this view, *Tit.* "embraces violence as a way of life" (92) and the logic of violence in the title character offers males a way of preserving their supremacy: by killing their daughters (93).

88. **Eliot, T.S.** "Seneca in Elizabethan Translation." In *Selected Essays.* London: Faber; NY: Harcourt, 1932. Part 2, 51–88 (pagination of this often-reprinted essay may vary).

Eliot's essay of 1927, which is primarily concerned with Seneca and includes discussions of Elizabethan Senecan plays, contains also a polemical denunciation of *Tit.* as "one of the stupidest and most uninspired plays ever written"; Eliot finds it "incredible" to think that Shakespeare had any part in its authorship (67). He argues that the play is hardly Senecan in any true sense of the term, although he concedes that there is ingenuity in the plotting (68). This essay was influential in discussions of *Tit.* that appeared during the middle years of the 20th century. (Eliot elsewhere expressed other views: see, for instance, "Shakespeare and the Stoicism of Seneca [1927]," *Selected Essays*, part 3, 107–20.)

89. **Godshalk, William Leigh.** *Patterning in Shakespearean Drama,* 13–16, 23–41. The Hague: Mouton, 1973.

Godshalk discusses patterns in image, theme, characterization, and action that recur in *Tit.* to convey plot continuity, establish irony, and give significance to dramatic situations. The author gives many examples, among them the recurrence of pairs: locations (for instance, Rome and the forest outside, which represent contrasting ideals); actions (Titus kills one of his children at the beginning and another at the end of the play); and details (Titus's hand, which blessed Lavinia, later kills her). Godshalk points out that such contrastive patterning nevertheless works for continuity: the dismemberment of characters may also signal the reintegration of Rome.

90. **Hunter, G.K.** "Seneca and English Tragedy." In *Dramatic Identities and Cultural Tradition: Studies in Shakespeare and His Contemporaries,* 174–213. Liverpool: Liverpool Univ. Press, 1978. (This essay appeared originally in

Seneca, ed. C.D.N. Costa, 166–204. London and Boston: Routledge and Kegan Paul, 1974.)

After discussing and rejecting the tendency of earlier scholars to treat the influence of Seneca as "a single and homogeneous quality" (177), Hunter argues that it was "possible in the Renaissance to think of Seneca as a man wholly acceptable in his moral outlook, and to view the fables of his plays therefore as wholly defensible didactic structures" (181). Titus is a martyr in a world where justice has disappeared, and gives in to the chaos of this "wilderness of tigers" (188), though he really knows what true justice is. This madness is atoned for, in Hunter's view, by the action of act 5, where justice returns to the world, giving comfort to the good and punishment to the wicked. Hunter provides eight English translations of Seneca's *Thyestes*, lines 391–403, published between 1557 and 1732 (209–13). Hunter compares *Tit.* with *Romeo and Juliet* and *King Lear* in another essay in this volume, "Shakespeare's Earliest Tragedies: *Titus Andronicus* and *Romeo and Juliet*," chap. 14, 319–34.

91. Marienstras, Richard. "The Forest, Hunting, and Sacrifice in *Titus Andronicus*." In *New Perspectives on the Shakespearean World*. Trans. Janet Lloyd. Cambridge: Cambridge Univ. Press, 1985. Chap. 2, 40–47.

In a book considering "the forest and hunting; the relations between the king, the kingdom, his subjects and foreigners; sacrifice and bloodshed" (1), Marienstras studies Shakespeare and two other dramatists of the period, using oppositions, especially those of nature/culture, near/far, continuous series/unique, disruptive event, sacrifice/the sacrilegious, pure/impure, and nurture/poison (1). In this critic's reading, *Tit.* opens with the sacrifice of an enemy of Rome, an act that sets in motion further acts of vengeance. Marienstras argues that Titus causes the calamities of Rome by making three mistakes: he sacrifices Alarbus (which the audience would have seen negatively as adherence to a pagan custom); he refuses the crown; and he sponsors Saturninus. As power falls into enemy hands, chaos (injustice, vengeance) at first holds sway, involving the forest world, which "symbolizes an instinctual, evil, and fatal force" (45), until, in this critic's reading, it is superseded by the new order of Lucius and the Goths. Marienstras studies *Macbeth* (chap. 4, 73–98), *Othello* (chap. 6, 126–59), *The Tempest* (chap. 7, 160–84), Marlowe's *Doctor Faustus* (briefly, 184–85), and John Ford's *'Tis Pity She's A Whore* (chap. 8, 186–201). Marienstras also provides an extensive bibliography covering a wide variety of topics including works of reference, political and social history, history of ideas, dramatic texts, sources and texts of reference, literary studies, and studies on the Elizabethan theater (240–66). (This book first appeared in French in 1981.)

92. Metz, G. Harold. *Shakespeare's Earliest Tragedy: Studies in "Titus Andronicus."* Madison, N.J.: Fairleigh Dickinson Univ. Press; London: Associated Univ. Presses, 1996.

In a series of detailed chapters, Metz surveys the history of the literary-critical and theatrical fortunes of *Tit.* from the earliest records to the 1990s, by which time the play was "reestablished in the Shakespeare canon and ... its theatrical values vindicated" (13). Metz reviews controversies over Shakespeare's authorship (chap. 1, 17-43) and then summarizes earlier scholarship on the following topics: literary criticism published during the 20th century (chap. 2, 45-109); debates about textual revisions and about the earliest texts (chap. 3, 111-24; chap. 4, 125-48); studies of sources, origins, and influences (chap. 5, 150-89), and of the date of composition (chap. 6, 190-97). In chapter 7, Metz describes significant theatrical productions between 1970 and 1994 (199-231). In the last three chapters, the author reviews scholarship on a number of ancillary topics: in chap. 8 (233-47), the Longleat manuscript (also known as the "Peacham drawing") that contains an illustration, c. 1594, "intended to represent action from *Titus Andronicus*" (233); in chap. 9 (248-55), the relation between *Tit.* and Thomas Nashe's prose narrative *The Unfortunate Traveller* (1593); and, in chap. 10 (255-61), the role of music in the play. Metz provides extensive notes (262-98) and a very full bibliography (299-306), together with a proper name index of all the scholars whose publications he has presented (307-09).

93. Price, Hereward T. "The Authorship of *Titus Andronicus*." *Journal of English and Germanic Philology* 42 (1943): 55-81. Repr. Kolin (no. 101), 75-97.

Price's interest in the issue of Shakespeare's authorship leads him to move from vocabulary tests and verbal parallels (to Robert Greene, George Peele, and Christopher Marlowe) to *Tit.*'s dramatic construction, which relies on the principle of contrast in the sequencing of dramatic units, whether plot or character, leading to a binding up and untying of the action in the fifth act. No other playwright of the period, Price argues, maintained such consistently strong control over his material, or portrayed figures like Titus, who falls due to a mixture of good and bad, whose very loyalty makes him vulnerable, and Aaron, a uniquely many-sided character, on the one hand a devil, dissembler, and hypocrite, yet also a loving father, able to speak romantic poetry.

94. Sommers, Alan. "'Wilderness of Tigers': Structure and Symbolism in *Titus Andronicus*." *Essays in Criticism* 10 (1960): 275-89. Repr. Kolin (no. 101), 115-28.

Sommers argues that the murder of Alarbus causes a split that widens out to include the conflict between an ordered Rome and the primitive barbarism of nature; this conflict questions Roman integrity, indeed the value of civilization itself. In Sommers' reading, characters come to prey on each other in a desperate attempt to live. Titus degenerates into a savage as a result of what he suffers, yet his revenge does, indirectly, lead to the restoration of order; he is masterfully portrayed in this early play, and foreshadows later Shakespearean tragic heroes.

95. Tricomi, Albert H. "The Mutilated Garden in *Titus Andronicus*." *Shakespeare Survey* 9 (1976): 89–105.

Tricomi argues that poetic ornament is successfully merged with a "coherent poetic matrix" as well as with the theatrical and thematic dimensions of *Tit.* (103). The earlier parts of the play set up positive associations for such natural terms as "park," "lily," "deer," and "fountain," and these are further associated with Lavinia. In this critic's view, the earlier idyllic atmosphere is destroyed by the fact that the forest is the setting for the tryst held by Tamora and Aaron and, most crucially, by the rape of Lavinia ("the metamorphosis of the pastoral forest is the metamorphosis of Lavinia writ large" [94]); the destroyed world is conveyed symbolically by the bubbling fountain. Tricomi identifies two large image clusters, of animals and mutilated plants (99), and relates them to issues of plotting and the theme of whether "civilized men can withstand the enormity of evil that the world contains and still retain their humanity" (96).

96. Waith, Eugene [M.]. "The Metamorphosis of Violence in *Titus Andronicus*." *Shakespeare Studies* 10 (1957): 39–49. Repr. in Waith's *Patterns and Perspectives in English Renaissance Drama*, 41–54. Newark: Univ. of Delaware Press, 1988. Repr. Kolin (no. 101), 99–113.

Waith argues that the dramatic violence and lofty literary style of *Tit.* are related by the presence of Ovid, especially the stories of Lucretia, Appius and Virginia, and Philomela. In this view, the emotions that destroy the characters lead to Ovidian metamorphoses (expressed in the imagery of metamorphosis that Waith analyzes) so that the play is both intensely involved in dramatic situations and also detached from them. In this reading, *Tit.* opposes moral/political chaos to the uniting forces of friendship and sound government; but the author feels that the unique achievement of the play is its success in showing that characters can go past their personal disintegration, even past the criteria of praise and blame: the appropriate audience response is therefore neither approval nor disapproval, but rather wonder (*"admiratio"*).

97. Willbern, David. "Rape and Revenge in *Titus Andronicus*." *English Literary Renaissance* 8 (1978): 159–82. Repr. Kolin (no. 101), 171–94.

Willbern's psychoanalytical approach discusses sexual, sadistic, and symbolic elements in *Tit.*, a play that enacts male fantasies of the rape and rescue of the "female" (daughter, mother, city); the play's action moves towards rescuing the female from the evil, devouring mother, who must be replaced by a benevolent one. The play is, in this view, consistently hostile towards women: Tamora portrays the orality of the pre-Oedipal destructive mother (expressed symbolically in images of pit, mouth, violated vagina, womb, tomb, and Hell), and Lavinia's rape brings together visually a cluster of closely related symbols including sexuality, death, dismemberment. Willbern also discusses several of the male roles in *Tit.*: Aaron tries but fails to maintain male integrity in the face of female peril; and Lucius, who is not a traitor, succeeds in a project of revenge that is retaliation against Rome.

98. Wynne-Davies, Marion. "'The Swallowing Womb': Consumed and Consuming Women in *Titus Andronicus*." In *The Matter of Difference: Materialist Feminist Criticism of Shakespeare*, ed. Valerie Wayne, 129–51. Ithaca: Cornell Univ. Press, 1991.

Wynne-Davies sees Tamora's sexual relationship with Aaron, and her bearing of a black child, as a challenge to Roman patriarchal society, which needed to control women's sexual expression. From this critic's feminist perspective, the play's imagery (of womb, pit, and wooded valley) associates female sexuality with danger and corruption for men, even with the threat of castration, and the play's action shows Rome as a mutilated female body which the male Roman principle of primogeniture is powerless to heal.

99. Zeeveld, W. Gordon. *The Temper of Shakespeare's Thought*, 205–10. New Haven: Yale Univ. Press, 1974.

Zeeveld rejects a simple moral reading of *Tit.* that sees Rome and Romans as superior to the Goths and Moors, arguing instead that both sides have positive and negative qualities: Tamora, though evil, yet has reasons for her actions; Aaron, though devilish, has positive human instincts; Titus, the preserver of Rome, must also be a private revenger whose actions undermine the order he would preserve; and Lucius, the future Emperor, justly vilifies Aaron, yet wants to act barbarously to torment his enemy. For this critic, any effective civility in the play's Rome is blotted out by Roman barbarousness.

See also nos. 31 and 101.

F. Stage History and Performance Criticism; Film Version.

100. Dessen, Alan C. *Titus Andronicus*. Shakespeare in Performance. Manchester and NY: Manchester Univ. Press, 1989.

Dessen surveys the historical record of a wide variety of stage performances of *Tit.* and relates them to the text's strengths and weaknesses. In Chap. 1 (5–23), the author discusses 17th-century allusions to *Tit.* and performances from Edward Ravenscroft's (1678) to Peter Brook's "landmark production of 1955" (1) starring Laurence Olivier. Here, as in the detailed discussions of post–1958 productions such as those by Gerald Freedman (NY Shakespeare Festival, 1967; chap. 2, 24–29) and Deborah Warner (Royal Shakespeare Company, 1987; chap. 3, 57–69), Dessen assesses the choices of directors (to stylize or not; to seek realism; to focus on bizarre features, possibly to treat the play as burlesque) and the effects of these choices on the audience's enjoyment and understanding. In chapters 4 and 5, Dessen focuses on the presentation of Titus (chap. 4, 70–89), commenting that no one "cares what happens to a cruel, stupid, reactionary old man" [72]); and the staging of the final scene (chap. 5, 90–110), where "the densest concentration of ... problems and anomalies" occurs (90). In the "Conclusion" (111–15), the author stresses ways directors have avoided unwanted laughter from the audience by cutting, adjusting, and stylizing, or, conversely, actually staging the atrocities; he acknowledges, however, that, if the play is to live on, some changes to the original text are necessary (115). Dessen provides a bibliography (116–17) and, in an appendix (118–20), lists of significant 20th-century productions and of the companies (with their principal actors) he has discussed.

100a. Taymor, Julie, director. *Titus.* 1999.

In this carnivalized adaptation of *Tit.* for the screen, Anthony Hopkins portrays a faithful but myopic Titus, while Jessica Lange creates a Tamora who is strong and sexual enough to be convincing as the author of Titus's downfall. Sets, costumes, and music are syncretistic blends from every period in history, representing Shakespeare's study of the horrors set in motion by the impulse to revenge as both timeless and timely. Harry Lennix's Aaron is a villain rich in the multiple dimensions of human love and hatred. Taymor's film, though intensely visual, also manages to give the language its full due. The DVD provides, as well, hours of commentary on the production from Taymor, the stars, and the music director, Eliot Goldenthal.

See also nos. 86, 92, and 101.

G. Teaching and Collection of Essays.

101. Kolin, Philip C., ed. *"Titus Andronicus": Critical Essays*. NY and London: Garland Publishing, Inc., 1995.

Kolin introduces the volume with *"Titus Andronicus* and the Critical Legacy" (Part 1, 3–55), which surveys "some significant trends and specific critics identified with them" (7) and adds specific groupings of criticism focused on Lavinia (19–26), Tamora (26–30), Aaron (30–34), Lucius (34–37), and Rome (37–40), before discussing essays on specific performances and performance traditions (41–48). The editor provides a full bibliography (48–55) for this comprehensive introduction. Kolin reprints the chosen critical essays in part 2 (59–372) and a variety of performance reviews and review-essays "informed by critical studies" (41) from the 17th century to the 1990s in many countries, not only England and the United States, but also Europe, China, and Japan, in part 3 (375–518). This book, which is not indexed, reprints a number of essays annotated in the present volume.

H. Bibliographies.

102. Sajdak, Bruce T., ed. *Shakespeare Index: An Annotated Bibliography of Critical Articles on the Plays 1959–83*. 2 vols. Vol. 1, Citations and Author Index. Vol. 2, Character, Scene, and Subject Indexes. Millwood, NY: Kraus International Publications, 1992.

Sajdak seeks to provide the student with a means to "quickly locate, amongst the thousands of possible sources, those few most relevant articles on specific ideas, characters, or scenes" (1.xi). He provides a statement of scope, a list of sources he consulted (xiii–xvii), and a guide on how to use the *Index* (xxi–xxii). Sajdak divides the *Index* into 48 chapters (arranged chronologically by date of publication), initially by research area, then by play title (arranged by period, genre, and title). For each entry, Sajdak gives full publication information and an annotation. There are indexes for authors and, beginning with vol. 2, for character (803–1033), scene (1035–1197), and subject (1199–1765), with extensive subdivisions. *Tit.* is covered in 1.703–10, items UU 1–67. This *Index* does not include chapters in books unless these were published separately as articles.

103. White, R.S. "*Titus Andronicus* and *Romeo and Juliet*." In *Shakespeare: A Bibliographical Guide*, New Edition, ed. Stanley Wells, 181–88 and 196–98. Oxford: Clarendon Press, 1990.

This volume, a rewritten, updated version of the first edition (1973), aims to provide a selectively critical guide to the best in Shakespearean scholarship and criticism. White's discussion of *Tit.* (182–88) surveys 20th-century approaches, distinguishing several main streams for critical comment, and giving examples of specific titles and authors: (1) after 1940, the Fredson Bowers view, placing *Tit.* in the tradition of the revenge plays and stressing the physical atrocities and the motiveless villainy of Aaron; (2) the Tillyard tradition, stressing his "Elizabethan World View" and its emphasis on approved order, control, and succession; (3) the poetic reading, emphasizing "complaint," "lamentation," and Ovidian material; (4) the play as melodrama or parody; (5) the ethical approach, stressing the idea of justice; and (6) the aesthetic approach.

V. JULIUS CAESAR

A. Editions.

104. Daniell, David, ed. *Julius Caesar*. The Arden Shakespeare, 3rd series. Walton-on-Thames: Thomas Nelson, 1998.

Daniell's introduction (1–147) consists of sections on the play, *JC* in London, 1599 (a historical, cultural, and theatrical context), language, structure, criticism, performance, and text. The introduction also offers 20 illustrations. The footnotes to the text of the play are fuller and more informative than in most critical editions; they are usually lexical, or accounts of what has been said about points of controversy. Insights about critical questions are sometimes offered. The appendices comprise excerpts from North's Plutarch (323–71), "Julius Caesar," "Marcus Brutus" including the "Comparison between Dion and Brutus," and "Marcus Antonius"; tables (372–85) of Abbreviations and References (the References are in effect a reading list); a useful index. Occasionally Daniell misses something significant (the source for the allegation of Caesar's deafness, e.g.) but on balance this is, with no.106, one of the two best separate editions of the play at the time of this writing. It replaces the Arden edition (1955, often reprinted) by T.S. Dorsch, which should be consulted for some points (e.g., history of the authorship controversy) not covered in Daniell's edition.

105. Johnson, S.F., ed. *The Tragedy of Julius Caesar*. The Pelican Shakespeare. Baltimore, Md.: Pelican Books, 1960.

Johnson's brief introduction (15–25) makes several original points about the play that later scholarship and criticism have been able to build on: focus falls on character, tone, style, and moral ambiguity. The text is conservative and uncluttered; conventional act-and-scene division is indicated, but asterisks inserted at the beginnings of scenes indicate scene division as Shakespeare probably intended it (e.g., 4.2 and 4.3 are a continuous scene in this notation). The notes are mainly lexical (including puns); a few useful facts about Roman customs also are included. This unpretentious but excellent edition is a good place for beginning students to start serious work on *JC*. The concise and incisive introduction and some of the excellent notes should be of interest to scholars, as well. The two limitations of the apparatus are the relative neglect of Shakespeare's response to Plutarch and a total neglect of theatrical values in the play. The General Editor, Alfred Harbage, offers some help with original staging of Shakespeare's plays (11–12), together with a basic and sensible life of Shakespeare (7–11) and an introduction to textual questions in the Shakespeare canon.

106. Spevack, Marvin, ed. *Julius Caesar.* The New Cambridge Shakespeare. Cambridge: Cambridge Univ. Press, 1988.

The text itself in this edition is more scholarly than that of any other critical edition of *JC* in the 20th century; it goes back in the textual tradition as far as the 17th century to rationalize the adopted readings. The commentary notes on this text are nearly all lexical from *The Oxford English Dictionary* or grammatical from E.A. Abbott (*A Shakespearian Grammar*, 3rd edition, 1870), and Wilhelm Franz (*Die Sprache Shakespeares in Vers und Prosa*, 4th edition, 1939), deliberately eschewing aesthetic or other bias. The introduction is more detailed, especially regarding date (1–6) and stage history (31–45, including 8 black-and-white pictures), than in any separate edition before it in the 20th century. Other sections in the conservative introduction are "Sources" (Spevack goes against the current trend by dealing only with Plutarch); and "The Play": "Frame," "Structure," "Theme," and "Persons and Politics." Appendices analyze the text (148–53) and reprint extensive excerpts from North's Plutarch ("Julius Caesar" and "Marcus Brutus," but not "Marcus Antonius," 154–83). A one-page "Reading List" completes the apparatus.

> See also no. 1, above, in which *JC* has some remarkably fine lexical notes and also an innovative reading at 1.2.124–25. Bevington's introduction emphasizes the position of the play between history and tragedy, the ambivalence of the political issues, and a sequence of protagonists in the mural-like design of the play.

B. Dating and Textual Studies.

107. Bowers, Fredson. "The Copy for Shakespeare's *Julius Caesar.*" *South Atlantic Bulletin* (now *South Atlantic Review*) 43, no. 4 (November 1978): 23–36.

A review of the controversy over the duplicate revelation of Portia's death in 4.3 (4.2 in Bowers' formulation) is the starting point for Bowers' argument that the copy text for F1 *JC* was a fair transcript of Shakespeare's foul papers, a transcript which was (as anomalies in exits and stage directions show) *not* the promptbook, but the clean copy that would normally be the basis for early rehearsals of a play. Bowers posits that into this copy were later (probably in rehearsal) inserted revisions of two kinds in 2.1 (one introduces the character of Ligarius into the play), and that also inserted was a rewriting of the original version of the revelation in 4.3 of Portia's death, with an indication (ignored by the F1 compositor) to delete the version in which Messala makes the revelation. Bowers sees Shakespeare as responsible for the revisions, but thinks they did not necessarily go to the F1 compositor in his handwriting; they *were* in a hand that differed from the hand of the copy for the rest of the play. This article, which assumes close knowledge of the play, can be regarded as authoritative, for the present. Even if its reasoning should later be modified, it will have shown that the prevalent notion that *JC* is a clean text without difficulties is plainly incorrect.

108. Schanzer, Ernest. "Thomas Platter's Observations on the Elizabethan Stage." *Notes & Queries* n.s. 3 [vol. 201] (1956): 465-67.

This note (by a native speaker of German) points out that other scholars, including Dorsch (see no. 104), have mistranslated the "slovenly form of Alemannic" (465) in which Thomas Platter, a traveler from Switzerland, expressed his eyewitness account of performances of a tragedy on Julius Caesar and of other plays in London in September 1599. The errors, Schanzer explains, have led to a number of misconceptions about the physical features of the Elizabethan stage and about the likelihood that what Platter saw on 21 September in the afternoon was indeed Shakespeare's *JC*. The play that Platter saw had 15 characters in it (not 15 actors playing parts, as scholars have incorrectly assumed). Shakespeare's play has 45 speaking parts. Schanzer offers evidence that Shakespeare's play should be dated between fall 1598 and fall 1599. Even if we join Schanzer in discounting Platter's evidence—for the reason that it may point to a hypothetical performance of another *JC* at the Rose Theater (also a thatched playhouse) on 21 September 1599—this document from the late 16th century is important to students of the Elizabethan theater. Schanzer's note is a valuable challenge to the virtually universal assumption that the Platter account, first published by Gustav Binz in *Anglia* in 1899, settles the question of the date of *JC* definitively. For a book-length argument that *JC* was the first play put on in the new Globe Theater on June 12, 1599, see Steve Sohmer, *Shakespeare's Mystery Play: The Opening of the Globe Theatre*. Manchester, England, and NY: Manchester Univ. Press, 1999. Sohmer uses evidence from almanacs, the calendar controversy, liturgical sources, and astrology to fix the likely date. The book is controversial, but, as Stanley Wells says in a "Foreword," it is clearly worthy of serious attention.

See also nos. 104–106.

C. Influences; Sources; Historical and Intellectual Backgrounds; Topicality.

109. Brower, Reuben A. "The Discovery of Plutarch." In *Hero and Saint: Shakespeare and the Graeco-Roman Heroic Tradition*, 204–38. Oxford: Clarendon Press, 1971.

In this chapter, the heroic language of *JC* and the stature of characters in the play are seen in terms of Classical heroism from Homer forward, as relayed to Shakespeare by Plutarch, especially the "hero and saint" touches lent to the character of Plutarch's Stoic Brutus by Sir Thomas North. Shakespeare's Brutus is seen as "an image of the Renaissance hero in perfection" (235); Cassius, Caesar, and Antony also are glanced at in light of Plutarchan heroism. Brower admits that Shakespeare would have seen the tragic potential in the assassination of Caesar without Plutarch's coloring, but he insists that Plutarch is clearly a "resource" for this potential as well as a "source" for the story. This chapter is a penetrating analysis of Plutarch (who valued Homer highly and quoted him in the "Life of Brutus"), Amyot, and North, as well as of *JC*. In an age of cynicism about Shakespeare's Brutus, Brower's positive view in historical perspective effectively swims against the tide of opinion.

110. Bryant, J.A., Jr. "*Julius Caesar* from a Euripidean Perspective." *Comparative Drama* 16 (1982): 97–111.

Bryant reasons that the "problems" that have been seen in *JC* (i.e., lack of a protagonist, whether this is a tragedy, how we are to judge the assassination) largely disappear if we place the play beside late Euripidean tragedy, especially *Hecuba* and *Iphigeneia at Aulis*. Shakespeare could have known both of these plays in Erasmus' Latin translations, Bryant points out; also relevant, he adds, is *The Bacchae*, which Shakespeare could not have known but which resembles *JC* in the blindness of Brutus and Pentheus to a supernatural dimension in their respective cultures-in-flux. The focus falls on Brutus and his strictly rational view of historical causality, but Cassius and Caesar receive attention, as well. To Bryant, the major point of contact among *Iphigeneia at Aulis*, *Hecuba*, and *JC* is human sacrifice to the gods, which causes outrage among mortals. Accordingly, a major theme of *JC* is a Euripidean theme: "the folly of affirming with certainty in ontological matters" (105). Bryant concludes that Shakespeare's vision in *JC* is more ironic than in his other tragedies—so that this tragedy (he insists that *JC* is not a "problem play" in the sense that Schanzer [no. 201] meant) resembles late Euripidean tragedies rather than the tragedies of Aeschylus or Sophocles.

111. Clarke, M[artin] L[owther]. *The Noblest Roman: Marcus Brutus and his Reputation..* Aspects of Greek and Roman Life. Ithaca: Cornell Univ. Press, 1981.

The first chapter of this book, "Brutus in History" (9–78), is a thorough account of Marcus Junius Brutus, the assassin of Gaius Julius Caesar, as he was in fact and as he seemed (ambivalent then as he is to us now) to his contemporaries. The rest of the book on later portrayals of Brutus (7 pp. on Shakespeare's *JC*) is superficial and out of date, and so cannot be recommended; however, Chapter 1 is a responsible and lucid distillation of ancient authorities, which anyone interested in the background of *JC* could benefit from reading with the play.

112. Jones, Emrys. "Shakespeare and Euripides (II): Tragic Sentiment." In *The Origins of Shakespeare*, 108–18. Oxford: Clarendon Press, 1977.

After brief remarks on elements in *JC* that can be seen to be modeled on scenes or groups of scenes in *2 Henry VI, Richard III, 1 Henry IV,* and Greene's *James IV,* this chapter focuses on the apparent imitation in the quarrel scene (4.3) of the quarrel between Menelaus and Agamemnon in *Iphigeneia at Aulis*. Jones emphasizes that the emotional or tonal structure of the scene is what Shakespeare borrowed, as brothers who love one another quarrel bitterly and then are reconciled. This scene in *JC* (or its source in Euripides and/or Erasmus' translation of the play into Latin) was imitated several times in the 17th and 18th centuries, as Jones observes. The chapter is an important example of Jones's innovative perception that a source may be identified for a form or even a tone, as well as for words or plot situations.

113. Liebler, Naomi Conn. " 'Thou Bleeding Piece of Earth': The Ritual Ground of *Julius Caesar*." *Shakespeare Studies* 14 (1981): 175–96.

Liebler identifies Plutarch's "Life of Romulus," the first Roman life in Plutarch's *Lives*, as the source for the morally significant use of the ritual of the Lupercalia in *JC*. Liebler recognizes that the Lupercal was a fertility rite that was performed to guarantee abundance in Rome; but, in the play, Caesarism is about to turn that Rome into a sickly wasteland. She recalls that important changes in the Lupercalian rituals were ordained by the historical Julius Caesar in 44 BCE; Marcus Antonius was appointed one of the *"Luperci Iulii"* as Caesar tried to appropriate the Lupercalia to his own political purposes. Liebler proceeds to explain in these historical circumstances Brutus's desire to elevate the assassination to a purgative ritual. It is not incidental, she thinks, that the play begins with the Lupercal. One of the portents, blood drizzling on the Capitol in 2.2., is found only in "Romulus." She points out also that "Romulus" leads toward the traditional Fisher King-Holy Grail ritual and the Elizabethan folk survivals of that ritual. This highly original and astute approach is the best of several that have proceeded (ultimately) from Brents Stirling's "Or Else This Were a Savage Spectacle" *PMLA* 56 (1951): 765–74. Liebler's interpretation makes coherent sense of the whole play, not just of Brutus.

114. Miola, Robert S. "*Julius Caesar* and the Tyrannicide Debate." *Renaissance Quarterly* 38 (1985): 271–89.

Constructing an extensively documented account of the theory of tyrannicide in Antiquity, the Middle Ages, and the Renaissance, Miola uses it to explicate many disputed passages in the play. He concludes that the moral ambiguity in the play reflects the vigor of the debate about whether one may assassinate a tyrant who has no title to the throne, as opposed to one who has a title but is tyrannous in use of power. Miola sees that both kinds of tyrant are found in Shakespeare's Caesar, yet Shakespeare's Caesar is not an egregious tyrant in his actions (as contrasted to Richard III and Macbeth). So the ambivalence deepens. Miola interprets the many invocations of the gods in the play to mean that the cosmos does not approve the assassination. In his view, the conspirators are portrayed as self-seeking. He brings forward the moral point that, when the upshot would be worse than the alleged tyranny, tyrannicide was forbidden; and we see in Antony's soliloquy about civil strife a foreshadowing of the evils yet to come, civil war (act 5) and Proscription (4.1) among them. This article is very thorough in citing backgrounds, and only a bit less so in citing modern secondary sources. It is a good place to put *JC* into a moral context.

115. Miola, Robert S. "*Julius Caesar*: Rome Divided." In *Shakespeare's Rome*, 76–115. Cambridge: Cambridge Univ. Press, 1983.

In this interpretation of *JC*, various characters either try to defy the movement of history or vainly try to make themselves the prime movers of history. In a Virgilian reading of the play, Miola sees Roman history as, like Aeneas, *"fata profugus"* (*Aeneid* I, 2), impelled by fate; though men play their roles in history, they do not control it. Virgil and a number of successors, including Plutarch, are shown to see history as fated (n. 25).

Themes that appear elsewhere in Miola's book are present in his analysis of this play: e.g., the role of the family as metaphor for the state and at the same time antagonist to the state; the sense that in deceiving others (the conspiracy, Antony's pose of friendship with his enemies), Romans deny their true selves. In one of the best readings in the chapter, Cassius' vision of himself as an alter-Aeneas carrying Caesar on his shoulder from the peril of the Tiber (1.2) is said to be a perverse distortion of Virgilian *pietas*. *Romanitas* is said to be a cold and all-demanding commitment to the State at the expense of one's private values, and indeed of one's humanity. In Miola's view, Shakespeare gives a hint in *JC* that he will eventually reject the lifestyle of Rome on humanistic grounds.

116. Miola, Robert S. "Shakespeare and His Sources: Observations on the Critical History of *Julius Caesar*." *Shakespeare Survey* 40 (1988), 69–76.

This essay begins with three pages of philosophical and semantic consideration of the plethora of terms for "source": "influence," "tradition," "subtext," "context", "background," "antecedent," "analogue," and others. The treatment that follows of *JC* in relation to North's Plutarch is arranged historically at first, then logically, as it carries over some of the categories to suggest how the play took shape in Shakespeare's mind in given passages. Miola sees Shakespeare as freely altering his sources for the play, regarding North as a subtext. This profound essay is valuable reading for anyone concerned with how artists work with "sources" to create art. It makes good points about *JC*, but should not be regarded as a comprehensive study of the play and its "sources."

117. Parker, Barbara L. "'A Thing Unfirm': Plato's *Republic* and Shakespeare's *Julius Caesar*." *SQ* 44 (1993): 30–43.

This essay sees the political syndrome of *JC* as a reflection of the political syndrome that Plato expounds in the *Republic*: the guardian of the state turns away from reason and toward will and passion, which leads to demagoguery and eventually to tyranny. The author notes that a carpenter and a cobbler are linked in the *Republic*, as they are in *JC* 1.1, and that the strategy of Antony's oration is prefigured in Plato's account of the demagogue; there are many other parallels. The question of direct or indirect access is left open. This fully documented and percipient argument places this article among the best studies of a background to the play beyond Plutarch.

118. Ribner, Irving. "Political Issues in *Julius Caesar*." *Journal of English and Germanic Philology* 56 (1957): 10–22.

This scholarly article considers the issue of monarchy vs. republic and oligarchy. It asserts that *JC* is not about the misguided assassination of a monarch, but about a military hero (Caesar) who dies because he would be king. The tension between tyranny and kingship is a second issue discussed here. A third is private vs. public commitments; a fourth is the "mixed state" (21) which, following Aristotle's *Politics,* proposes a combination of monarchy, aristocracy, and republic. Despite the prominence of Caesar in this schema, Ribner believes that Shakespeare turned toward Brutus as the more dramatic character. Ribner defends Brutus at just the period of *JC* criticism in which denigration of him rose to fashion. Ribner's view of Caesar is traceable to Renaissance Caesar plays, of which Ribner cites several. The essay also considers a background to *JC* in the political issues of the last years of Elizabeth I's reign. This essay can be taken as representative of a large body of criticism that sees the play as a two-man action and sides with either Brutus (here) or Caesar.

118a. Rose, Mark. "Conjuring Caesar: Ceremony, History, and Authority in 1599." *English Literary Renaissance* 19 (1989): 291-304.

This essay interprets elements prominent in the first half of *JC* as allusions to the struggle in the 1590s between Puritans and English Church authorities about "ceremonies," including vestments, statuary, rituals, holidays, portents, and exorcism. The point is emphasized that anyone in Shakespeare's audience in 1599 would be struck by familiar English religious controversy portrayed in ancient Rome. The conspirators, except Brutus, are said to be anti-ceremony, while Caesar and his associates adhere to respect for ceremony. Brutus' authority forces a certain ceremonious character on the assassination. The "mysterious" dimension of the world of the play is said to proceed from and heighten the portrayal of the controversy over ceremony in the action. The magical becomes "embedded" in history as the play progresses. There are comments late in the essay on the replacement of papist "ceremonies" in England with iconography of Elizabeth I, including some hints in *JC* itself. Cf. David Kaula. "'Let us be Sacrificers': Religious Motifs in *Julius Caesar.*" *Shakespeare Studies* 14 (1981): 197-214; also Liebler, no. 113.

118b. Teague, Frances. "Letters and Portents in *Julius Caesar* and *King Lear.*" *Shakespeare Yearbook* 3 (1992): 87-104.

An intertextual analysis of 1.3 of *JC* (and other scenes in the play before the assassination) with *Lear* 1.2, Plutarch, and Sidney's *Arcadia* throws light on *JC* and indeed on all four of the intertexts. The forged letters of *JC* 1.3 (not forged in Plutarch) recur in the forged letter of *Lear* 1.2, and the ambiguous portents in 1.3 and elsewhere in *JC* also are an element in the *Lear* scene, making it clear, in Teague's view, that Shakespeare rewrote two motifs from *JC* in writing *Lear.*

119. Vawter, Marvin L. "'Division 'tween Our Souls': Shakespeare's Stoic Brutus." *Shakespeare Studies* 7 (1974): 173-96.

Vawter sees Shakespeare's Brutus as a portrait of the Stoic Wise Man, one who disjoins mind from heart and body: Brutus neglects food, sleep, and carnal intimacy (2.1) in favor of rational arguments for killing a friend, and he also suppresses emotion systematically. The portrait here is constructed from close reading of passages which the tradition has interpreted differently: from the "soul/sole" pun in 1.1 to "Brutus with himself at war" (1.2), to the confrontation between Brutus and Portia in 2.1, and the sickness imagery in the play. Vawter posits that Shakespeare knew the anti-Stoic tradition that can be traced to Cicero (who, he points out, has sometimes been called a Stoic, but was critical of Stoicism). The difficulty with such a reading is that it makes Brutus a caricature, not a character. Indeed, we might say that Brutus is a failed Stoic, and that his failure makes him a whole person. This stricture considered, the article is a very intelligent approach to the play, philosophical, not political; it is an overstatement of a profound approach to *JC*.

120. Velz, John W. "Clemency, Will, and Just Cause in *Julius Caesar*." *Shakespeare Survey* 22 (1969): 109-18.

The argument here is that *JC* is informed by a passage in Seneca's *De clementia*, which distinguishes between valid kings and tyrants by portraying the latter as wronging others at will, while the former are harsh only for just cause. In this article, the Senecan passage is used as a guide to the politico-moral issues of *JC*; a detailed analysis concludes that Shakespeare exploits the tension between kingship and tyranny as, respectively, Caesar's self image and the conspirators' view of him.

120a. Williams, George Walton. "Antique Romans and Modern Danes in *Julius Caesar* and *Hamlet*." *Literature and Nationalism*, ed. Vincent Newey and Ann Thompson. 41-55. Liverpool: Liverpool Univ. Press, 1991.

Williams perceives that, as the spirit of Pompey hovers fictively over the action of *JC*, referred to in acts 1, 3, and 5, the spirit of Julius Caesar hovers over the action of *Hamlet*, referred to in acts 1, 3, and 5. This analogy is fully explored in the essay, which extends to a comparison of Brutus with Hamlet, notably in 1.2. of the respective plays and in the closet scene of *Hamlet*. The argument eventually reaches out to Lucius Junius Brutus as well. A number of perceptions are conveyed only in the learned notes. This is the most probing of the essays that have commented on the peculiar allusions to Julius Caesar and to *JC* in *Hamlet*.

See also nos. 35, 39, 115, and 137.

D. Language and Linguistics.

121. Fuzier, Jean. "Rhetoric versus Rhetoric: A Study of Shakespeare's *Julius Caesar* III.2." *Cahiers Élisabéthains* 5 (Avril 1974): 25–65.

This is a detailed and technical analysis of the orations of Brutus and Antony in 3.2, as built from the Classical rhetorical figures that appear in Renaissance treatises and schoolbooks. Shakespeare is shown to be a master of the formulas and their uses in oratory. The article is therefore also an introduction to the study of Renaissance figures of speech and of rhetorical strategy generally. The learned notes and appended lists of figures of speech also assist such study, as does the bibliography. Brutus' oration is so sculpted that it can be, and is, laid out in a three-page diagram that accounts for every word. Antony's speech is seen as less technical but equally at home among the rhetorical devices of oratory. Fuzier shows that, between them, Antony and Brutus use 66 of the approximately 200 figures of speech that a Renaissance writer would have studied in school. This is a formidable analysis and should be read with a *JC* text open beside it, but it is lucid and entirely comprehensible. One emerges with respect for the power of traditional rhetoric, a sense of Brutus' Stoic restraint (even unappealing stiffness), and a sense of Antony's deviousness. The comparison between the two speeches is masterful. There is an *excursus* on Brutus' Stoicism as reflected in his choice of figures and a thoughtful reflection on why Shakespeare chose prose for Brutus and verse for Antony. Of those who have found Brutus' oration unappealing by comparison with Antony's, Fuzier is the most documentary, the most persuasive.

122. Velz, John W. "*Orator* and *Imperator* in *Julius Caesar*: Style and the Process of Roman History." *Shakespeare Studies* 15 (1982): 55–75.

The focus in this stylistic analysis is on the manipulative techniques of the orator, here rhetorical questions and *ad hominem* argument, and on the contrasting address of the commanding officer, suitably imperative, not persuasive but declarative and commanding. The thesis is that oratory and the emotions it stirs are the energizer of historical change in the world of the play, and the *Imperium* is the goal of history. The detailed analysis shows that oratory is evident not only in 3.2, but nearly ubiquitous in the first three acts of the play—except in Caesar, who (though Plutarch called him the second man in Rome for oratory) restricts himself to the *imperator*'s style before the *Imperium* is in his hands. Late in the play Octavius is seen to show signs of a tactful variation on Caesar's blunt style, suggesting that Octavius has the potential to retain power in a world where oratory creates political opportunities.

See also nos. 119, 124, 131, 132, 138, 139, 151a, 152, and 153.

E. Criticism.

123. Blits, Jan H. *The End of the Ancient Republic: Essays on "Julius Caesar."* Durham, N.C.: Carolina Academic Press, 1982.

The four close readings in this book (the first two of which appeared in 1981 in respectively *Interpretation* and *The Journal of Politics*) place emphasis on questions of character and ethics: Chapter 1 focuses on the meaning and limitations of manliness and friendship in *JC*; Chapter 2 argues for the prefiguration in 1.1 of the collapse of the Republic, in the preference for the personal instead of public spiritedness; Chapter 3 deals with Brutus's strengths and weaknesses as a "republican"; Chapter 4 outlines Caesar's attempts in 1.2 and 2.2 at a self-apotheosis that adumbrates the self-declared divinity of the Caesars to come. Chapter 4, though argued at the greatest length, considers too subtextually and is the least convincing of the four. The documentation is more likely to be primary than secondary in this book; the reader will need to supply the interpretive criticism of the 1970s, which is largely ignored. This book is a suitable place for beginners to grasp, and for scholars to refine their understanding of, the political and historical issues of the play.

124. Bonjour, Adrien. *The Structure of "Julius Caesar."* Liverpool: Liverpool Univ. Press, 1958. Repr. n.p.: Folcroft Press, 1970.

This slender (81 pages) but ambitious book lays out three structural principles that provide coherence to *JC*: balance in character and role between Brutus and Caesar; the repetition of motifs (the supernatural ["superstition"], suicide, and sleep); and recurrent verbal imagery of rise and fall. Bonjour can be said to have opened a door for other commentators (see Rabkin [no. 134] and Velz, [no. 140]) into the complexities of a play that is not as simple as it was once thought to be.

125. Brockbank, [J.] Philip. "*Julius Caesar* and the Catastrophes of History." In *On Shakespeare: Jesus, Shakespeare and Karl Marx and Other Essays*, 122-39. Oxford: Basil Blackwell, 1989.

Brockbank applies catastrophe theory—the analysis of a dynamic equilibrium that builds to instability ("on the cusp") and then to catastrophic divergence—to the history and drama that meet in Shakespeare's play. The essay is philosophical, yet informal, and it ranges broadly to embrace Georg Büchner's *Dantons Tod* and Antonio Gramsci's *Prison Notebooks*, religion (the creation and slaying of gods), and psychoanalysis, as well as history and politics in the play. The essay is wise, paradoxical, and intellectually provocative, e.g., in its application of the theory to Brutus' soliloquy (134-35).

126. Edwards, Philip. *Shakespeare: A Writer's Progress.* London and NY: Oxford Univ. Press Opus Books, 1986.

This brief, deft comment on *JC* (132–33) defends Brutus and Cassius from charges that they are respectively self-deceiving and conniving. In this book, intended for students and the general public, a defense of Cassius rests on interpreting the "He" in "He would not humour me" (1.2.315) as referring to Caesar. Of Brutus, it is said, "It is the enterprise to which he commits himself that makes all his best qualities appear meretricious."

127. Fortin, René E. "*Julius Caesar*: An Experiment in Point of View." *SQ* 19 (1968): 341–47.

The moral ambivalence other critics had noticed in *JC* is interpreted here as the theme of the play, epistemology: judgment is not absolute but rests in the point of view. Mildred E. Hartsock ("The Complexity of *Julius Caesar*." *PMLA* 81 [1966]: 56–62), argued earlier than Fortin that the play is about relativity in values. Fortin's article shows that various characters are seen in various ways by multiple observers; this structural principle makes for irony throughout. It follows in Fortin's rationale that, if the character sees others in a skewed fashion, he also fails to see himself aright. In this reading, the play puts its audience into the same epistemological frame that the characters are in. Fortin's article could have been longer and more detailed; we are left to supply some of the evidence ourselves.

128. Garber, Marjorie. "A Rome of One's Own." In *Shakespeare's Ghost Writers: Literature as Uncanny Causality*, 52–73. NY and London: Methuen, 1987.

In *JC*, Garber reasons, we find not history but a quotation of it. She sees the Ghost as the implied author of the play, because it sets the consequences of Caesar's assassination in motion. She points out that the confusion about the identity of the Ghost heightens the sense that the play is contingent. Garber draws on Walter Benjamin, Sigmund Freud, Karl Marx, and Friedrich Nietzsche for her sense of history as a quotation from the past, a "revenant" (65), a returner from the past—as it were, a virtual reality. Garber interprets a constellation of Julius Caesar allusions in plays from *1 Henry VI* to *Hamlet* to support her thesis. This chapter is useful in pointing out Shakespeare's metatheatricality in *JC*, his objective distance from the world of his own play.

129. Jones, Emrys. *Scenic Form in Shakespeare.* Oxford: Clarendon Press, 1977.

JC receives attention in analyses of several scenes and groups of scenes:

1.2 (18-23), where Greene's *James IV* is brought up for comparison; 1.1 — 3.3, where continuity is threatened by apparent haste and compression; 2.1 (43-50); 4.1, arguing for its placement with events of act 3, giving Octavius the last word in each of the two parts of the play (76-78); 5.1 (91-93), where Jones brings in *Othello* and *3 Henry VI* for comparison; 1.2 and 3.2 as sources for the design of *Othello* 3.4 (139-41). The design of *JC* as a whole is chosen for the climax to Part I of the book (106-13). There Jones considers the form of *JC* in relation to his rough model, *2 Henry VI*, and he reflects with originality on the place of *JC* in the Shakespeare canon. The criticism is perceptive and imaginative; Jones was first to show that form precedes language in a Shakespearean play, and that form can be borrowed, as language and plot can be.

130. Kernan, Alvin [B.] "The Plays and the Playwrights." In *The Revels History of Drama in English: Vol. III 1576-1613*, by J. Leeds Barroll, Alexander Leggatt, Richard Hosley, and Alvin Kernan, 361-83. NY: Harper & Row, Barnes & Noble, 1975.

In this formulation, *JC* (362-66) belongs to a group of plays (1595-1602) in which absolutes are held up but shown to be tragically untenable; as in *Romeo and Juliet, Troilus and Cressida*, and *Hamlet*, the characters in *JC* believe in the power of mind over matter and over the ideals of others. However, as this chapter sees it, such belief comes short of the more mundane realities of life. There are comments on Portia and Cassius, and fuller analysis of Brutus and Caesar, who are seen to be—despite apparent differences—quite alike in that they "worship and die for an unchanging image of themselves" (363): Brutus's principles and Caesar's will to power are equally fatal.

131. Knight, G. Wilson. "The Eroticism of *Julius Caesar*." In *The Imperial Theme: Further Interpretations of Shakespeare's Tragedies, Including the Roman Plays*, 63-95. Rev. edition. Oxford: Oxford Univ. Press, 1951.

In Knight's view of the play, love (defined much more broadly than the title suggests) is the theme of the play. He sees Caesar, "imperial theme" (93), "sublime figure-head" and "man, weak, egotistical, petulant" (64), at the center of the theme, although love in various forms pervades the play (Cassius' for Brutus, Brutus' for Lucius, etc.). In Knight's view, Cassius thinks Caesar too trivial for a heroism that can be loved; "impossible" (81) Brutus splits the world of the play between love and rigid ethical honor; Antony reintegrates the play by loving Caesar, his hero, as practically as Cassius hates Caesar, mere mortal. The essay, a very close reading, is misguided at odd moments but especially percipient at others; e.g., Knight places Brutus/Cassius beside Angelo/Duke (in *Measure for*

Porta Aurelia
Porta Portuensis
Circus
Riuulus Tiberis
Portus Ostiensis.
Templ. Neronis
Sepulchrum Numae
MONS
Templum Iani.
Porta Laurentina
Por. Ostiensis
Pons Aemilius.
T
I
Pons
Pons Palatinus siue Senatorius.
INSVLA
OSTIA TIBERINA.
Porta Trigemina
Porta Trigonia
Casa Rhemi.
Porta Naualis
Armilustrum.
Templum Dianae
Cohors
Domus
vigilum
Sacerdotis
Pons Fabritu
TEMPLV
Iouis
Ara
ARX
Asylum.
Porta Sancualis
Porta Naeuia
MONS SAVENTINVS.
Ara Dianae.
MONS CAPITO
MERIDIES.
Por. Radusiulana
Regia Saturni
TEMPLVM
Apollinis cum Bib
Porta Camena siue Capena.
Saeptum Herculis.
Augusti
Dom Tib
Porta Latina
MONS PALAT
Porta Labicand
Porta Gabina.
Porta Querquetulana siue Caelimontana.
Porta Triumphalis siue sacra.

ASVS
Porta Septimiana.
Porta Valeria.
Templum Apollinis.
Templum Februi
Templ. Carmente.
S
Pons Miluius
I
R
E
B
VLVS ET VATICANVS
Porta Flumentana siue Flaminia
Porta Rhutumena siue Veientana.
Porta Rhomanula.
Hic adhuc una porta pingi debebat nomine Collatina.
Pons Hadrianus.
Pons Vaticanus.
DOMVS Aurea Neronis.
Domus Pastorum.
Porta Collina
Por. Catullaria
Templum Isidis
Templ. Sarapidis
Castra Mesenatium.
Templum Quirini
Por. Quirinalis
MONS EXQVILINVS.
META veneris siue sudãs
Nympheum publ.
SEPTENTRIO
MILIARIVM AVREVM.
MONS QVIRINALIS.
Por. Viminalis
AMPHITHEATRVM.
Porta Lauernalis
Castra peregrina.
Templ. Claudiorum.
Castra prætoria.
Porta Piacularis.
Curia hostilia.
Armamentum publ.
Porta Salutaris.
MONS CELIVS.
Porta Exquilina.
Porta Minutia.
Porta Mutia.
Porta Tiburtina.

Measure): abstract virtue is found wanting by a demanding scrutiny (82–84). Another of many fine moments is the interpretation of 1.2.308–15 (86). Knight has often been accused of overstating his case for the emotional side of literature, but this essay and "The Torch of Life" (see no. 132) may be said to have been first to give the lie to Dr. Johnson's shibboleth that *JC* is stiff and spare because Shakespeare kept too closely to "Roman [Stoic, unemotional, and verbally sparse] manners" (afternote to *JC* in Johnson's edition of 1765).

132. Knight, G. Wilson. "The Torch of Life: An Essay on *Julius Caesar*." In *The Imperial Theme: Further Interpretations of Shakespeare's Tragedies, Including the Roman Plays*, 32–62. Rev. edition. Oxford: Oxford Univ. Press, 1951.

In an essay that builds to a discussion of the relation between body and spirit in *JC*, Knight sees the body as associated with animals and metals, the spirit with blood and fire. He detects a body-spirit link in the pun on "mettle." As Knight understands it, the spirit (life force) triumphs over bodily sickness and infirmity that is nearly everywhere a factor in the play; the body is made vivid for us in many animal images and in the motif of slaughter, but the play always comes back to the spirit. Despite his "ailing, puny body" (51), Caesar's spirit, in his blood, triumphs even after the assassination, which is not "gruesome" as the blood and slaughter are in *Macbeth*, perhaps because Caesar's *Imperium* and order live on as his spirit does; though men fear supernatural chaos in his play, the spirit triumphs. The play emerges from this close scrutiny very rich in images, including also hearts of gold, weeping, and the objects and activities of daily life; Knight finds positive values in them all. The essay begins with evidence that the style of *JC* is simple and unadorned; but the richness of the play's texture is amply demonstrated in what follows. (See also preceding entry.)

133. Palmer, John. *Political Characters of Shakespeare.* Chap. 1, pp. 1–64. London: Macmillan, 1945. Repr. in no. 153.

The chapter is the first of five analyses of tragic figures (Marcus Brutus, Richard of Gloucester, Richard II, Prince Hal, and Coriolanus), each in a political context. Palmer presents Brutus in a detailed exposition as a man whose temperament is unsuited to the evolving political situation in which he finds himself. Brutus is said to be a reclusive character, of divided mind, not a man to take decisive public action, reluctant to get involved politically, and yet transparently honest and a traditional republican. The essay might well have been titled, "Brutus and Cassius," since it offers Cassius repeatedly as a foil to Brutus (5–9, etc.). Late in the play we are shown a Cassius of emotional depth. Caesar and Mark Antony are discussed more briefly. Palmer's essay had a major influence on the interpretation of *JC* in the last half of the 20th century; if his approach seems familiar, it is because so many have adopted it. The best single perception: "Brutus ... has the eye and disposition of a poet" (4, alluding to 1.2.183-88). There are no footnotes or bibliography, but the text shows awareness of some of Palmer's precursors in criticism of *JC*: Voltaire, Coleridge, Bradley. This sympathetic response to Brutus can profitably be contrasted with Gordon Ross Smith's hyperbolic denigration (no. 136).

134. Rabkin, Norman. "Structure, Convention, and Meaning in *Julius Caesar*." *Journal of English and Germanic Philology* 63 (1964): 240-54. Repr. in Rabkin's *Shakespeare and the Common Understanding*, Chap. 3, pp.105-21 (NY: The Free Press; London: Collier-Macmillan,1967) and in no. 153.

Rabkin's essay was the first to analyze 2.1 and 2.2 together to show the remarkable similarity between Brutus and Caesar. Both men are shown as "flawed giants" (246); and the similarities between them suggest to Rabkin the futility of Brutus' planned assassination. Rabkin goes on to point out another pivot in the play, Antony's soliloquy that ends 3.1 and calls for a revenge that the second half of the play works out. A third approach to the play in this article is to posit a determinist cosmos in the play, a set of cause-and-effect events to which idealism and moral philosophy are irrelevant. This is the first essay to see *JC* as a revenge structure; it remains for modern scholars to make a larger study that will interpret the whole early tragic canon as revenge stories.

135. Sanders, Norman. "The Shift of Power in *Julius Caesar*." *A Review of English Literature* 5, no. 2 (April 1964): 24-35.

In Sanders' formulation, *JC* is about political power—how it shows itself, how it is perceived, how it is transferred from one person to another. For Sanders, Brutus' notion of power is abstract, Cassius's concrete. Sanders' Antony, like the conspirators, has a negative, destructive, view of power (see his soliloquy in 3.1), and he never attains political power in his own right, as Octavius does in act 5; the negativity of power in the play is underscored by the mob, also a power holder, which is merely destructive. Sanders was first to suggest that Caesar and Octavius might be doubled on stage, to suggest the shift of power from the one to the other; this attractive casting would imply that Shakespeare wrote 3.3, the death of Cinna the Poet, to cover the costume change from Julius to Octavius, who first appears onstage in 4.1. (See also Stuart M.

Kurland, "'No Innocence Is Safe, When Power Contests': The Factional Worlds of *Caesar* and *Sejanus*." *Comparative Drama*: 22 [1988]: 56–67; in this article the transfer of power is (with dynasty) seen as one of two themes of *JC* treated also in *Sejanus*.)

135a. Schanzer, Ernest. *The Problem Plays of Shakespeare: A Study of "Julius Caesar," "Measure for Measure," "Antony and Cleopatra."* Chap. 1, pp. 10–70. NY: Schocken, 1963.

In Schanzer's view the "problem" in *JC* is ambiguity about the morality of the assassination. The first section of the chapter shows that all of Shakespeare's possible sources for the play—from Cicero through Plutarch, Appian, Suetonius, and certain medieval and Renaissance commentators and playwrights—see Gaius Julius Caesar himself as an ambivalent figure. Section 2 shows Shakespeare's Caesar to be ambiguous, sometimes vainglorious, sometimes heroic, reflecting those sources (his earliest allusions to Caesar were all positive); section 3 treats Cassius, Antony, and (briefly) Casca, the first two negatively, the third as implausibly inconsistent; sections 4 and 6 see Brutus as a typical Shakespearean tragic protagonist (the traits of which are sketched in section 5), a hero with inner conflict which none of the other characters in *JC* have. As Schanzer sees it, Shakespeare shrewdly makes Brutus, as in Shakespeare's sources, tragically of two minds about Caesar. The essay has become a reference point as criticism of the play has become since 1963 more and more contingent.

136. Smith, Gordon Ross. "Brutus, Virtue, and Will." *SQ* 10 (1959): 367–79.

This psychoanalytic study of Brutus is perhaps the most famous negative criticism of the character. It has had many followers, especially among postmodern critics, but few as vigorous in condemnation of Brutus as this essay, which, it may be said, distorts small details in the play to denigrate Brutus as more willful than virtuous.

137. Stirling, Brents. *The Populace in Shakespeare*. NY: Columbia Univ. Press, 1949. In Chap. 2, 25–34, and *passim*. Repr. in no. 153.

Stirling comments on crowd manipulation in the two orations of *JC* act 3 and on the important role of the populace in the play, which is signaled in 1.1 but largely absent from Plutarch's relevant *Lives*. He notes that, here and in other plays, the crowd is judged by cynical choric characters. Stirling was essentially first to give serious attention to the "unstable" plebeians in *JC*, and his book still has importance for its shrewd perceptions, especially about Shakespeare's changes in his sources, and for awareness of 20th-century literary analogues to the fickle-crowd motif in *JC*.

138. **Thomas, Vivian.** *"Julius Caesar."* Harvester New Critical Introductions to Shakespeare. NY and London: Harvester Wheatsheaf, 1992.

A preface (xi–xxiv), making a balanced judgment of post-modern methods of criticism, is followed by a survey (xxvi–xxxvii) of stage history of *JC* (based largely on Ripley, no. 149) and a brief comment (xxxviii–xli) on points of controversy in the criticism of the play. It then offers chapters on "Textual Issues" (1–8), "Genre and Unity" (9–24), "Shakespeare and Plutarch"(25–72), "Style" (78–101), and a conclusion asserting that the play is deceptively simple, and in reality is rich and subtle (102–10). The bibliography (121–34) is a valuable resource. Thomas should not be accepted unquestioningly: he places undue faith in flawed works (notably the Oxford *JC*, ed. A. H. Humphreys) and sometimes states as facts opinions that are open to challenge (e.g., *JC* as the first play to appear in the Globe Theatre in 1599). Read with caution, the book is helpful. The chapter on genre and unity explains Shakespeare's *Romanitas* effectively. The analysis of the play in relation to Plutarch is perceptive, identifying the source in the "Life of Brutus" of Brutus's "breathtaking naiveté" in *JC* (38). The interpretation of Brutus's soliloquy recognizes that the audience enters it *in medias res*; the analysis of Brutus' state of mind about the assassination and its aftermath is excellent (51–63 especially), although Plutarch is gradually forgotten here.

139. **Traversi, Derek A.** *An Approach to Shakespeare.* In Chap. 11, pp. 492–512. 3rd edition, revised and expanded. Garden City: Doubleday, 1969.

This section is a *seriatim* commentary on *JC* which offers interpretations of the principal characters: Caesar, Brutus (especially), Cassius, Antony, and Octavius; and it points also to the often ironic ethical meaning of the action. This approach, though conventional for its time, is based on an acute close reading that is frequently innovative and profound. There are no notes and very little hint of the *Romanitas* lying behind the events of the play, and Plutarch is mentioned only in passing. Chapter 11 is written elegantly in a slightly old-fashioned style. It is a model of what an intelligent close reading can do for a familiar text by touching at times a "subtext."

140. **Velz, John W.** "Undular Structure in *Julius Caesar*." *The Modern Language Review* 66 (1971): 21–30. Repr. in *Shakespearean Criticism*, ed. Mark W. Scott. Detroit: Gale Research Corporation, 1988.

This article argues that *JC* is neither a one-man play nor a clash between two powerful men; rather, it is built on a succession of rises and falls of ambitious Romans, from Pompey to Octavius (by way of Caesar,

Brutus, and Antony). The article sees this open-ended pattern enlarging the world of the play—from a dead past to a future yet unseen. The interpretation goes on to note that the subplot partially imitates the mainplot, as it repeatedly shows Brutus crescent in the conspiracy and its aftermath, and Cassius cadent. This structure is characterized as wave-like, the term deriving from several references to rising water, waves, tides, and storms at sea. Velz argues that Shakespeare arranges the play so as to make the Caesareans and the republicans say the same kinds of things, all unaware of the inherent irony; a philosophical point about the futility of political ideology is enforced, and in a larger sense the audience is made to feel the brevity of human glory. The analogies between successive "waves," between speakers on the rise, are also a major force for coherence in the play.

140a. Willson, Robert F., Jr. *"Julius Caesar*: The Forum Scene as Historic Play-within." *Shakespeare Yearbook* 1 (1990): 14–27.

After a prologue that points out the profound meanings of theatrical metaphors in *Hamlet, Macbeth, Richard III,* and other Shakespearean plays, Willson argues that the conspiracy and the assassination in *JC* are metaphored in theatrical terms, the conspiracy being an acting company and Mark Antony in 3.1 being a hired extra for a particular minor role who unexpectedly takes over the plot of the play-within, making it into a revenge play. The Forum scene is discussed fully in these terms. A coda to this interpretation discusses 3.3. as also a play-within in which an intended funeral is turned into a riot. It is significant, Willson reasons, that it is a poet who is murdered by the mob; the playscripts of history are in the hands of poets. Antony has, therefore, he concludes, overplayed his part in more than one sense.

See also nos. 34, 43, and 45.

F. Stage History and Performance Criticism; Adaptations.

141. Barton, John. *Playing Shakespeare*. London and NY: Methuen, 1984.

This book is based on a nine-part BBC-TV series (1984), in which Barton, a founder/director of The Royal Shakespeare Company, used 21 RSC actors in conversation and recitation to explore and debate problems in delivering various kinds of speeches in Shakespeare. Speeches from *JC* are discussed on pp. 53–54 (Antony's oration); 62–64 (Calphurnia and Caesar in 2.2); 78–80 (Brutus' prose oration); 121 (irony in Antony's oration); 139–41 ("passion and coolness" in Brutus' soliloquy and 2 others of his speeches in 2.1); 204-05 (Brutus' largely monosyllabic eulogy over Cassius's body in 5.3). The book as a whole is an excellent resource for learning how to "speak Shakespeare."

142. Booth, Stephen. "The Shakespearean Actor as Kamikaze Pilot." *SQ* 36 (1985): 553-70.

This essay treats four Shakespearean roles that defy actors to succeed: Cleopatra, her Antony (554-64), Brutus (564-68)—and Prince Hal. Booth affirms that, in each of the four, the character is either passively worked on (Brutus); or upstaged (Brutus; Antony); or divided against himself (Brutus "with himself at war" [1.2.46]; Cleopatra, queen and coquette; Antony, heroic warrior and roué). These roles are, as Booth points out, almost always misunderstood by reviewers, who fault actors for not being (whatever) enough. Booth's point is that Shakespeare leaves the audience dissatisfied with the performance so that they can contrive in their own imaginations a more perfect Antony, Cleopatra, Prince Hal, or Brutus. When "an actor go[es] down in flames as Antony or Cleopatra, or Brutus or Hal" we are to think that he or she has succeeded in doing to us exactly what Shakespeare intended to do (570).

143. Cohn, Ruby. *Modern Shakespeare Offshoots.* Princeton, N.J.: Princeton Univ. Press, 1976.

George Bernard Shaw's *Caesar and Cleopatra* (1898) is discussed (327-31) as a deliberate response to both *JC* and *Ant*. Shaw complained of Shakespeare's Caesar that he says not a word worthy of the historical Gaius Julius Caesar; Shaw determined to make his own Caesar an intelligent and detached man who has none of the romantic notions of Antony with Cleopatra, nor suffers the betrayals that Shakespeare's Caesar undergoes. Elsewhere in Cohn's book (313-15) the *JC* (1971) of Steve Rumbelow is seen as experimental theater, an attempt to make a living sculpture of Shakespeare's complex action. Rumbelow reduced the cast to five actors, and the production, aimed at a sophisticated audience, drew on the director's training as a painter to portray body movements in the cast. The Ghost of Caesar stabs Brutus on the battlefield in a deliberate reminiscence of Brutus' thrust at Caesar in 3.1 of Shakespeare's play. The Rumbelow version of the play begins with the battle scenes and ends with them, again scoring a moral point.

144. Gielgud, John. "Foreword to *Julius Caesar.*" In *The Guild Shakespeare,* ed. John F. Andrews, vii-xi. GuildAmerica Books, vol. 4. Garden City, NY: Doubleday, 1989.

The remarks on *JC* as a stage vehicle come from an actor who remembers productions back as far as 1916, including some, notably the Houseman/Mankiewicz film of 1953, in which he acted. The focus is on the characters, about most of whom he makes pithy remarks. He also discusses costume, objecting to the legacy of the Mercury Theatre production of 1937, in which Orson Welles dressed Caesar's faction as Mussolini's Black Shirts (actually Nazi uniforms). The comments on the difficulty of staging the anti-climactic battle scenes are cogent, though perhaps too pessimistic.

145. Granville-Barker, Harley. "From *Henry V* to *Hamlet*." In *More Prefaces to Shakespeare*, ed. Edward M. Moore, 135–67. Vol. 6. Princeton: Princeton Univ. Press, 1974 (repr. in no. 153). Revised and corrected version of the British Academy Annual Shakespeare Lecture, 1925. *Proceedings of the British Academy* 11 (1924–25), 283–309. London: Humphrey Milford for Oxford Univ. Press, 1926.

The scope of this lecture is broader even than its title suggests; though it is focused on *JC* as a hinge in the Shakespeare canon, it ranges from early plays to late and always from a seat in the director's chair. The audience and the actor are always on Granville-Barker's mind, and his sense of Shakespeare's success as theater is astute. Therefore this lecture is a mini-history of the Shakespeare canon, seen in terms of the actor's art. *Henry V* in this lecture is heroic (external) drama; *JC*, like *Hamlet*, which followed it more perfectly, is tragic (internal) drama. Granville-Barker may have been the first to reason that Shakespeare's art developed as a response to theatrical needs. He also may well have been first to recognize the crucial position of *JC* in the canon: looking backward to the histories and forward to the tragedies. Moody E. Prior ("The Search for a Hero in *Julius Caesar*." *Renaissance Drama* n.s. 2 [1969]: 81–101) also argues for this central place in the Shakespeare canon, but without the theatrical dimension. The earlier essay on *JC* in Granville-Barker's *Prefaces to Shakespeare*: First Series (1927) advances a similar interpretation of play and characters, but covers less canonical ground and is less focused on the actor and his audience. Beginners in theater history as well as students of Shakespeare from non-theatrical points of view can use this British Academy Lecture as an introduction, taking note that Granville-Barker may be incorrect about the dates of *Measure for Measure*, *Othello*, *Macbeth*, and *King Lear*.

146. Houseman, John. *Front and Center*. NY: Simon and Schuster, 1979.

This account (382–409) from the producer's point of view of the circumstances surrounding the production of the film of *JC* (1953), which Joseph Mankiewicz directed, is very much in the style of Houseman's earlier *Run-Through* (see no. 147), anecdotal, sometimes amusing, and factual. The misadventures with the battle scenes; the decision to cast Marlon Brando, who had no "Classical" acting experience, as Mark Antony; the respect of John Gielgud (Cassius) for Brando and Brando's rejection of a contract that Gielgud offered him afterwards to co-star with Paul Scofield in a tour of Shakespeare repertory; the difficulty that Orson Welles was planning a film of *JC* in Europe at the same time (it did not materialize), and the stringency of the filming budget; all and more are fully recounted. Reading the surrounding text will provide an important introduction to the workings of Hollywood in the period after World War II. It is sometimes said that the Houseman/Mankiewicz film was first to recognize the dramatic structure of *JC* that elevates given roles to prominence at given moments, then pushes them successively into diminuendo. However, the all-star cast was partly dictated by the fact that MGM had a number of the actors under contract. (Cast also included James Mason [Brutus], Deborah Kerr [Portia], Louis Calhern [Caesar], Greer Garson [Calphurnia].) Houseman seems not to have understood the literary critical implications of the film he worked so hard on. (See also Velz, no. 150.)

147. Houseman, John. *Run-Through: A Memoir.* NY: Simon and Schuster, 1972.

An excerpt (285–321) from Houseman's extended memoirs of a life in the theater focuses on the founding of the Mercury Theater in an abandoned theater building on Broadway in 1937, and the sensation the first production, *JC*, made among the reviewers and at the box office. Houseman, who produced the show, sees Orson Welles (Brutus) and the rest of the cast with a fond but critical eye. The production dressed the Caesar faction in Nazi-style uniforms and portrayed Brutus as the sort of liberal who is always destroyed by revolutionaries. The production is famous for its reshaping of *JC* to make points about mid-20th-century political life. Houseman's anecdotal style brings to life the production itself, and the struggle to fund it. This is a close-up account of one of the two most important productions of *JC* in the twentieth century (for the other, see nos. 146 and 150).

147a. Nettles, John. "Brutus in *Julius Caesar*." In *Players of Shakespeare 4: Further Essays in Shakespearian Performance by Players with the Royal Shakespeare Company*, ed. Robert Smallwood, 177–92. Cambridge: Cambridge Univ. Press, 1998.

Nettles finds Brutus enigmatic, inconsistent, one who is gentle, and kindly, and honorable in his private life but much closer to corruption in his public life; he acts out of envy of Caesar's greatness. Nettles (and presumably the director, Sir Peter Hall, in the 1995 *JC* at Stratford) commits himself wholly to a widespread contemporary vision of Brutus as a self-deceiver who fails to recognize his motives in public life for what they are. Nettles' Brutus seems shifty because he succeeds in convincing himself of the rightness of his position even when he will contradict that position moments later. At the same time, we see his high-mindedness in personal relationships. We witness his decline "from the moral uplands of honour, love, and gentleness into the dark pit of murder, terror, and civil war" (188). The role, seen in these terms, is a difficult one to play, and Nettles admits to having struggled with it in rehearsal. The chapter is illustrated by black-and-white photographs of Nettles with Cassius in 1.2 and with Strato at Brutus's suicide in 5.5.

148. Pickup, Ronald. *"Julius Caesar." Shakespeare in Perspective* Vol. I: 65–72. London: BBC Ariel Books, 1982.

Pickup, who played Cassius in 1977 at the National Theater with John Gielgud as Caesar and John Schlesinger directing, takes a view of the play which is mildly negative, modern, and theatrical. There is a comment on Marlon Brando's Antony (MGM film, 1953) as played with "stealth" (69). Cassius is spoken of as "the explosive force that gives the play its dramatic lift-off" (67) in 1.2. Pickup fastens on the comparison of the conspirators' army to "sickly prey" (5.1.90), as indicative of the contingent final state of the action: "The world is still 'sickly prey' to the opportunists" (72).

149. Ripley, John. *Julius Caesar on Stage in England and America, 1599–1973.* Cambridge: Cambridge Univ. Press, 1980.

In twelve narrative and descriptive chapters, major actors and theater managers are discussed, some (J. P. Kemble, Tree, Benson, Bridges-Adams) at chapter length, and all informatively. Prominent is Chapter 6, focused on Edwin Booth, Lawrence Barrett, E.L. Davenport, and several others during a span (1871–91) that saw thousands of *JC* performances in America. Often a scenario is given for a major production, and often acting technique and stage design are discussed in detail, but trends and the social history they reflect are also prominent. Supporting apparatus includes a brief guide to 18th- and 19th-century stage terms (xiii); 17 black-and-white photographs; a performance list (287–311), which should not be taken as comprehensive, especially for early productions. Including cogent analytical comments, this now-standard stage history of *Julius Caesar* is truly a history, not merely a reference book.

G. Afterlife.

150. Velz, John W. "*Julius Caesar* 1937-97: Where we are now; How we got there." In *The Shakespearean International Yearbook, 1: Where Are We Now in Shakespearean Studies?*, 257-65. London: Ashgate, 1999.

This article discusses the two productions of *JC* that were the work of John Houseman: the Mercury Theater stage *JC* (1937), starring Orson Welles as Brutus; and the MGM film of 1953 with an all-star cast. The latter production is shown to have had a major influence on subsequent literary criticism of the play, and the former is shown to lie behind the now popular convention of costuming Shakespeare's characters in modern military uniforms to score political points. The article also traces the history of *JC* interpretation since 1937, in characterization, structure, style, genre. The suggestion is made that contingent criticism of *JC* in the 1960s had a part in shaping the postmodern reading of Shakespeare that came later. Beyond literary criticism, there is an account of scholarship of various kinds about this play in the given period, e.g., sources and text. The conclusion is that the play is now seen as more complicated, more ambiguous, and more subtle than was thought in the preceding three centuries. (See also nos. 146 and 147.)

151. Walch, Günther. "The Historical Subject as Roman Actor and Agent of History: Interrogative Dramatic Structure in *Julius Caesar*." In *Shakespearean Illuminations: Essays in Honor of Marvin Rosenberg*, ed. Jay L. Halio and Hugh Richmond, 220-36. Newark: Univ. of Delaware Press; London: Associated Univ. Presses, 1998. See also "Postscript," 237-41.

The publishing history of this essay is complex, and germane to its interpretation. It was written in 1988 and 1989, and published in German in 1990. It thus straddles the celebration in the German Democratic Republic of the anniversary of the French Revolution of 1789, and coincidentally the fall of the Berlin Wall and the collapse of the GDR itself. The essay suggests meaningful parallels between the fall of a dictator (Caesar) or the ultimate failure of a temporarily successful elite oligarchy (the conspiracy) and events in Germany from the fall of Hitler to the collapse of the Marxist oligarchy. These analogies are only hinted at in the original essay itself, partly because of official censorship, which caused Walch to write in an "Aesopian" (indirect) mode. But his analogies are openly presented in the "Postscript," which was written from a retrospective stance in 1995 and published as an afterword (237-41) to the essay. The continuing relevance of *JC* to human history is emphatically reinforced in this essay about a set of events in the late 20th century that ironically replicate the events of Shakespeare's play. The play interrogates the history of our time, as it does the history of late-18th-century France, and perhaps the late Elizabethan era (the Essex Affair) as well.

H. Teaching and Collections of Essays.

151a. Bitot, Michel, ed. *Shakespeare/Julius Caesar: Texte et representation.* Actes du Colloque de Tours ... novembre 1994. Tours: Univ. François Rabelais, 1995.

This book comprises an introduction and 15 new essays by well-known scholars, mainly French; essays in English are by Stanley Wells, "*Julius Caesar* in Its Own Time" (11–31); Jean Dubu, "Mantle, Vesture, and Undress in *Julius Caesar*" (57–70); Malgorzata Grzegorzewska, "The Death of an Orator: The Use of Rhetoric in *Julius Caesar* (139–51); Jean-Marie Maguin, "Rhetoric and *Julius Caesar*: What Is at Stake?" (167–75); Colin Ellwood, "Directing *Julius Caesar*: The Event on Stage" (237–51).

152. Charney, Maurice, ed. *Shakespeare's Roman Plays.* Discussions of Literature. Boston: D.C. Heath, 1964.

This paperback anthology of essays on the Roman plays reprints three well-known studies of *JC*: Richard G. Moulton, "How the Play of *Julius Caesar* Works to a Climax at the Centre: A Study in Passion and Movement," from Moulton's *Shakespeare as a Dramatic Artist*, 1885/1906, (40–52); Harold S. Wilson, "The Order of Nature: *Julius Caesar*," from Wilson's *On the Design of Shakespearian Tragedy*, 1957 (title of this selection provided by Charney, 53–64); Ernest Schanzer "The Tragedy of Shakespeare's Brutus," from *English Literary History 1500–1900* 22 [1955]: (65–76). In addition, there is Edward Dowden on "The Character of Caesar," a brief excerpt from Dowden's *Shakspere: A Critical Study of His Mind and Art*, 1875/1881 (title of this selection supplied by Charney, 37–39). Not to be overlooked are two further essays on more general subjects which give significant attention to *JC*: T.J.B. Spencer, "Shakespeare and the Elizabethan Romans" (1957): 1–15 (also in no. 42), and Maurice Charney, "Style in the Roman Plays" from his *Shakespeare's Roman Plays: The Function of Imagery in the Drama* (1961), 16–36.

153. Dean, Leonard F., ed. *Interpretations of "Julius Caesar": A Collection of Critical Essays.* Englewood Cliffs, N.J.: Prentice-Hall, 1968.

This is the most ambitious of the resource collections to appear in the 1960s. It includes excerpts from major essays by Mark Van Doren, John Palmer (see no. 133), Harley Granville-Barker (see no. 145), Leo Kirschbaum, Arthur Sewell, Brents Stirling (see no. 137), L.C. Knights, R.A.

Foakes, Ernest Schanzer, David Daiches, Maurice Charney, Sigurd Burckhardt, Robert B. Heilman, Geoffrey Bullough, Northrop Frye, Hugh M. Richmond, and Norman Rabkin (see no. 134). The collection is rounded off with a previously unpublished essay by William and Barbara Rosen, "*Julius Caesar*: 'The Specialty of Rule,'" (109–15). The essays take a variety of approaches: characters, style, genre, tone, sources, theme, structure. Dean's editing sometimes gives no hint of deletions. His introduction is unfortunately offhand, and it implies that *JC* is "largely useless" (7), i.e., has outlived its relevance; this remark seems, in long retrospect, ludicrous, as it was made toward the end of a decade of political assassination in America. The book went through several printings and can be found in many college and university libraries which have other volumes in the "Twentieth Century Interpretations" series, edited by Maynard Mack.

154. Harrison, G. B., compiler. *Julius Caesar in Shakespeare, Shaw and the Ancients.* NY: Harcourt Brace, 1960.

This paperback collection, intended for students, is about (and by) Caesar including both ancient sources and George Bernard Shaw's *Caesar and Cleopatra*. It focuses almost entirely on primary sources: Plutarch (3 Lives); Cicero (*Letters* and *Philippic II*); Gaius Julius Caesar (*The Civil Wars*); Suetonius, *Lives of the Caesars*; and Appian, *The Civil Wars*. In addition, the texts of Shakespeare's *JC* (lightly annotated) and Shaw's *Caesar and Cleopatra* (unannotated) are reproduced. Apparatus includes end-paper maps, a list of suggested research topics (207–09), a short reading list (209), a timeline for Caesar's life, and a glossary.

154a. Lomonico, Michael, and Nancy Goodwin, editors. "Teaching *Julius Caesar*: Are We to Praise Caesar or Bury Him?" *Shakespeare* 2, issue 3 (Fall, 1998): 7–15.

This feature, in an issue of the magazine devoted almost exclusively to teaching *JC*, comprises brief essays: on using living statues to deliver monologues written for the various characters in the play (Katherine Utley); on using Plutarch as a platform from which to observe Shakespeare's play (Joe Bonfiglio); on using *Troilus and Cressida* and *Cor.* and other timely plays instead of *JC* to examine Shakespeare's political ideas (Joshua Cabat); on using a performance of *Ant.* as a way of teaching *JC* (Brian J. Kelley). The editors of *Shakespeare* review the Orson Welles *JC* production of 1937, the Joseph Mankiewicz production of 1953, and the RSC production of 1993. In a separate article in the same issue, "What Portia Knew," Naomi C. Liebler argues that Portia is a strong character, negating the traditional assumption that she is weak. According to Liebler, "She may be the only female character in Shakespeare who tolerates, even invites, physical pain while refusing to put up with emotional rejection" (18).

155. Wilders, John. "Dramatic Structure and Dramatic Effect in *Julius Caesar*." In *Teaching with Shakespeare: Critics in the Classroom*, ed. Bruce McIver and Ruth Stevenson, 42–51. Newark: Univ. of Delaware Press; London and Toronto: Associated Univ. Presses, 1994.

Eschewing ideology, literary criticism, and textual explication, Wilders divides the central scenes of *JC* into movements in the manner of music. His sense of the flow and careful timing of the action derive from his own student days at Cambridge, where he played Caesar (among several other roles). This lucid account of the emotional design of the play also draws its strength from indications of what happened to him and his students, who were actors in the classroom. The essay ranges broadly and makes passing remarks on dramatic strategies in other plays.

I. Bibliographies.

156. Sajdak, Bruce T., ed. *Shakespeare Index: An Annotated Bibliography of Critical Articles on the Plays 1959-83.* 2 vols. Vol. 1, Citations and Author Index. Vol. 2, Character, Scene, and Subject Indexes. Millwood, NY: Kraus International Publications, 1992.

This bibliography contains 150 entries on *JC* (1: 401–16) arranged chronologically 1959–1983, and alphabetically within years. No books or chapters are included. Sajdak represents a range of stances from source study to ritual interpretation and from psychological analysis to aesthetic criticism (of characters). Two bibliotextual essays on *JC* are included, but theater criticism is not. Annotation is usually in the form of paraphrase without evaluative comment.

157. Velz, John W., compiler. *A New Variorum Edition of Shakespeare: The Tragedy of Julius Caesar: A Bibliography to Supplement the New Variorum Edition of 1913.* NY: Modern Language Association of America, 1977. Published separately in paperback; also in hardback with analogous bibliographies, compiled by others, for *Richard II* and *1 Henry IV*.

This bibliography, more or less comprehensive within its stated limits, contains 1256 entries (some works are listed in two classifications). It has a cut-off date of 1972, although it did not appear until five years after that date. It is classified as follows: Editions since 1913; Commentary (i.e., explications and comments on limited segments of the play); Text; Date; Sources (backgrounds of all kinds); Criticism; Staging and Stage History.

Brief bracketed annotations indicate principal emphases of most entries. An index to authors and editors is provided. The compiler's Prefatory Note offers explanation of the classification system and a caveat about some categories of omission: collected editions; novelty and miniature editions; book and theatre reviews; "most inaugural dissertations and all Schulprogramme"; "commentary and editions intended primarily for secondary-school teachers or students"; abridgments and paraphrases of *JC*; most translations; and some psychoanalytic and some anti-Stratfordian approaches.

158. Weis, R. J. A. "*Julius Caesar* and *Antony and Cleopatra*." In *Shakespeare: A Bibliographical Guide*, New Edition, ed. Stanley Wells, 275–94. Oxford: Clarendon Press, 1990.

The introductory remarks on Shakespeare's response to the ancient world (275–78) are an appropriate place to begin consideration of this subject. The discussion of *JC* (texts and criticism) is also helpful. The emphasis in the present Pegasus bibliography falls on other critical aspects of the play than those Weis holds out for consideration. This is all the more reason to draw also on his observations, and on the 30 works he lists under "*Julius Caesar*: Criticism" (291–92).

VI. ANTONY AND CLEOPATRA

A. Editions.

159. Bevington, David, ed. *Antony and Cleopatra*. The New Cambridge Shakespeare. Cambridge: Cambridge Univ. Press, 1990.

In the introduction (1–70), Bevington studies date of composition (suggesting 1606), sources (especially the range of Renaissance attitudes about the key characters), "contrarieties of critical response" from important critics (13–16), especially on the gap between word and action in the play (16–30), and discusses genre, structure, and style (30–40). Bevington offers an analysis of the drama in terms of stage issues, for instance, juxtaposition of scenes, stage picture, the use of messengers, and the "monument scenes" of 4.15 and 5.2 (40–44) as well as a history of British stage performances from the late 17th century through the 1960s (44–70). After a brief note on the text (71–73) of the 1623 Folio, which provides the copy text of his edition, Bevington prints the play (78–258) with notes to and on the text, including copious glossing of difficult words and phrases, with background information and critical commentary, at the bottom of each page. In conclusion, Bevington gives a brief supplementary note (259), an analysis of the Folio text (261–70), and a suggested reading list (271–74). The New Cambridge Shakespeare succeeds "The New Shakespeare," under the editorship of Sir Arthur Quiller-Couch, John Dover Wilson, et al., that began publication in 1921. See also no. 211.

160. Neill, Michael, ed. *Anthony and Cleopatra*. The Oxford Shakespeare. Oxford: Clarendon Press, 1994. The World's Classics. Oxford and NY: Oxford Univ. Press, 1994.

After giving a chronology of historical events from 82 to 30 BCE (x–xi) and a map on the following page, Neill summarizes critical assessments of the play from Coleridge to the 1970s (1–5), reviews recent controversies over the meaning of such terms as "sources," "influences," and "analogues" (5–6), relates *Ant.* to *JC* (7–9), and discusses Shakespeare's use of and variance from Plutarch and earlier 16th-century dramatizations of the material. Neill dates the first performance of the play to "late 1606 or early 1607" (22) and surveys many stage performances (23-67) from the later 17th century to 1991, with illustrations. Neill offers an account of important past literary-critical and performance-oriented interpretations (67-89), using details of performance to highlight critical interpretation, including a discussion of Enobarbus as "choric fool" (87-94) and a series of critical discussions on nostalgia (94-100), the balancing of hyperbole with harsh reality (100-07), the ambivalences of suicide (107-11), properties of the self, both male and female (112-23), and the ambiguous end of Cleopatra and the play (123-30). Following a discussion of editorial procedures (131-41), Neill presents the play (143-325) with notes to the text and on the text at the bottom of each page. Neill provides the following additional material: in Appendix A, excerpts from North's translation of Plutarch's *Lives* (327-62); in B, notes on the staging of 4.16 and 5.2 (363-67); in C, a note on pronoun usage in the 17th century (368-69); in D, editorial problems in lineation (370-78) and a list of such changes. Last, in the Index Neill provides a "guide" to words and phrases glossed in the commentary and a selection of the names and topics discussed in the Introduction and commentary (379-88).

161. **Spevack, Marvin,** ed., with Michael Steppat and Marga Munkelt, associate eds. *Antony and Cleopatra*. A New Variorum Edition. NY: Modern Language Association, 1987.

Spevack provides the text of *Ant.* based on the 1623 Folio (1-344), with notes to the text and on the text that "explicate its language ... and summarize the notes that a long succession of editors and commentators has written on it" (xiii), and an appendix reproducing or summarizing general discussions of the play, together with material and opinions too long for inclusion elsewhere in the volume. Spevack and his editors provide emendations suggested (345-60), an analysis of the Folio text (360-79), a discussion of the date of composition (378-84), of sources, influences, analogues, and excerpts from Plutarch and others (384-459), including a full transcription of such earlier texts as Robert Garnier's *Antonius* (1592) and Samuel Daniel's *Cleopatra* (1594), with other versions of the story (459-611). Spevack provides surveys of earlier criticism under various headings, such as "General Assessments," "Genre," and "Other categories," which include "Themes and Significance," "Technique," and specific characters (611-727). Spevack and the other editors also analyze ways in which *Ant.* has been reshaped for printed acting versions from the 18th century onward (727-58) and give an account of performances from the late 17th to the 20th century, together with speculations about ways in which selected scenes might have been staged in Shakespeare's theater (727-93), ending with a bibliography (794-848) and an index (compiled by Sabine U. Buckmann-de Villegas, 849-85).

162. Wilders, John, ed. *Antony and Cleopatra.* The Arden Shakespeare, 3rd series. London and NY: Routledge, 1995.

In the introduction, Wilders presents the play as centered on the title figures, who seek to "perpetuate their legendary status" (4) in a play that is also about international politics. The editor discusses the play's construction, its distinctive language and style, its sources, date of composition, and the text; Wilders describes early Jacobean conditions of performance, its aural as well as visual nature, and casting practices (5-12), and summarizes earlier studies of the play's disregard for "Aristotelian" unities, blending this topic with accounts of ways in which it was staged from the 18th century to 1980 (12-26), by which time critics "began to consider the construction of *Ant.* on its own terms" (26). Wilders studies the "question of structure" (26-38), stressing shifts of location, contrasts and contradictions within scenes as expressed by characters, a radical instability within the characters themselves, also expressed by imagery (31-36), bringing in early writers on the subject of instability (36-37) and stressing the contrary pull toward stability (37-38). Wilders reviews a few earlier critics who discussed the issue of moral judgment (38-43), deciding that the play demands "the extreme of skepticism ... balanced by an extreme of assent" (43; quoting Adelman, no. 176, [110]). Wilders criticizes A.C. Bradley's reservations about the play's status as a great tragedy (43-49), and discusses language and various aspects of style (49-56). Wilders studies Shakespeare's use of sources (56-69) and his technique of associating the characters with "mythological archetypes" (64-69). Wilders ends the introduction with discussions of date of composition (probably completed by 20 May 1608 [74]), and the nature of the Folio text; following the text of the play (86-301) Wilders adds "longer notes" (303-05), an appendix listing passages in which his edition differs from the Folio in lineation, a list of abbreviations used and earlier editions collated (305-16), a bibliography (316-27), and an index to the introduction and commentary (328-31). This edition replaces the earlier Arden edition by M.R. Ridley (1954).

B. Authorship, Dating, and Textual Studies.

163. Spevack, Marvin. "On the Copy for *Antony and Cleopatra.*" In *"Fanned and Winnowed Opinions": Shakespearean Essays Presented to Harold Jenkins,* ed. John W. Mahon and Thomas A. Pendleton, 212-15. London: Methuen, 1987.

Spevack argues against earlier bibliographical studies, chiefly those by John Dover Wilson, that emphasized the approach to textual scholarship in terms of Elizabethan orthography, and that believed the Folio text of *Ant.* was set from a manuscript in Shakespeare's hand. Rather, Spevack proposes the ultimate indeterminacy of these issues, and despairs of ever identifying the copy underlying the Folio text.

See also nos. 159–62.

C. Influences; Sources; Historical and Intellectual Backgrounds; Topicality.

164. Barroll, J. Leeds. *Shakespearean Tragedy: Genre, Tradition, and Change in "Antony and Cleopatra."* Washington, D.C.: Folger Books; London: Associated University Presses, 1984.

In Part 1, Barroll shows that in the Classical and Christian traditions as expressed in dramatic and non-dramatic works (including Homer, Sophocles, Aristotle, Plato, Plutarch, St. Augustine, Boethius, Chaucer, and a variety of 16th-century writers), it is the protagonist's breaking of social and moral norms that leads to tragedy; in drama, where the authorial voice is essentially absent, the dramatist must devise a means of making clear the freedom of choice, and the responsibility, of the protagonists, indirectly (chap. 1, 15–56). After a second chapter on the nature of tragic drama (chap. 2, 57–79), Barroll focuses on the developing action of the plot, and interaction of character, in *Ant.* In Part 2, chap. 3, 83–129, the critic follows Antony's role, especially stressing his uniqueness and separation from conventional moral valuation (90), his strengths and limitations as a commander, his suicide, and his final silence. Then, in chapter 4, 130–87, the critic similarly follows Cleopatra's "infinite variety" (130) and role as tragic protagonist who pursues a goal that is, finally, "only a metaphor" (153), analyzing in particular her role in the battle of Actium and its aftermath (he provides a detailed discussion of Cleopatra's fidelity, 161–68). Part 3 consists of chapters on the military/political setting (chap. 5, 191–242); on other important characters, such as Caesar, Octavia, Enobarbus, and Lepidus (chap. 6, 243–78); on the nature of Shakespearean tragedy and the relation of *Ant.* to Shakespeare's other plays (chap. 7, 279–88). Barroll concludes with a bibliography (289–99) and an index (301–09).

165. Bono, Barbara J. *Literary Transvaluation: From Vergilian Epic to Shakespearean Tragicomedy.* Berkeley: Univ. of California Press, 1984. Chap. 4, 140–219.

In the context of a study of literary transvaluation ("an artistic act of historical self-consciousness that at once acknowledges the perceived values of the antecedent text and transforms them to serve the uses of the present," 1), Bono studies *Ant.*'s "conscious reversal of the values of Vergil's *Aeneid*" (1). After three chapters that cover such earlier writers as Virgil, St. Augustine, Dante, Spenser, Robert Garnier, and Christopher Marlowe, and, in chap. 4, after a brief survey of earlier Shakespearean plays (140-50), Bono argues that, by means of Cleopatra, *Ant.* exhorts its audience "to tolerant synthesis, in harmony with those late humanist, eirenic movements in Shakespeare's day that assumed a liberal, conciliatory attitude toward the remnants of the past, toward the discoveries of the present, and toward the areas of cultural conflict generated between them" (151). Bono stresses Antony, following the development of his experience of himself as a Roman and descendent of Hercules (153-67). She argues that Cleopatra, associated with Venus (167-90), draws Antony "beyond the tragic paradox of his own nature, infusing his death with the full transcendent thrust of the *Hercules Oetaeus* [by Seneca; see discussion, 159-67]; and turning *Ant.* from a love tragedy to love triumph" (166-67). In this change, Bono points out, an important element is the play's "divided catastrophe" (218-19). In addition to Hercules and Venus, Bono discusses mythic material about Isis and Osiris (about whom Plutarch wrote at length), tracing Medieval and Renaissance knowledge of them, and showing how this knowledge enriches the play for audiences (191-213).

166. Cantor, Paul A. *Shakespeare's Rome: Republic and Empire.* Ithaca: Cornell Univ. Press, 1976. Part 2, 127-208.

Cantor treats *Cor.* and *Ant.* as "companion pieces" (207) that share an "inner unity" (205-08) and dramatize Rome at different epochs (Republic and Empire), arguing that in *Ant.* Republican values such as the respect of one's equals and the ideal of public service are weak but have not been replaced; thus, Antony is surrounded by a spiritual vacuum (136). Cantor studies this deterioration, which renders the traditional evaluation of action difficult (148-54); love is disjoined from marriage (159) and linked with death (163-80). Cantor studies the protagonists' love for each other at length, and finds the play's final scenes suffused with an aura of uncertainty and mystery.

167. Davies, H. Neville. "Jacobean *Antony and Cleopatra.*" *Shakespeare Studies* 17 (1985): 123-58.

Davies understands this play of 1606 in the context of the political world of King James, who had acceded to the English throne three years before: James's supporters associated the king with Antony, and the visit in 1606 of King Christian IV of Denmark highlighted the relationship since the Danish king was, like Antony, an attractive military hero who enjoyed his pleasures, especially drinking, fully.

168. MacCallum, M[ungo]. W., *Shakespeare's Roman Plays and Their Background*, 300-453. London: Macmillan, 1910.

MacCallum positions *Ant.* in Shakespeare's development after the period of the great tragedies (300-17); he stresses Plutarch as a source for both plot and verbal details (318-43), studies the characterization of minor characters (friends, 344-67; enemies, 368-90), especially Enobarbus (349-59), before devoting a chapter to Antony (391-412), emphasizing the love of excess and pleasure, and the failure, the realization of degradation, and suicide, and one to Cleopatra (413-38), emphasizing the unreliability, fearfulness, yet achievement of a "new dignity and strength" (431) at the end. In the last chapter of this section (439-53), the critic argues that the protagonists' love leads to both shame and glory (445), that each is incomplete without the other, and that the audience must admire them.

169. Miles, Geoffrey. *Shakespeare and the Constant Romans*. Oxford: Clarendon Press, 1996. Chap. 9, 169-88.

In accordance with his aim to provide "a closer analysis of [Roman] 'constancy' that acknowledges the complexity of its meanings and the tangled roots from which it springs" (vii), Miles sees Antony as a contrast to Coriolanus, one who, in a mutable world, "chooses to embrace 'the benefit of inconstancy'" (169). For Miles, change has become paramount in the Rome of this play: the human soul, even truth itself, is unstable, and the poetry expresses images of instability. Antony, in this critic's reading, tries to combine discordant elements, to embrace mutability (embodied by Cleopatra), thus reaching beyond categories in an attempt to redefine them (especially self-consistency, 182-85). Antony's death is a tragicomic attempt to attain a stability that the play undercuts (185). Miles argues that Cleopatra's suicide combines her "un-Roman, un-Stoic qualities—emotionalism, sensuality, frivolity, capriciousness, changeableness"—with "a new Stoic dignity and resolution" (187).

170. Miola, Robert S. *Shakespeare's Rome*. Cambridge: Cambridge Univ. Press, 1983. Chap. 5, 116-63.

In this book, which chronicles how Shakespeare's treatment of Rome changed both as he developed as a playwright and as he dramatized different historical periods of Roman history, Miola argues that *Ant.* is a "daring excursus" that reaches beyond "the boundaries of drama and beyond those of life itself" (117) and warns against trying to find in the play a single-minded moral or political teaching. Miola comments on the play's action from beginning to end, drawing attention to similarities to *JC*, to character patterning, and to Classical and mythic associations. In Miola's view, Shakespeare emphasizes the lovers and yet is unsympathetic with them; however, he also presents the transcendence of love, largely verbally through Cleopatra's mythic associations, culminating in her death scene (154) and its emblematic staging (154-58).

171. Simmons, J.L. *Shakespeare's Pagan World: The Roman Tragedies.* Charlottesville: Univ. Press of Virginia, 1973. Chap. 4, 109-63.

Simmons argues that *Ant.* "evokes ideals that ... are incapable of realization but that ennoble man" (111): "the ability to transcend the clay is still the distinction between beast and man" (163). After reviewing Renaissance treatments of love by Spenser, Shakespeare (*Midsummer Night's Dream, Much Ado About Nothing*, 115-17), and Sidney, Simmons comments on Shakespeare's sources, and concludes that the conflicts in this play are between lust and love, and between political power and honor (124). For Simmons, Antony finds himself repeatedly in a position where he must choose, yet he is not wholly involved in this need, and his understanding of his own tragedy is similarly inadequate; ultimately, its nature is "contingent upon [Cleopatra's] enigma" (149), an enigma that results from the co-existence of comedy and tragedy. For Simmons, "our comic expectations are fulfilled in the tragedy, but not by Antony" (154); they are fulfilled rather by Cleopatra, who "is poetically restoring nature to its original perfection" (161), and whose "sleep of death ... is now filled with life" (161).

172. Thomas, Vivian. *Shakespeare's Roman Worlds.* London and NY: Routledge, 1989. Chap. 3, 93-153.

Opening with a discussion of Shakespeare's alteration of his sources in characterization (especially Caesar, Antony, and Cleopatra, 93-106), Thomas emphasizes the resulting multiplicity of perspectives generated, and applies this perception to many aspects of the play, such as the inscrutability of Caesar's intentions, the amazed responses of minor characters, Antony's indecision, the opposed values of Rome and Egypt, public and private views of characters, and judgments of characters about others (121-38). In act 5, Thomas argues, the play's tone alters as Caesar changes from "the busy civil servant to historian and iconographer" (138) and the audience is presented with multiple views of earlier action and characterization, a situation reflected in the contrasting perceptions of literary critics, and of theater audiences. For Thomas, the play "disconcerts because it explores the guile and folly of reality along with the attainment of immortality and the *process* of the creation of myth" (153).

173. Yachnin, Paul. "Shakespeare's Politics of Loyalty: Sovereignty and Subjectivity in *Antony and Cleopatra.*" *Studies in English Literature 1500-1900* 33 (1993): 343-63.

In an essay that builds upon the new historicist focus on the "theatricality of power and the power of theatricality" (343), Yachnin examines the conflict between absolutism and the latent power of the governed in *Ant.* This controversy, Yachnin claims, emerged "into the consciousness of the members of its 1606-1607 audiences" (345). Yachnin argues that Shakespeare's use of the "rhythm of command and response" (346) undermines authority in both of the protagonists, and that Caesar "parallels King James's absolutist fantasy" (350); a variety of characters (Lepidus, Seleucus, Enobarbus, Menas, and Philo) helps the play "to display ideological contradiction rather than to propagandize in favor of state positions" (355). Yachnin links Cleopatra's inscrutability to King James and his divine right arguments for the absolute supremacy of the monarch. Relying in part on Francis Bacon's *Advancement of Learning* (1605), this critic concludes that the play reassigns political victory from King to subject, who "finds himself free to determine his own allegiance"; as a result, the subject "stands and has always stood on even ground with his 'sovereign'" (360-61).

See also nos. 46, 176, 181, 186, 194, 197, 199, 201, 204, and 205.

D. Language and Linguistics.

174. Charney, Maurice. *Shakespeare's Roman Plays: The Function of Imagery in the Drama.* Cambridge: Harvard Univ. Press, 1961. Chap. 4, 79-141.

Charney discusses *JC, Ant.,* and *Cor.,* paying primary attention to verbal images and their dramatic context, to character action, and to the unfolding of dramatic action in time. In his analysis of imagery in *Ant.,* Charney stresses hyperbole in action and language (for instance, the word "world," 82-93). Charney also studies images of the Nile and serpents, eating and drinking, hotness, indolence, and vanity, as well as hyperbole in the "heightening of Cleopatra" (112-25); he discusses the tragic ends of the protagonists (125-41); for Cleopatra at the end, "the conflict between Egypt and Rome ceases to exist, and the hard 'visible shapes' of Rome are dissolved into an ecstatic, poetic reality" (141).

175. Colie, Rosalie. *Shakespeare's Living Art.* Princeton: Princeton Univ. Press, 1974. Chap. 4, 168–207. Excerpt repr. Bloom (no. 213), 57–85.

Colie stresses magniloquence, or hyperbole, and shows that it is not merely a rhetorical ornamentation, but an integral part of the play, an aspect of life that reveals "personality, values, and ethics" (178). Colie stresses the explicit sexuality of the lovers and Cleopatra's imaginative power, which can invert the conventional: "the larger world has been contracted into the limits of Antony's body (normally a microcosm), and Antony's body in turn enlarged encompasses and surpasses the macrocosm" (192). Colie associates qualities of language with the gods (Mars, Hercules, Venus, and Isis, 195–99) and with natural fertility; after citing many examples throughout the play, and relating them to the characters of the protagonists, Colie concludes, "By their manner of dying, these figures are known," for both Antony and Cleopatra "die as they had lived, beyond definition, in expectation of more" (206).

See also nos. 29, 176, 181, 188, 190, 192, 196, 198, 199, and 203.

E. Criticism.

176. Adelman, Janet. *The Common Liar: An Essay on "Antony and Cleopatra."* New Haven: Yale Univ. Press, 1973. Excerpts in Bloom (no. 213), 5–34, Drakakis (no. 216), 56–77.

Adelman studies the relation of character to symbolic design, allowing the play to "teach us how to see it" (11); *Ant.* uses varying perspectives, all of them shifting, inconclusive, and temporary, on character and action: "We do not know how to regard *Ant.*: for the play is essentially a tragic experience embedded in a comic structure. In that sense it is as treacherous and painful as life itself" (52). Adelman highlights sources, especially Ovid, Virgil, Horace, and Tacitus (53–59), images, especially of horse, crocodile, and serpent (59–68), and myths, especially of Dido and Aeneas and Mars and Venus (68–101), and grounds these studies in the play's structure of doubt and paradox. For Adelman, the play itself invalidates the tendency to judge characters and experience, and questions the validity of making such an attempt. Adelman concludes the volume with Appendix A, "Plutarch and Shakespeare" (173–76), Appendix B, on verbal resemblances with Marlowe's *Dido, Queen of Carthage* (177–83), and Appendix C, on "Cleopatra's Blackness" (184–88).

177. Adelman, Janet. *Suffocating Mothers: Fantasies of Maternal Origin in Shakespeare's Plays, "Hamlet" to "The Tempest."* London and NY: Routledge, 1993. In chap. 7, 174–92.

Adelman's psychoanalytical approach stresses the contrast between female bounty ("the common mother's promiscuous generativity," 175) and male scarcity: "Longing for that heroic masculinity [absent in Shakespeare's output since *Hamlet*] is ... at the center of the play" (177); it is recovered in Cleopatra's dream of Antony in act 5, which is "the great generative act of the play" (183). For Adelman, masculinity is integrated with its female source (177), although this return is devastating. For this critic, Caesar, who is the spokesman of scarcity/masculinity, has Oedipally-tinted, complex feelings about the elder Antony's voluptuous completeness (178-81). Adelman stresses the connection of Cleopatra and the goddess Isis; bringing Antony to rest in her monument, Cleopatra evokes the ambivalence of the mother-infant bond, which is expressed in the play verbally in images of dissolution, as where such terms as *dragon, bear, lion, rock,* and *trees* become "temporary shapes wrested from vapor" (189). Adelman concludes by arguing that the play's realignment of masculinity with the maternal is a liberating imaginative achievement.

178. Bamber, Linda. *Comic Women, Tragic Men: A Study of Gender and Genre in Shakespeare.* Stanford: Stanford Univ. Press, 1982. Chap. 2, 45-70. Repr. Bloom (no. 213), 109-35.

Bamber isolates three Cleopatras: one represents Egypt (ambiguous, unknowable, 46); one is the "other," opposition to which leads to tragedy; and one is the character in the play's action. For Bamber, Rome has decayed and Egypt is the New World in which Antony must make his way—with new values that do not denigrate the female (as Rome has done) but prize relatedness. Cleopatra's ambiguity, in this critic's view, stems from the audience's never seeing her inner life; she is a performer, one who refuses to be defined by others (in contrast to Octavia, who allows this). Bamber stresses the role of nature, which the two main characters deal with differently: Antony sees it as "humanistic, synthesizing, responsible" (66), whereas Cleopatra sees it as a challenge which she meets with an identity as hard and "unyielding as Nature herself" (69).

179. Barton, Anne. "'Nature's Piece 'Gainst Fancy': The Divided Catastrophe in *Antony and Cleopatra*." In Bloom (no. 213), 35-55. (This paper first appeared as "Inaugural Lecture," Bedford College, London, 1973.) Revised version in Barton's *Essays, Mainly Shakespearean* (Cambridge: Cambridge Univ. Press, 1994), 113-35.

Barton argues that three of Sophocles' tragedies use the technique of the "divided catastrophe" to "force reappraisal, a radical change of viewpoint" at the end of the play, when the audience is tempted "to feel superior or even dismissive" (37). Barton studies earlier treatments of the

Antony and Cleopatra story (42–44) and gives examples of the "divided catastrophe" technique in Elizabethan-Jacobean drama (45–46). For Barton, the play's tragedy seems achieved with the death of Antony, and she explores the effects of the continuation: the audience wishes for Cleopatra to die, and is satisfied in a way that modifies its "feelings about the entire previous development of the tragedy" (51) as Cleopatra's death, in which "comedy simply flowers into tragedy" (52), "transfigures its earlier, more suspect stages" (53), thereby bestowing upon Antony "an heroic identity so colossal ... that it will defeat Time" (54).

180. Bradley, A.C. "Shakespeare's *Antony and Cleopatra.*" In *Oxford Lectures on Poetry*, 279–308. Oxford: Oxford Univ. Press, 1905. Second edition, 1909. Repr. Brown (no. 215), 63–87.

For Bradley, *Ant.* is not so great as the other major Shakespearean tragedies; acts 3 and 4 are marred by a disconcerting series of fragmented scenes, and the earlier half of the play does not contain sufficient passion and stage action. In Bradley's reading, Antony's inner struggle against his passions is not shown; nor is his final embracement of that passion shown with sufficient grandeur. Bradley notices the presence of irony: this quality prevents Antony from reaching the full tragic nature of other Shakespearean tragic heroes; Cleopatra achieves it, but only at the very end of the play.

181. Brower, Reuben. *Hero and Saint: Shakespeare and the Graeco-Roman Tradition.* Oxford: Oxford Univ. Press, 1971. Chap. 8, 317–53.

Brower reviews "anticipations" of Shakespeare's treatment in earlier plays (319–24) and stresses the imagery and its interaction with drama within *Ant.* (324–28), drawing attention to images of darkness, the fall and rise of Antony's nobility (328–37), and the "nobler life" expressed by Cleopatra's dream (337–46). Brower discusses the death scenes in detail (346–53), consistently emphasizing mythic parallels. For Brower, Antony represents nobility in its most complete form; Cleopatra's love rises to nobility, and "her vision and death renew our certainty of his greatness" (318). In Brower's reading, Shakespeare presents "the tragedy of the heroic and the heroism of love" while simultaneously showing love's "sensuous fullness and gaiety" and heroism's "pomp and self-aggrandizement, even to the point of burlesque" (318).

182. Cartwright, Kent. *Shakespearean Tragedy and Its Double: The Rhythms of Audience Response.* University Park: Pennsylvania State Univ. Press, 1991. Chap. 5, 227–70.

Cartwright argues that a number of Shakespeare's plays invite audience engagement (especially in terms of acting and theatricality), expressed as a "surrender of self-awareness through empathy, sympathy, or identification," and audience detachment (especially in terms of character and action), expressed as "doubt, evaluation, mediated emotion" (ix). In this critic's reading, the protagonists star in a *"theatrum mundi,"* and "are always performing their relationship for supernumeraries" (229): chief among their audience are Caesar, who moves from detachment to engagement, and whom the audience sees as "witnessing, listening, reacting ... watching, abhorring, desiring, envying" (241), and Enobarbus, who moves from engagement "to (attempted) detachment" from Antony following the defeat at Actium, and whom the audience sees with increasing "distanced superiority" (242). Cartwright traces audience responses to Antony in detail through his suicide, stressing the "ambivalent connotations" of self-compromise and parody in that event (259–64), and argues that in Cleopatra's last scenes these negative qualities become "self-enhancing and even noble," eliciting engagement on the part of the Romans onstage, who come to be actors but must become spectators, moments before the cast of the acting company will "bow before the applause of the performing playgoers" (270).

183. Cavell, Stanley. "Introduction." In *Disowning Knowledge in Six Plays of Shakespeare*, 18–37. Cambridge: Cambridge Univ. Press, 1987.

Cavell's "intuition is that the advent of skepticism as manifested in Descartes's *Meditations* is already in full existence in Shakespeare," that is, "how to live at all in a groundless world" (3). In this interpretation, the play presents "the repudiation of assured significance, repudiation of the capacity to improvise common significance, of the capacity of individual human passion and encounter to bear cosmic insignia" (19). Cavell discusses the play's presentation of love, which he relates to God, Christianity, seduction, the idea of marriage (a paradox in which two is one), and "satisfaction," both female and male (34–35).

184. Charnes, Linda. *Notorious Identity: Materializing the Subject in Shakespeare*. Cambridge and London: Harvard Univ. Press, 1993. Chap. 3, 103–47. Revised version in *Shakespearean Tragedy and Gender*, ed. Shirley Nelson Garner and Madelon Sprengnether, 268–86. Bloomington: Indiana Univ. Press, 1996.

Charnes argues that of the various forms that fame can take in plays one is notoriety, with its associations of being "noted, annotated, indicted, widely and overly known, obsessively talked and written about" (3), which create the pathological form "notorious identity," in which the dramatized character to some extent opposes the "persons or figures it 'originally' designates" (3). For Charnes, the real opposition in *Ant.* is between Egypt/Cleopatra and Rome/Caesar and is fought out by a combination of "strategy" and "tactics" (defined 109-10) "across the terrain of Antony's identity" (112). In this reading, Antony, Enobarbus, messengers, and various reporters make contact between the two antagonists; indeed, identity is constructed by those receiving reports and participating in discussions about them (Enobarbus's role is important, 119-25); the lovers are destroyed, therefore, not only by political and military events, but also by "representational politics" (146). For Charnes, a character with traits unreported to others cannot exist, and both lovers are devoted to their own existence as legends. Charnes discusses the revisionism involved in the transformation of what was for the Renaissance "a notorious story about politics on every level" (133) into a love story (133-47).

185. Danby, John F. *Poets on Fortune's Hill: Studies in Sidney, Shakespeare, and Beaumont and Fletcher.* London: Faber and Faber, 1952. Chap. 5, 128-51.

Danby stresses the play's swiftness of action in time and space, the ambiguity of character assessment by others, and the "co-presence of opposed judgments" (132) in this play, the central process of which is the juxtaposition, mingling, and "marrying" of opposites (132). Danby analyzes the first three scenes in detail (132-39) and studies Octavia, Caesar, and Cleopatra before concentrating on the play's tragic figure, Antony. For this critic, the play's uniqueness is that Shakespeare has constructed "a world without a Cordelia" (149).

186. Dickey, Franklin M. *Not Wisely But Too Well: Shakespeare's Love Tragedies.* San Marino: Huntington Library, 1957. Chaps. 10-12, 144-202. Excerpts in Brown (no. 215), 144-57.

Dickey recapitulates the Classical view of *Ant.* from Cicero to Sidonius (1st Century BCE to the 5th century CE), which stressed their lust and extravagance (144-52); the Medieval to 16th-century tradition, which saw Cleopatra as a warning against living for pleasure (152-60); and a variety of earlier Renaissance dramatic treatments in France and England, which Shakespeare knew and used, particularly Jodelle's *Cléopatre Captive*, 1552; Garnier/Sidney's *Antonius* (Garnier, 1578; Sidney, 1592); and Daniel's *Cleopatra*, 1594 (161-76). In chapter 12, Dickey denies that the play presents a celebration of transcendent love, highlighting negative qualities that undermine Cleopatra's positive ones (she is destructive, cruel, tyrannical, lustful, and proud, 187-88); in her death scene, she is preoccupied by visions of her impending humiliation at Rome.

187. Dollimore, Jonathan. *Radical Tragedy: Religion, Ideology, and Power in the Drama of Shakespeare and His Contemporaries,* 204-17. Chicago: Chicago Univ. Press, 1984. Repr. in Wofford (no. 218), 197-207, Bloom (no. 213), 137-49, and Drakakis (no. 216), 248-61.

For Dollimore, in *Ant.* "we are shown how the ideal in question constitutes not only the authority of those in power but their very identity" (204); in this play, which was first produced at a time when the titular aristocracy was declining in power, *virtus* (virtue, with additional connotations of self-sufficiency and autonomous power, 209) was praised, but Antony, especially in his death, shows that it was already obsolescent (212). Dollimore stresses the element of "power" in the language of the love of the protagonists and argues that the two "actually experience themselves in the same terms" (215). Neither the play nor the protagonists achieve a world beyond history, Dollimore claims: "if *Antony and Cleopatra* celebrates anything it is not the love which transcends power but the sexual infatuation which foregrounds it" (217).

188. Grene, Nicholas. *Shakespeare's Tragic Imagination.* NY: St. Martin's, 1992. Chap. 10, 223-48.

Grene's point of departure is his sense that in Shakespeare's last three tragedies (*Macbeth, Ant.,* and *Cor.*) "there were similar thematic concerns, similar preoccupations ... the relation of power to legitimating authority ... or of male and female roles in the imagination of [male] heroic endeavour" (ix). Following chapters on the English history plays and the earlier tragedies, Grene points out that in *Ant.* there is no pure evil and that the role of history is minimized, freeing the characters to "make themselves" (248). For Grene, despite the "transsexual antics" of the lovers and their dismissal of Rome, the play presents "as an open question ... what constitutes the nobleness of life" (227) in a world without stable moral standards. Grene studies the play's language, especially on imagination ("dissolution" and "dream" are important terms) and shows how it contributes to the effect of "imaginative expansiveness" (241). In this critic's reading, characters imagine themselves and others; Cleopatra recreates Antony so that his death becomes "a moment of transcendent significance" (244) and her suicide "is a pure histrionicism which defies disbelief and succeeds in imposing upon an audience a dream of apotheosis" (247).

189. Holloway, John. *The Story of the Night: Studies in Shakespeare's Major Tragedies.* Lincoln: Univ. of Nebraska Press; London: Routledge and Kegan Paul, 1961. Chap. 6, 99-120. Repr. Brown (no. 215), 179-200.

Holloway argues that nobility, or greatness, is for Antony and Cleopatra a role that they must live up to (102); this is a task they accomplish through many statements and actions; the two characters inspire each other with the "spectacle of greatness," intense, exuberant physical eulogy that issues from sexuality (105). For Holloway, each of the protagonists finds greatness within, and within the other; the "developing ordeal" of the two (112) is acted out against a backdrop of fluctuations and alternations (109–13). Both characters are, for Holloway, forced by circumstances into conduct that may be exalted or abject, and both are reduced to the level of "unaccommodated man," yet only Cleopatra's death scene presents in detail the continuation of greatness and humanity at its most primitive level: "it is the ordeal of the great and alienated who are pursued by life until they are sacrificed" (120).

190. Knight, G. Wilson. *The Imperial Theme: Further Interpretations of Shakespeare's Tragedies Including the Roman Plays.* Rev. edition. Oxford: Oxford Univ. Press, 1951. Chaps. 7–10, 199–350.

In chap. 7, Knight discusses the poetry of the play and shows how the repetition of key words helps create a theme of magnificence and eroticism, the idea of "blending" in nature, which reflects the love theme, and, finally, the spiritual or transcendent values in that love theme (205–62). In chap. 8, concentrating more on human qualities, Knight discusses the absence of evil, the "oscillating tendency" of the play (263–65), reflected in "a wavering, a failing of trust in love's unreason, a swift and beauteous recovery in death" (274); Cleopatra, "infinite woman" (313), becomes "love absolute and incarnate" in death (318). In chap. 9, Knight argues that *Macbeth* and *Ant.* have the "similarity of exact opposition" (327), and in chap. 10 he discusses the play's positive life-vision.

191. Lindley, Michael. *Hyperion and the Hobbyhorse: Studies in Carnivalesque Subversion.* Newark: Univ. of Delaware Press; London and Cranbury: Associated Univ. Presses, 1996. Chap. 6, 137–56.

Lindley argues that it is impossible to understand, in *Ant.* 4.15, "Cleopatra's ability to combine Venus, Isis, the maid that milks, the progenitive slime of the Nile, and the Virgin Mary—without recourse to the carnivalesque" (139). Arguing against earlier, polarizing interpretations, Lindley proposes a "carnivalesque paradigm" (141) that "inscribes a shifting, dialectical relationship between the two poles" (141). For Lindley, Cleopatra actively advances her own interests, suggesting a world in which women are independent (and opposed primarily by Octavius, who "epitomizes a Roman mentality," 144), many-faceted, and subversive (the connection of subversion and punning is discussed, 145–46). With regard to Antony, Lindley stresses the distinction between the individual and the "armor" ("the collective and unstable judgment of his community," 148);

the truly heroic Antony exists in Cleopatra's mind (149); in effect, Antony's manhood is relocated in Cleopatra, who is consistently "identified" with fluidity (sea, Nile, mud).

192. Markels, Julian. *The Pillar of the World: "Antony and Cleopatra" in Shakespeare's Development.* Columbus: Ohio State Univ. Press, 1968.

For Markels, equally valid but contradictory assessments of the moral natures of Antony and Cleopatra make the characters amoral; further, there are no clear villains in the play, and the evil to be conquered is not external but internal, inseparable from positive qualities. By contrast, Markels shows that in Shakespeare's history plays, from *Richard II* to *Henry V* and *JC* (chap. 3, 51–85), and in *Hamlet* and *King Lear* (chap. 4, 87–122), the opposition "between public appearance and private reality" is only one among many aspects of each play (51). In chap. 5 (123–51), Markels studies Antony (123–40) and Cleopatra (140–47) and argues that Antony's actions, which lead to death, achieve "the equation of love and honor," for his adversities "have enlarged him to a point where he is able to contain those public and private loyalties that were formerly opposed" (139). For Markels, Shakespeare's "symbolic treatment of death as apotheosis" (150) is a milestone in the dramatist's career. In chap. 6 (153–76), Markels studies language and relates it to theme: for instance, a "jerky discontinuity" between phrases or sentences "serves to isolate consecutive statements, and consecutive speakers, from one another," whereas flowing, integrated movements bind up "wholes that are greater than the sums of their parts" (159). Markels concludes with a brief postscript on *The Tempest* (171–76), an Appendix on the implications of his studies for the dating of some of Shakespeare's plays (177–79), a "Bibliographic Note" combining the author's indebtednesses with suggestions for further reading (181–83), endnotes (185–88), and a brief index (198–91).

193. Mason, H.A. *Shakespeare's Tragedies of Love*, 229–76. NY: Barnes and Noble, 1970.

In the first part of the study of *Ant.* (229–53), Mason acknowledges that his arguments have elicited "acrimony" from some, for he finds Antony a "professional clown, the hired entertainer of a courtesan" (234). Mason analyzes the opening scene (231–35) to establish this negative view, and finds that the following scenes of act 1, and the play's action from the beginning of act 2 to 3.7, is "emptiness" (241), expressing an unhealed division between "substance and shadow, dramatic reality and imaginative play" (245), despite the "characteristic strength" of many of the play's best known moments (246), which he analyzes in detail. In "Telling *versus* Shewing" (254–76), Mason finds that Antony is "unreal" after Actium (262); that the prominence of Enobarbus is "a symptom of Shakespeare's failure to focus his mind" (262); and that, since the high view of Antony expressed by Cleopatra's dream is told but never shown in earlier action, Shakespeare never achieves the promise of the play, despite moments of undoubted imaginative and poetic expression (276).

194. McAlindon, T. *Shakespeare's Tragic Cosmos.* Cambridge: Cambridge Univ. Press, 1991. Chap. 9, 220–57.

McAlindon studies *Ant.* as a tragedy of Fortune ("inevitable change in the cyclic order of history and nature," 223) in the light of Ovid's *Metamorphoses* (224–29) and Plutarch's essay "Isis and Osiris" (229–32); the play has a positive attitude even toward tragic change in its "sense of renewal in death, of eternity in time, and of the divine in flawed human greatness" (232). In this reading, Antony's conflict is between responding to the changing demands of time and desire to lose himself in it, and achieving a time-reckoning that transcends minutes and hours (238), an attempt associated with myth and alchemy; the many dualities in the play, remarked in analyses of Antony, Octavius, Cleopatra, and Octavia, are all resolved and fully harmonized (241–57).

195. Mills, Laurens J. *The Tragedies of Shakespeare's "Antony and Cleopatra".* Bloomington: Indiana Univ. Press, 1964.

For Mills, this play presents two separate tragedies, for "the fate of Cleopatra is foreshadowed by that of Antony and the tragedy of Antony is vividly remembered while that of Cleopatra is in enactment" (5). In chap. 2, Mills compares Antony as he is in Rome (7–22) with the later Antony at Actium and after (22–35). Cleopatra in the second half of the play is, for Mills, transfigured, and is tragic: "It is pathetic and tragic that a beginning of anything other than sensual self-interest comes when there is neither the opportunity nor the time for growth to ensue" (61). Mills concludes with a note on Enobarbus, whom he sees as "Roman" in his criticism of Antony's neglect of his responsibilities.

196. Nevo, Ruth. *Tragic Form in Shakespeare.* Princeton: Princeton Univ. Press, 1972. Chap. 9, 306–55.

Nevo argues that the protagonists' love, far from being opposed to the world, seeks to enjoy it, but the course of tragedy makes an irreconcilable opposition between them and the world (318). Act 3, in this reading, marks the *peripeteia*, the "reversal of the lovers' fortunes at the very moment when they are together again" (324). Nevo stresses the role of Enobarbus, a tragic figure, and analyzes Cleopatra's imagination through its language (339–55). For Nevo, the clown plays an important role, emphasizing the double catastrophe; the clown, "perhaps the most daring of all his [Shakespeare's] clowns" (353), in his word play allows Cleopatra to transcend baser life, yet also "casts a final ironic and pitiful light upon Cleopatra's self-created situation" (353).

197. Nochimson, Richard L. "The End Crowns All: Shakespeare's Deflation of Tragic Possibility in *Antony and Cleopatra*." *English* 26 (1977): 99-132.

For Nochimson, Shakespeare has deliberately reduced the tragic elements inherent in the Antony and Cleopatra story as much as possible. He sees Shakespeare's Antony as "blind to his own defects" (102), stubborn and childish (105), "pathetic" (107) rather than tragic; Enobarbus, upon whose comments many critics rely, provides ambiguous and even inaccurate guidance on Antony (111-13). In Nochimson's reading, Cleopatra is changeable, an actress, "a pitiable, a comically pathetic character" (114-16). The critic argues that for Cleopatra, potentially the more tragic of the two, "life ... consists of eating dung and the only way to achieve greatness is to master Fortune by committing suicide" (121); her view that life is meaningless makes it valueless and therefore reduces the tragic impact on readers and audiences. Throughout, Nochimson supports his argument with analysis of Shakespeare's use of and departures from various sources: Plutarch, Garnier, and Samuel Daniel. In focusing on the play's death scenes, he emphasizes the Shakespearean motif of the contrast between dying of a broken heart and dying in an ignoble manner—through contrast between the ways in which Antony and Cleopatra say they will die and the ways they actually die, and through contrast between the ways that they die and the ways that Enobarbus and Iras die (117, 124).

198. Rackin, Phyllis. "Shakespeare's Boy Cleopatra, the Decorum of Nature, and the Golden World of Poetry." *PMLA* 87 (1972): 201-12. Repr. Drakakis (no. 216), 78-100.

For Rackin, this play is a reckless, daring dramatic composition that challenged neo-Classical standards of dramatic composition. Rackin focuses on many aspects of Shakespeare's daring—for instance, the illegitimacy of the protagonists' love, the inconsistency of Cleopatra's character, the episodic structure of action (the jumping from continent to continent and the passage of years), and the variousness of the language (which combines Latinisms, mixed metaphors, highly refined rhetoric, and slang).

199. Riemer, A.P. *A Reading of Shakespeare's "Antony and Cleopatra."* Sydney: Sydney Univ. Press, 1968.

In chap. 1, Riemer surveys the "background" of *Ant.* (especially

Garnier, Daniel, and Plutarch) and argues that Plutarch's major contribution was a "liberality of attitude" (20). For Riemer, this play ultimately breaks free from an "overpowering" and "constricting" world of tragedy: tragic possibilities are part of the play's dialectic that brings public and private worlds into complex and uneasy interrelation (110-11). Riemer provides detailed commentaries on language, character, and structural patterns—for instance, the pattern of reversals running from 1.1 to 1.3 (29-37); the sequence of units running from 1.4 to 3.6 (37-47); the creation of ironic distancing and simultaneous focus on Antony in the section 3.7-the end of 4 (49-61); and the language of Cleopatra in 5 (62-77). In chap. 3, Riemer reviews the arguments of a number of earlier critics and engages with some of them on the interpretation of character and on language (78-115), developing comments he had made earlier in this book.

200. Rosen, William. *Shakespeare and the Craft of Tragedy.* Cambridge: Harvard Univ. Press, 1960. Chap. 3, 104-60.

Rosen contrasts Antony's past, "the only unquestioned ideal in the play" (112), with Cleopatra's ideal of "magnetic sensuality" (117); Antony must choose between recreating this past and succumbing to a temptress. Rosen discusses the play's structure, stressing the patterning of departures and reunions and Antony's exposure to "vying demands" (123); the play presents "opposing values and beliefs ... held in tenuous balance" (147). For Rosen, Antony's death is a final commitment to his reputation and honor; Cleopatra's is an attempt for a comparable vision, but she is unable to sustain it (158-59) and hence her death cannot be seen as idealistic transcendence (153).

201. Schanzer, Ernest. *The Problem Plays of Shakespeare: A Study of "Julius Caesar," "Measure for Measure," and "Antony and Cleopatra."* NY: Schocken, 1963. Chap. 3, 132-83.

Schanzer discusses the structural pattern of parallels and contrasts, especially Rome/Egypt and Antony/Cleopatra (the latter, for instance, consists of "echoes of each other by the lovers, both in words and actions ... similarities in descriptions of them ... parallels in relations with them" (133), all of which bring out the essential likeness, or near-identity, of the lovers. Schanzer reviews earlier dramatic treatments of "Antony's choice" (155), and then studies its unique treatment in *Ant.* by comparison with the choice of Hercules in myth, between Pleasure and Virtue, and that of Aeneas, between Dido and the fulfillment of his divine mission to found Rome (155-67). Schanzer concludes by studying the play as a tragedy from three perspectives (formal, experiential, and affective, terms defined in chap.

1, 57–63), contrasting it to Garnier's *Antonius* and Daniel's *Cleopatra*; *Ant.* is, for Schanzer, "Shakespeare's problem play *par excellence*" (145), presenting "opposed evaluations" that exclude a single response.

202. Simonds, Peggy Muñoz. "'To The Very Heart of Loss': Renaissance Iconography in Shakespeare's *Antony and Cleopatra*." *Shakespeare Studies* 22 (1994): 220–76.

Drawing on a wealth of earlier scholarship, Simonds attempts to "arrive at a Renaissance reading of the tragedy" (223), using an iconographic approach to words and stage imagery to demonstrate Cleopatra's close association with the goddess Fortuna (nine attributes, 224–46); Antony, who foolishly trusts Fortune, is "caught like a fish on a hook baited with female sexuality and beauty" (223) and then sacrificed (246–61). For Simonds, the play ends in ambiguous tragedy, as Cleopatra immortalizes her performance as Fortuna in a "transcendent artistic work of marble statuary" (223; 261–71). To support her analysis, Simonds uses a large number of illustrations from emblem books from the Renaissance period as analogues to images and ideas presented in the play.

203. Steppat, Michael. *The Critical Reception of Shakespeare's "Antony and Cleopatra" from 1607 to 1905.* Bochumer anglistische studien 9. Amsterdam: Verlag B.R. Gruner, 1980.

After a brief summary to 1660 (chap. 1, 1–4), Steppat presents the period of the restoration and 18th century under aspects and themes such as "nature and art," and "poetic justice" (4–47), giving copious quotations from a wide variety of English and Continental critics, some in the original languages. In chapter 3, Steppat introduces Romantic criticism, its approaches and values (48–71), and summaries, often with excerpts, of such critics as A.W. Schlegel, Goethe, Coleridge, and Tieck; in chapter 4 (72–205), the author divides English post-Romantic criticism according to approach, for instance "moral" and "later Romantic," with special attention to A.C. Bradley (150–60) and critics writing on individual characters (for instance Cleopatra, 161–81). Steppat surveys French and German criticism in chapter 5 (206–317) and in chapter 6 (318–26) follows developments from Bradley to Schücking. Steppat also provides a "Topical analysis" of the material he presented earlier: "general assessments" and who expressed them (328–36); the themes critics have stressed and who stressed them (337–48); discussions of the relation of the play to history (349–72); and two sections devoted to Technique (structure and language, 373–96) and characters (397–484). Steppat concludes with end notes and a full bibliography, 1607–1977, an index of names, and one of "Terms" and characters.

204. **Waith, Eugene M.** *The Herculean Hero in Marlowe, Chapman, Shakespeare, and Dryden.* NY: Columbia Univ. Press, 1962. In Chap. 5, 113–21.

In the course of studying the protagonists of seven Shakespeare plays in the light of Herculean heroism (" ... the poet who associates his hero with Hercules shows him, momentarily at least, in a pre-existing heroic form" [50]) to which the typical response is admiration, a "range of responses from awe to astonishment" [53]), Waith argues that, although Cleopatra is important in the play, and Antony's final commitment to her makes the play "something other than the tragedy of a Herculean hero" (113), it is nevertheless a major treatment of the type. Waith focuses on the different images of Antony given by Caesar and Cleopatra, and on his bounty and rage (115–20), the latter a characteristic of this kind of hero; these are a large part of Antony's heroic nature. In Waith's reading, Antony's suicide is noble, the "recognition of the impossibility of achieving Cleopatra's ideal in the world," and a "dedication of himself to Cleopatra, the final custodian of his heroic image" (121).

205. **Weber, A.S.** "New Physics for the Nonce: A Stoic and Hermetic Reading of Shakespeare's *Antony and Cleopatra.*" *Renaissance Papers 1995*: 93–107.

Weber draws on a wide variety of Classical sources (especially Greek and Roman Stoicism and Hermetic literature, itself influenced by Stoicism) that appealed to Renaissance readers concerned with "the crumbling Aristotelian-Ptolemaic" astronomy, to emphasize the origins of *Ant.*'s "Christian resurrection symbolism, alchemical imagery, and Herculean cosmic allegory" (94). Weber argues that Stoic cosmology, in opposition to Christian-Aristotelian thought, made no essential distinction between celestial and terrestrial phenomena (97), thus problematizing subject-object dichotomies. These strands of thought are expressed in Cleopatra's dream of Antony's apotheosis (5.2), which Weber interprets in terms of "the pneuma itself, the Stoic force and material operating through tonic expansion and contraction" (101). Weber argues that Antony is associated with both Hercules and Bacchus, a generative force, and suggests that the apotheosis may be read as a "figure of hermaphroditic joining of active and passive ... the complete man who harmonizes desire (love) and the violent destructive impulse" (103).

206. **Wilcher, Robert.** "*Antony and Cleopatra* and Genre Criticism." In "*Antony and Cleopatra,*" ed. Nigel Wood, 95–120. Theory in Practice Series. Buckingham and Philadelphia: Open Univ. Press, 1996.

Wilcher, whose essay is one of four touching more and less directly on *Ant.* from varying perspectives, positions the play by means of discussions of two earlier theorists, Jonathan Culler and Northrop Frye (95–104). For Wilcher, the play is divided into three phases: the first mingles different generic elements, especially tragedy, comedy, and history (106–11); the second, following the defeat at Actium, is transitional, and in it "the carnival world of Egypt" has been destroyed (113); and the third leads to the double catastrophe, the deaths of the protagonists, when, following Cleopatra's death, the audience is brought up sharply "against the impossibility of distinguishing between 'perfect honour' and 'excellent dissembling'" (115). This volume, which is part of a series that seeks to "bridge the divide between the understanding of theory and the interpretation of individual texts" (xi), includes a guide, "How to Use This Book" (xiv–xv), a general theoretical statement by Wood (1–8), who also introduces each essay (92–95 for Wilcher), and also appends to each a brief interview with the critic (120–24), and an endpiece (125–27).

See also nos. 31, 34, 36, and 43.

F. Stage History and Performance Criticism; Adaptations.

207. Cohn, Ruby. *Modern Shakespeare Offshoots*. Princeton: Princeton Univ. Press, 1976. Chap. 7, 321–39.

"Almost all art builds on previous art," Cohn observes, "but much modern art builds *with* previous art" (x); with this idea in mind, the author studies how Shakespeare plays have been points of departure for later dramatists. Cohn admits that she cannot prove that Shaw's *Caesar and Cleopatra* (1898) derives from Shakespeare's *JC* and *Ant.* (327). Nevertheless, Cohn's discussion compares them: Shaw's play is "unromantic" and eliminates "love and revenge" (329): the strong, sensual Antony is replaced by a "keen, balding, intelligent Caesar" (329), and Shakespeare's "unwithered and infinitely various Cleopatra is ... replaced by a charming and capricious adolescent" (329). At the play's end, Cohn argues, the comic note foreshadows tragedy, for Caesar promises to send Cleopatra the young, handsome Antony. Cohn concludes that Shaw composed *Caesar and Cleopatra* "consciously or unconsciously ... in reaction to (and against)" *JC* and *Ant.* (331), a point supported by Shaw's preface, "Better than Shakespear?" (1912). For Cohn, Shaw's play displays the author's "most creative use of the Bard" (331), and she notes that some theaters in the 20th century have presented *Ant.* and *Caesar and Cleopatra* together as a pair (331).

208. Goldman, Michael. *Acting and Action in Shakespearean Tragedy.* Princeton: Princeton Univ. Press, 1985. Chap. 6, 112–39. Repr. Wofford (no. 218), 249–67.

Goldman observes that the word "action," when used to describe a play's action, really refers to three different kinds of action: "the actions the characters perform; the action of the audience's mind in responding to and trying to possess the events it watches; and finally the actions by which the actors create and sustain their roles" (12). He studies all three meanings, and hence combines a literary with a theatrical approach. The author studies *Ant.*'s idea of greatness ("a way of experiencing life," 112) as "primarily a command over other people's imaginations" (112), ranging from self-dramatization to the overcoming of "time, death, and the world" (113). In Goldman's view, greatness affects a variety of characteristics of the play, such as the large number of reports, which measure a character's greatness by showing how thinking about him or her "dominates and controls the mood of others" (117). Goldman also discusses problems in acting, and finds the actor must realize that the protagonists' love radiates a "larger process that is everywhere at work in the play" and has a transforming effect, exerting "a transforming force on the apparently more substantial and valuable world" (123). Goldman studies transformation in the poetic language (124–33) and its complex effect on the audience: "we identify with audiences, with Antony and Cleopatra as each other's audience, with ourselves as audience, and with the audience characters on stage" (138).

209. Granville-Barker, Harley. *"Antony and Cleopatra." Prefaces to Shakespeare I.* Princeton: Princeton Univ. Press, 1947. 367–458.

For Granville-Barker, *Ant.* is a play of action rather than spiritual insight (367) which keeps the audience interested by its mixes of character and action. This critic stresses the sweep in space and time conveyed by the absence of authorial stage directions, concentrates on the three days following the defeat at Actium and the confrontation of Cleopatra and Caesar. Granville-Barker discusses scenery, costuming, verse, characterization, and the fact that Cleopatra was played by a boy actor; Cleopatra is "quick, jealous, imperious, mischievous, malicious, flagrant, subtle, but a delicate creature, too" (438), and she dies "defiant, noble in her kind, shaming convenient righteousness, a miracle of nature that ... will not be reconciled to any gospel but its own" (447).

210. Lamb, Margaret. *"Antony and Cleopatra" on the English Stage.* Rutherford: Fairleigh Dickinson Univ. Press; London: Associated Univ. Presses, 1980.

Lamb surveys productions of *Ant.* from Shakespeare's day to the Peter Brook 1978 production for the Royal Shakespeare Company. Beginning with a chapter on what little is known about productions before the Restoration (23-34), Lamb comments briefly on the 1660-1759 period, when the play was apparently not performed at all, and then highlights David Garrick's innovations (44-51), and those of the 19th and early 20th centuries, whose many productions (from John Philip Kemble's 1813 revival through those featuring Helen Faucit and William Charles Macready, and culminating in Herbert Beerbohm Tree's of 1906) made use of new possibilities in scenery and had an interest in period costuming (52-98). Stressing the radical changes of staging available after this period, Lamb surveys "continuous action" productions between the wars (101-30), "star" productions between 1946 and 1953 (131-54), and the most recent period of "repertory and experiment" (155-79), emphasizing politics and "cinematic" techniques of "cross-cutting, dissolves, close-ups and overlaps" (161). Throughout the discussion of the various productions, Lamb emphasizes how the actors seem to have understood the characters they played. Lamb concludes with Appendix A, notes on the staging of 4.15 (180-85), Appendix B, a list of the productions referred to (186-88), endnotes (189-221), and a very substantial selected bibliography (222-35).

211. Madelaine, Richard, ed. *Antony and Cleopatra.* Shakespeare in Production. Cambridge: Cambridge Univ. Press, 1998.

Madelaine reprints Bevington's text (see no. 159), substituting his glossing, background information, and critical commentary with "a comprehensive dossier of materials—eye-witness accounts, contemporary criticism, promptbook marginalia, stage business, cuts, additions and rewritings—from which to construct an understanding of the many meanings" (ix) that *Ant.* has carried since its composition, a procedure that offers many glimpses of live performances of the past. The editor's introduction (1-138) is an extended stage history, beginning with miscellaneous topics, for instance ways of separating scenes, earlier habits of cutting or Bowdlerizing text, reflections on the demands of the role of Cleopatra on actresses, and the fascination of Europe with Egypt (1-14). Madelaine then discusses (14-66) the play in terms of Jacobean and later theater practices, showing how it was produced and acted from the Restoration to the recent past, highlighting productions by J.P. Kemble (1813), W.C. Macready (1833), and H.B. Tree (1906). Madelaine then surveys 20th-century productions, both stage and film (74-138), before giving Bevington's text (141-325), prefaced by brief remarks on speaking, acting, and the significance of the first scene (141–44). The editor provides a bibliography (326–37) and an index (338–58).

212. Scott, Michael. *Antony and Cleopatra.* Text and Performance. London: Macmillan, 1983.

In Part 1, "Text," after giving a brief synopsis of the play's action, Scott analyzes the role of Cleopatra, "one of the greatest challenges to an actress" (11); she is "Queen of Love," transcending petty accusation, while Antony is divided between allegiance to Mars and to Venus, and dies unsure and divided (19–25). For Scott, the lesser characters create an atmosphere of paradoxical experience (25–30) such that even the queen's death is surrounded by "paradoxes, ambiguities and deceits" (37) in which fantasy and reality fuse. In Part 2, "Performance," Scott discusses how the play has been staged, and how Cleopatra and Antony have been interpreted by players in major performances from 1951 to 1978. Scott adds brief notes comparing the productions (71–73), a postscript on one of 1982 (73–75), a reading list (76–78), and an index.

G. Teaching and Collections of Essays.

213. Bloom, Harold, ed. *William Shakespeare's "Antony and Cleopatra."* NY: Chelsea House, 1988.

This useful volume publishes excerpts from critical discussions, some of them annotated in the present volume.

214. Bloom, Harold, ed. *Cleopatra.* Major Literary Characters. NY: Chelsea House, 1990.

This useful volume publishes excerpts from critical discussions, some of them annotated in the present volume.

215. Brown, John Russell, ed. *Shakespeare: "Antony and Cleopatra": A Casebook.* Casebook Series. London and Nashville: Aurora Publishers, 1970.

This collection, which has been reprinted frequently since its first appearance, is noted here because it contains essays that have been annotated in the present volume.

216. Drakakis, John, ed. *"Antony and Cleopatra": William Shakespeare.* New Casebooks. NY: St. Martin's; Basingstoke: Macmillan, 1994.

This useful collection reprints many critical discussions, some of which are annotated in the present volume.

217. **Rose, Mark,** ed. *Twentieth Century Interpretations of "Antony and Cleopatra": A Collection of Critical Essays.* Englewood Cliffs, N.J.: Prentice-Hall, 1977.

This useful collection reprints critical essays, many of which are annotated in the present volume.

218. **Wofford, Susanne L.,** ed. *Shakepeare's Late Tragedies: A Collection of Critical Essays.* Upper Saddle River, NJ: Prentice-Hall, 1996.

This collection contains critical essays, many of which are annotated in the present volume.

219. **Wood, Nigel,** ed. *"Antony and Cleopatra."* Theory in Practice Series. Buckingham and Philadelphia: Open Univ. Press, 1996.

This collection reprints a critical essay annotated in the present volume.

H. Bibliographies.

220. **Bains, Yashdip S.,** ed. *"Antony and Cleopatra": An Annotated Bibliography.* NY and London: Garland, 1998.

Bains introduces this volume with a short history of the interpretation of *Ant.* (xi–xxi): in the 17th and 18th centuries, literary critics concentrated on the plot, the sprawling geographical range, the large number of scenes, the sources, and the disregard for the Classical unities, whereas in the Romantic period they stressed the "organic unity" (xii) of the plot and the difficulty in passing judgment on the lovers (Cleopatra was found a troublesome female by some but admirable by others, and Antony intemperate by some and warm and vigorous by others). More recently, Bains argues, critics have concentrated on the nature of the love that unites Antony and Cleopatra, and, for some, this love transcends all earthly considerations. The editor arranges this bibliography into sections devoted to Criticism, whether separately-published essays or chapters in books (3–317, items 1–1152); Sources and Background (319–38, items 1153–1233); Textual Studies (339–46, items 1234–66); Bibliographies (347–53, items 1267–96); Editions (355–81, items 1297–1405); Translations (383–93, items 1406–1509); Stage History (395–459, items 1510–1755); Major Productions (461–68, items 1756–1813); Films (469–73, items 1814–27); Music (475–79, items 1828–46); Television (481–83, items 1847–55); Teaching Aids (chiefly audio- and videotapes, 485–87, items 1856–80); Adaptations and Synopses (489–91, items 1881–95); Additional Entries (493–500, items 1896–1922); and an Index (501–27). The editor concentrates on the years 1940–95 (including some significant items that appeared before and after that date) and arranges the entries chronologically, then alphabetically within the year.

221. Sajdak, Bruce T., ed. *Shakespeare Index: An Annotated Bibliography of Critical Articles on the Plays 1959-83*. 2 vols. Vol. 1, Citations and Author Index. Vol. 2, Character, Scene, and Subject Indexes. Millwood, NY: Kraus International Publications, 1992.

Sajdak seeks to provide the student with a means to "quickly locate, amongst the thousands of possible sources, those few most relevant articles on specific ideas, characters, or scenes" (1.xi). He provides a statement of scope, a list of sources he consulted (xiii–xvii), and a guide on how to use the *Index* (xxi–xxii). Sajdak divides the *Index* into 48 chapters (arranged chronologically by date of publication), initially by research area, then by play title (arranged by period, genre, and title). For each entry, Sajdak gives full publication information and an annotation. There are indexes for authors and, beginning with vol. 2, for character (803–1033), scene (1035–1197), and subject (1199–1765), with extensive subdivisions. *Ant.* is covered in 1. 209–29, items P 1–204. This *Index* does not include chapters in books unless these were published separately as articles.

222. Weis, R.J.A. "*Julius Caesar* and *Antony and Cleopatra*." In *Shakespeare: A Bibliographical Guide*. New Edition, ed. Stanley Wells, 275–94. Oxford: Clarendon Press, 1990.

This volume, a rewritten and updated version of the first edition of 1973, aims to provide a selectively critical guide to the best in Shakespearean scholarship and criticism. Weis's up-to-date discursive bibliography (the hallmark of the Wells guide) discusses Shakespeare and Roman history (275–78), *Ant.* texts, and the history of criticism from Coleridge through the mid 1980s (284–90); Weis also provides a bibliography for further reading (292–94).

See also nos. 161, 203, 210, 211.

VII. CORIOLANUS

A. Editions.

222a. Bliss, Lee, ed. *Coriolanus.* The New Cambridge Shakespeare. Cambridge: Cambridge Univ. Press, 2000.

In the introduction (1–100), Bliss dates the play (composition, winter 1607–08; first performance between March and late July 1608 [4]), discusses its relation to the other Plutarchan plays (5–17), relates it to contemporary events of "death, riots, rebellions" (17–27), and, via Plutarch, to such political issues as elections and the roles of the Roman Senate and English Parliament (27–33), finding in the careers of Sir Walter Ralegh and the Earl of Essex contemporary models that "would have made this relatively obscure Roman soldier immediately 'recognizable'" (33). Following this background material, Bliss offers a scene-by-scene reading of the play, stressing politics and ethics, and arguing that the possibility of viable compromise rests in adherence to Menenius's fable of the belly and the members (46). Bliss focuses on the Coriolanus-Volumnia relationship, cautioning against understanding it in too modern a way (48–52), and offers a range of possible responses to the final scenes (56–61). Bliss ends the introduction with a survey of the play's theater history to 1994 (63–98). Bliss then prints the play, with notes to and on the text, glossing difficult words and phrases, and offers further specific background information and critical commentary at the bottom of each page. The volume ends with a bibliographical analysis of the text (275–300), and a list of suggested readings (301–03).

223. Brockbank, Philip., ed. *Coriolanus.* The Arden Shakespeare, 2nd series. London: Methuen; Cambridge: Harvard Univ. Press, 1976.

In the introduction (1–89), Brockbank studies the text, date, and sources of the play, providing in two appendices passages from North's *Plutarch* (313–68) and Camden's 1605 *Remaines* (369–70). The editor argues that the 1623 Folio text was set from Shakespeare's ms. and dates the play 1607–08 on the basis of the quality of the verse and the political ideas expressed, especially in that it dramatizes the confrontation of an individual, a hero who identifies valor with virtue, in crisis with a particular and hostile political situation. Brockbank provides notes to the text and on the text at the foot of each page, with not only glosses on difficult words and phrases but also background information and critical commentary.

224. Furness, Horace Howard, Jr., ed. *A New Variorum Edition of Shakespeare: The Tragedie of Coriolanus.* Philadelphia and London: Lippincott, 1928.

In his preface (v–xi), Furness accepts the 1623 Folio as the only copy text, although he views it as corrupt (v); he reviews Shakespeare's use of Plutarch and his anti-democratic bias (vi), and argues for a composition date of 1607–09 (viii). The editor provides notes to the text and on the text on each page, with the comments of 18th- and 19th-century scholars and critics (1–583). In the appendix (587–738), Furness groups together a wide variety of material: he studies issues concerning the text, reprints an excerpt from J.P. Collier's "Trilogy" (1874), and presents selections from earlier criticism on the play's date of composition and sources (he includes passages from North's *Plutarch*, 621–45). Furness also discusses criticism of the play and of specific characters (649–701), as well as the issue "Shakespeare and the masses" (701–15); he also provides an account of dramatic "versions" of Shakespeare's play (716–25) and a stage history, including quotations from significant actors and from theatergoers (730–38). Furness ends the volume with a bibliography (739–48) and an index (749–62).

225. Parker, R.B., ed. *Coriolanus.* The Oxford Shakespeare. Oxford: Clarendon Press; NY: Oxford Univ. Press, 1994.

Parker's introductory material (1–154) discusses the date of composition, the play's place in the development of Shakespeare's political thought (which he links to Shakespeare's various presentations of Rome in his work), the sources (17–33), events in Jacobean England that might account for Shakespeare's treatment of the people (33–43), a critical discussion of the political, psychological, and existential levels on which the play operates (43–70), and an exploration of the play's language and style (70–86). Parker dates the play's original production to 1609–10 (87); discusses fully what is known of its original staging, including stage properties, music, blocking, acting cues in the text, silence, gesture; and frequently refers to later acting traditions (89–115). Parker surveys *Cor.*'s stage history (115–36) in terms of specific critical interpretations (for instance, ideological, right- and left-wing, anti-heroic, post-modernist). The editor discusses the nature of the 1623 Folio text (the copy text of this edition) and editorial procedures (136–54); the play is printed (157–

359) with textual notes, glosses of difficult words and phrases, background information, and critical commentary at the bottom of each page. Parker ends the volume with Appendix A, a listing of this edition's departures from the Folio lineation (361–66), Appendix B, summaries of, and excerpts from, chief sources and analogues (367–77), and the Index (379–88).

B. Authorship, Dating, and Textual Studies.

226. Clayton, Thomas. "Today we have Parting of Names: Editorial Speech-(Be)Headings in *Coriolanus*." In *Shakespeare's Speech-Headings: Speaking the Speech in Shakespeare's Plays*, ed. George Walton Williams, 61–99. Newark: Univ. of Delaware Press, 1986.

In this essay, Clayton studies the difficulties caused by problematic speech-headings in the Folio text of *Cor.*; Philip Brockbank, in his 1976 edition of the play (see no. 223), identified "sixteen-plus cruxes and editorial variants" which are "editorial—and bibliographical—problems because they were first critical [ones]" (65), and a decision on them must be made by readers and actors alike. Clayton divides these cruxes into four groups: the first is concerned with the meaning of "all," "some," and "other"; the second, which he terms "citizen which," raises the issue of distinguishing between "1 Cit." and "2 Cit."; the third analyzes situations where it is not clear whether Coriolanus or Cominius is to speak; the fourth, a final "miscellany" (65–82), concludes that "abbreviation…, ambiguity, misplaced SHs [speech headings], and occasional illegibility in an autograph MS possibly used as a 'prompt-book,' seem as likely an explanation as any other of most of the SH cruxes discussed above" (83). Clayton provides Brockbank's list of editorial variants, a collation of that list with "recent scholarly editions" (85–87), facsimiles of selected Folio pages (88–93), notes, and a bibliography (94–99).

See also nos. 223–25 and 264.

C. Influences; Sources; Historical and Intellectual Backgrounds; Topicality.

227. Barton, Anne. "Livy, Machiavelli, and Shakespeare's *Coriolanus*." *Shakespeare Survey* 38 (1985): 115–29. Repr. in Barton's *Essays, Mainly Shakespearean* (Cambridge: Cambridge Univ. Press, 1994) 136–60.

Although agreeing that the primary source for *Cor.* is Plutarch, Barton argues for Shakespeare's recourse to Livy's *Ab urbe condita* and Machiavelli's

Discorsi (commentaries on Livy): Livy's stress was less on the biographies of famous heroes than on the development of the city of Rome and of its people (116). For Barton, *Cor.*, "unique in the canon for its tolerance and respect" for the citizens of Rome (117), is a play in which the protagonist learns "certain necessary truths about the world in which he exists, but dies before he has any chance to rebuild his life in accordance with them" (128). In her reading, Shakespeare "looked attentively at the young Roman republic ... and chose to emphasize what was hopeful, communal and progressive in it" (129).

228. Cantor, Paul A. *Shakespeare's Rome: Republic and Empire.* Ithaca: Cornell Univ. Press, 1976. Part 1, 55–124.

Cantor contrasts *Cor.* with *Ant.* as dramatizations involving Rome at different epochs and with differing values: *Cor.* presents Republican Rome ruled by patricians who emphasize loyalty to the city and who treat the people with contempt. In Cantor's analysis, which devotes considerable space to language (110-16), the class conflict works itself out by trial and error (71), but Coriolanus, who is inflexible in his criticism of the Republic (79), ultimately tries to live in isolation. For Cantor, Coriolanus "seeks honor but dislikes the requirement of having other men to honor him" (95): he learns (chiefly by the claims of his family) that he cannot live without Rome, and the Romans learn they cannot exist without him (120); the radical incompatibility is fatal to both.

229. Dollimore, Jonathan. *Radical Tragedy: Religion, Ideology, and Power in the Drama of Shakespeare and His Contemporaries*, 218–30. Chicago: Univ. of Chicago Press, 1984.

For Dollimore, Shakespeare and the other contemporary playwrights undercut Tudor-Stuart values by expressing criticism of the dominant ideologies in a camouflaged way, a tactic which enabled them to oppose such ideas as the harmonious resolution of dramatic action through retributive, or therapeutic, providence. Dollimore argues that *Cor.* questions militaristic ideals, and thereby highlights the more complex conflicts in society and politics that such ideals silence without recognizing their validity. In Dollimore's reading, Shakespeare treats the plebeians and their powerlessness sympathetically and the play expresses the social construction of the self (a topic often stressed by New Historicist criticism). When Coriolanus goes to Antium, Aufidius recognizes only his public name, not his individual, and human, face.

230. Huffman, Clifford Chalmers. *"Coriolanus" in Context.* Lewisburg: Bucknell Univ. Press, 1972.

Huffman outlines the balanced, or "mixed," state, a form of government recognized by Aristotle and championed by some Classical writers (especially Polybius, 31-34), and argues that Elizabethan dramatic treatments of Rome (3 non-Shakespearean treatments, 50-72, and *Tit., Luc., JC*, and the later *Ant.*, 34-50) presented favorably values that promoted the welfare of this form of government in Rome and condemned activity that could result in single (monarchic) rule (65). Huffman presents a variety of Medieval and Renaissance writers, both in England (chap. 3, 73-96) and on the Continent (chap. 4, 97-136) to document sympathy with the mixed state idea; however, beginning in 1603 the new king, James I, expressed displeasure with the mixed state and especially with tribunes; and those dependent on the Court, including Shakespeare, followed suit (chap. 5, 137-70). In chap. 6, Huffman presents a scene-by-scene reading of *Cor.* from this perspective (171-222): up to act 3, the play reflects Jacobean political situations, and after that it becomes "a warning to the audience of ... consequences of the patrician failure to achieve balance" (199-200). Huffman adds an epilogue (223-29) suggesting that in *Catiline* (1611) Ben Jonson provided a "counterstatement" to *Cor.* (223).

231. Liebler, Naomi Conn. *Shakespeare's Festive Tragedy: The Ritual Foundations of Genre.* London and NY: Routledge, 1995. In chap. 4, 155-72.

Basing her discussion on Derrida's *pharmakon* (both poison and remedy), and focusing on different ways in which "body" is presented in *Cor.* (grotesque; sick; ritual/combat-heroic), Liebler relates the pattern and language of the plays to accounts of the mummers' plays (including sword-dances, morrises, and St. George plays, all ultimately derived from "ancient agrarian rituals of purgation, fertility, and seasonal renewal" [158]). Liebler especially discusses the St. George play pattern and relates moments of similarity to the career of Coriolanus, a character of "heroic complexity" (158) and "ambiguity and transcendence" (162), who is ultimately a dismembered sacrificial victim (171) whose death leaves Rome in a state of crisis.

232. MacCallum, M[ungo] W. *Shakespeare's Roman Plays and Their Background.* London: Macmillan, 1910. Repr. with a foreword by T.J.B. Spencer. London and Melbourne: Macmillan, 1967. Pp. 454-627.

MacCallum, who is credited with first isolating the Roman plays as a distinct group within Shakespeare's output, emphasizes the political worlds inhabited by Coriolanus. Early chapters, in the book's "Introduction" (1-167), treat 16th-century Roman plays (1-72), Shakespeare's treatment of historical material (73-94), and his use of (and departures from) Plutarch, Amyot, and North (95-167) and pave the way for analyses of *JC, Ant.*, and *Cor.* In his study of *Cor.*, MacCallum argues that the plebeians are famished and chaotic, the tribunes selfish and manipulative, while the patricians are disorganized, indecisive, selfish, and unresponsive; only Rome itself is presented as a worthy ideal (547). For MacCallum, the only great man among the patricians is Coriolanus, but he is flawed by the harshness he has learned from Volumnia; he is proud, and his ideals are out of step with the conflicted political situation. The author analyzes many aspects of Coriolanus's character and finds him honest, magnanimous, unselfish, honorable, modest, patriotic, and loyal to his family (571-97).

233. Miles, Geoffrey. *Shakespeare and the Constant Romans.* Oxford: Clarendon Press, 1996. Chap. 8, 149-68.

In accordance with his aim to provide "a closer analysis of [Roman] 'constancy' that acknowledges the complexity of its meanings and the tangled roots from which it springs" (vii), Miles discusses *Cor.*'s "testing of the limits of constancy" (viii), a quality made up of two elements, steadfastness and consistency (150-51); Coriolanus "towers above humanity as a Herculean and godlike figure," yet he also "is tied to his society as Rome's soldier-servant" (157), and plays the role of the heroic warrior. Miles argues that attitudes towards Coriolanus are presented clearly by the play's language (he is compared to a god, a rock, an animal, and a statue) and that skepticism (traced, like Stoicism, to Classical authors and Montaigne) is an important element. In this critic's reading, Coriolanus is constant even when he turns against Rome (163-64) in a play that is "Shakespeare's definitive critique of the contradictions of 'constancy'" (168).

234. Miola, Robert S. *Shakespeare's Rome.* Cambridge: Cambridge Univ. Press, 1983. Chap. 6, 164-205.

In this book, which chronicles how Shakespeare's treatment of Rome changed both as he developed as a playwright and as he changed the plays' dramatic times of action, Miola argues that in *Cor.* Shakespeare presented problems inherent in the concept of civilization itself: in this view, Coriolanus's arrival and presence in Rome, together with his later departure, epitomize this radical uncertainty.

235. Thomas, Vivian. *Shakespeare's Roman Worlds.* London and NY: Routledge, 1989. Chap. 4, 154-219.

For Thomas, the varying Romes of the Roman plays express a continued dramatic concern with social values and politics, the result of Shakespeare's reading of Plutarch. Thomas meticulously compares Plutarch's account of Coriolanus with Shakespeare's play to show details the dramatist introduced, or changes he made ("Shakespeare ... transfers the fable of the belly and Menenius's key role to the political crisis which occurred three years after the retreat to the Sacred Mount. The Menenius of history was already dead by then" [157]). Thomas argues that Shakespeare "locates the source of the tragedy in the ethos of the society" (175–76); thus in interpretation neither character nor politics, neither individual nor social values, can be considered most important, for "the power and fascination of the play resides in their complex interaction" (181). After a scene-by-scene study, Thomas concludes, "At the heart of the play lies the question of values" (219).

See also nos. 45, 243, 248, 257, 258, 260, 264, and 271.

D. Language and Linguistics.

236. Barton, Anne. "*Julius Caesar* and *Coriolanus*: Shakespeare's Roman World of Words." In *Shakespeare's Craft: Eight Lectures*, ed. Philip H. Highfill, Jr., 24–47. Carbondale and Edwardsville: Southern Illinois Press for George Washington University, 1982.

For Barton, *Cor.* portrays a Rome in which oratory (ambiguous, since it can persuade either to truth or to falsehood) has more power than action: without this skill, one is condemned to silence or death. Barton argues that Coriolanus's reluctance to speak represents a fear of language, and his skill in fighting (admired only by the relatively primitive Volscians) is anachronistic. In this critic's reading, Coriolanus experiences two climactic moments when he must try to use language: one with Volumnia (5.3) and a second in explosive response to Aufidius (5.6).

237. Charney, Maurice. *Shakespeare's Roman Plays: The Function of Imagery in the Drama.* Cambridge: Harvard Univ. Press, 1961. Chap. 5, 142–96. Excerpt in Brockman (no. 268), 118–28 and (from an earlier version) in Phillips (no. 270), 74–83.

Charney discusses *JC, Ant.*, and *Cor.*, paying primary attention to verbal images and their dramatic context, to character action, and to the unfolding of dramatic action in time. For Charney, the imagery of *Cor.* is dominated by food and eating (Menenius's fable of the belly and the members notably uses food to present a view of social order), disease and animals, acting and theater, and isolation, the last especially communicated by visual details of costume and staging.

238. Coote, Stephen. *William Shakespeare: "Coriolanus."* Penguin Critical Studies. Harmondsworth: Penguin, 1992.

Coote discusses *Cor.* in terms of the Humanist tradition (2–11), placing its politics and literary construction in the context of the Classical tradition. Coote stresses rhetoric, and this subject provides the structure of the book, which is divided into four "basic units" of rhetoric: the *Protasis* (*Cor.* 1.1–3; 12–26); the *Epitasis* (*Cor.* 1.4–10; 27–35); the *Catastasis* (*Cor.* 2.1–4.2; 36–57); and the *Catastrophe* (*Cor.* 4.3–end; 58–85). Coote provides abundant incidental commentary on characters (for example, Menenius's fable of the belly and the members, 14–17; the Tribunes, 52–57; Volumnia, 73–78). Coote concludes by contextualizing the play in 17th-century English politics and values (86–97) and adds a brief bibliography (98).

239. Danson, Lawrence. *Tragic Alphabet: Shakespeare's Drama of Language.* New Haven: Yale Univ. Press, 1974. Chap. 7, 142–62. Repr. Wheeler (no. 271), 123–42.

Danson's focus is on linguistic inadequacy in its various dramatic manifestations; he observes that in *Cor.* the more general term metonymy (the use of the name of one thing to represent another thing with which it is associated) and the more specific term synechdoche (the part for the whole, the species for the genus, etc.) are rhetorically dominant, replacing simile and metaphor, which are more usual in literature. In Danson's view, the effect of this strategy is fragmentation, chaotic grasping for power, and usurpation. Coriolanus, in this critic's view, responds to fragmentation by asserting his own wholeness; only Cominius's naming of him "Coriolanus" bridges this gap (the name "most nearly identifies the doer with his deeds," 150), but, being a social gift, the action fails. Danson also notes that Shakespeare provides an unusually large amount of information about Coriolanus's childhood (152–55) and that the Coriolanus who responds violently to Aufidius's insult "Boy" is, in fact, still a child (159–62). (For another study relating language to dramatic action, see Michael Platt, *Rome and the Romans According to Shakespeare* [Lanham, Md.: Univ. Press of America, 1983].)

239a. Kermode, Frank. *Shakespeare's Language.* NY: Farrar, Straus, Giroux, 2000.

Kermode traces "what happened in the fifteen years or so between *Titus Andronicus* and *Coriolanus*" (13), initially contrasting the two plays (7–14), the earlier with its overly literary quality and the later one with "its extraordinarily forced expressions, its obscurity of syntax and vocabulary, its contrasts of prose and harsh verse, its interweavings of the domestic and the military" (14). In the chapter on *Cor.* (243–54), which he characterizes as "probably the most difficult play in the canon" (244), Kermode expands on these topics, stressing the presence of passages that have never been satisfactorily interpreted, in which obscurity may be related to character, and he compares these to obscurity in other plays (244-46). Kermode focuses on the words "voice," "report," "name," "fame," and " noble" (246-54).

See also nos. 29, 225, 228, 248, and 263.

E. Criticism.

240. Adelman, Janet. "'Anger's My Meat': Feeding, Dependency, and Aggression in *Coriolanus*." In *Shakespeare: Pattern of Excelling Nature*, ed. David Bevington and Jay L. Halio, 108-24. Cranbury N.J.: Associated Univ. Presses, 1978. Repr. in *Representing Shakespeare: New Psycho-analytic Essays*, ed. Murray M. Schwartz and Coppélia Kahn, 129-49. Baltimore and London: Johns Hopkins Univ. Press, 1980. Repr. Bloom (no. 267), 75-89. Revised version in Adelman, *Suffocating Mothers: Fantasies of Maternal Origin in Shakespeare's Plays, "Hamlet" to "The Tempest,"* 146-64. NY: Routledge, 1992. Repr. in Wofford (no. 272), 134-67.

In Adelman's psychoanalytic interpretation, *Cor.* enacts audience fantasies, but causes its audience anxiety by keeping the protagonist at an emotional distance and by withholding resolution of the conflicts. For Adelman, hunger caused by the withholding of food is of central importance in the play and radiates outward: the uprising of the people is a sexual threat; political leveling (inherent in permitting the people to elect Tribunes) is the threat of losing potency (sexual as well as political). Adelman identifies Rome with Volumnia: both are non-nourishing mothers; to need to be fed, in this view, is to be vulnerable, a condition Rome and Volumnia despise. Coriolanus's response to this coldness is to reject food and unconsciously try to overcome his vulnerability by rage and aggression.

241. Bradley, A.C. "*Coriolanus*." *British Academy, Annual Shakespeare Lecture*, 1912. Proceedings of the British Academy, 1913 [1911-12]: 457-73. NY: Oxford Univ. Press, 1912. Repr. Folcroft, Penn.: Folcroft Press, 1970. Repr. in Bradley's *A Miscellany*. London: Macmillan, 1929, 73-104. Repr. Wheeler (no. 271), 25-45. Repr. Brockman (no. 268), 53-72.

Bradley ascribes *Cor.*'s lack of popular success to the choice of essentially undramatic material, which excludes love interest, the supernatural, and nature. Bradley stresses further negative qualities, primarily the play's anti-democratic bias and the coldness of the main character, whose inner motivations are veiled: Coriolanus is unjustifiably rigid with regard to the common people and is lacking in introspection and self-control. For Bradley, Menenius is a comic figure (13-14), while the crude Aufidius is the play's chief weakness (14-15); Coriolanus's yielding to his mother is "the conquest of passion by simple human feelings" (468), but it inevitably leads to his death.

242. Bristol, Michael D. "Lenten Butchery: Legitimation Crisis in *Coriolanus*." In *Shakespeare Reproduced: The Text in History and Ideology*, ed. Jean E. Howard and Marion F. O'Connor, 207-24. NY: Methuen, 1987.

In Bristol's view, the issue of legitimacy in *Cor.* resides neither in Coriolanus's claims to be consul nor in the Tribunes' opposition; rather, the play asks what kind of government should exist, and Menenius's fable of the belly and the members expresses an ideal model according to which society is a single living existence made up of subordinated, but actively contributing parts. For Bristol, Coriolanus's refusal to show his body to the people, an expression of his rejection of this view, makes him into a victim of a kind of popular festival (the Battle of Carnival and Lent, 215). Bristol urges critics to study the play outside itself and its time, and to pay attention to the history of its reception and the earlier responses' understanding of it as endorsing an ideology of repression.

243. Brower, Reuben. *Hero and Saint: Shakespeare and the Graeco-Roman Tradition.* Oxford: Oxford Univ. Press, 1971. Chap. 9, 354-81. Excerpts repr. Brockman (no. 268), 197-224.

Brower places Coriolanus in the tradition of Classical heroism as presented in pre-Shakespearean literature: Coriolanus, whose heroic values resemble those of Homer's Achilles, exists in a fully articulated civil society, a situation which tests his *virtus*, and which ultimately causes him to choose isolation and death. Brower stresses limitations in Coriolanus's character: he has no Achilles-like idealism and no personal conscience; he upholds no qualities that could fit a Christian worldview.

244. Burke, Kenneth. "Coriolanus—and the Delights of Faction." *Hudson Review* 19 (1966): 185-202. Repr. in Burke's *Language as Symbolic Action: Essays on Life, Literature, and Method.* Berkeley: Univ. of California Press, 1966, 81-97. Repr. Bloom (no. 267), 33-49. Excerpts appear in Phillips (no. 270), 100-01, and Brockman (no. 268), 168-81.

In Burke's view, Coriolanus's outspokenness sharpens inherent political conflicts and makes him a perfect sacrificial victim for the play's tragic action; other characters, for instance Menenius, are far more moderate. This behavior of Coriolanus's is, for Burke, linked to his aristocratic origins: the hero must of necessity interact with the nation, and his pride makes the situation worse. In this critic's reading, the play does not resolve its conflicts; the audience achieves some degree of relief by Coriolanus's invective, although the play's conclusion is thereby made grotesque.

245. Cavell, Stanley. *Disowning Knowledge in Six Plays of Shakespeare.* Cambridge: Cambridge Univ. Press, 1987. Chap. 4, 143–77. Earlier versions appeared in Cavell's "'Who does the Wolf Love?' Reading *Coriolanus*," *Representations* 1.3 (1983): 1–20; and *Themes Out of School: Effects and Causes* (San Francisco: North Point Press, 1984), 60–96; also in *Shakespeare and the Question of Theory*, ed. Patricia Parker and Geoffrey Hartman, 245–72 (NY and London: Methuen, 1985); repr. Bloom (no. 267), 99–122 and Wofford (no. 272), 168–87.

In seeing food, its presence and absence, and the linked concepts of hunger and cannibalism as dominant in *Cor.*, Cavell studies Menenius's fable of the belly and the members as a key to interpretation of the play: since words = food, people depend on others for both and the play embodies a social vision of mutual interdependence; the author expands these ideas in the "Postscript" (169–77). Cavell makes several comparisons of Coriolanus with Christ (for instance, Coriolanus's refusal to show his wounds to the people is like Christ's refusal to show His wounds to prove His resurrection, 158–61): Coriolanus is the sacrificial lamb butchered to feed an undeserving Rome (the analogy Cavell presents is Euripides' *The Bacchae*, 161–62). In Cavell's view, the play's end is not truly tragic. This essay has been influential in recent criticism.

246. Gordon, D.J. "Name and Fame: Shakespeare's *Coriolanus*." In *Papers, Mainly Shakespearian*, 40–57. Edinburgh: Oliver and Boyd, 1964. Repr. in *The Renaissance Imagination: Essays and Lectures by D.J. Gordon*, ed. Stephen Orgel, 203–19. Berkeley: Univ. of California Press, 1976.

Gordon stresses the ambiguities and conflicts involving fame: in *Cor.*'s Rome, honor is won by deeds, but is paradoxically dependent on fame (as expressed by the people's stinking breath). This problem, discussed by the Classical writers Cicero and Seneca, becomes crucial toward the end of the play: Gordon notes that the name "Coriolanus" expresses the individuality of the character, but must be discarded because conferred by Rome; and yet, a human without a name is a monster. In Gordon's view, the only possibility of a solution would be for Coriolanus to accept the family, which he does when he agrees to spare Rome; yet, paradoxically, this action causes his death.

247. Jagendorf, Zvi. "*Coriolanus*: Body Politic and Private Parts." *SQ* 41 (1990): 455–69.

After reviewing earlier political writing that emphasized the opposition between wholeness and fragmentation, Jagendorf approaches the Rome of *Cor.* as a "well-equipped, sharply lit laboratory for research into the nature of politics" (457) and studies especially the "presence of the body [particularly the body of the people and that of the hero, 462] and the impression of the body's language" (457), emphasized at first in the bread riot and Menenius's fable of the belly and the members (459). The critic relates Coriolanus's dislike of playing a part, or acting, to his obsession with wholeness and unity, and suggests the related point that the communal role of play acting in a theater undermines the acting of constancy (468). In Jagendorf's reading, "voice" (shouts, flourishes, votes, and cries), market-place demands, and rituals all contribute to the fall of Coriolanus, whose torn body is "a powerful tragic emblem" that is violent but also therapeutic (468).

248. King, Bruce. "*Coriolanus.*" Critics Debate. Basingstoke: Macmillan Education; Atlantic Highlands, N.J.: Humanities Press International, 1989.

In accordance with the aim of the Critics Debate series "to help delineate various critical approaches to specific literary texts" (7), King surveys, in Part One (13–58), the following critical approaches to *Cor.*: the contextual (13–17); textual and formal, particularly those emphasizing character and imagery (17–31); religious, social, and anthropological (31–43); interdisciplinary (43–50); and performance (50–58). In Part Two (59–107), King discusses the "advantages and problems of various critical methodologies" (59), often probing the critics' work for unstated assumptions and weaknesses in logic or consistency, in a large number of categories such as "the crowd" (63–64), "distancing" (66), "language and acting as deception" (75), "Coriolanus and his mother" (76–80), power (90–93), the play's conclusion (93–95), and the hero's death (95–97). King ends the volume with a list of references, divided by type of critical approach (108–10), a brief selected bibliography (111), and an index (112–13).

249. Knights, L.C. *Shakespeare's Politics: With Some Reflections on the Nature of Tradition.* Oxford: Oxford Univ. Press, 1958. Repr. in *Further Explorations*, 11–32. London: Chatto and Windus, 1965. Excerpts repr. in Charney (no. 269), 114–19.

Knights stresses Shakespeare's treatment of an important theme in English Renaissance culture, that of the governor (20). In Knights's view, *Cor.* dramatizes the ruler's need to coexist with other parts of the commonwealth; because the relation is interactive, the community will of course have an effect on the ruler. For Knights, the tragedy stems both from Coriolanus's limitations and also from Rome's fragmented condition.

250. Kott, Jan. *Shakespeare Our Contemporary.* Trans. B. Taborski. Garden City: Doubleday, 1964. In part I, 179-210.

In Kott's reading, the Rome of *Cor.* is radically divided by a class struggle between Coriolanus and the patricians on the one hand, and the common people on the other. Kott views Menenius's fable of the belly and the members as reductive rhetoric serving patrician interests only; Coriolanus's rudeness is more honest. Kott's perspective allows him to stress political elements such as the play's occasional objectivity about war, the similarity between a Roman and an English mob, and the role of history in condemning Coriolanus as a traitor.

251. Murry, John Middleton. "A Neglected Heroine of Shakespeare." In *Countries of the Mind: Essays in Literary Criticism*, 19-50. First series. London: Collins, 1922.

In the course of an analysis of the austere beauty of *Cor.*, which expresses the Roman values of relentlessness and inevitability, Murry finds a warm human touch in the brief portrayal of Virgilia, who elicits from Coriolanus his only moments of genuine humanity; she expresses herself even more in her moments of silence than in her speeches, and, in this way, provides the play with a human alternative to Roman brutality.

252. Nevo, Ruth. *Tragic Form in Shakespeare* Princeton: Princeton Univ. Press, 1972. Chap. 10, 356-404.

Nevo constructs a five-stage dramatic pattern of action for the Shakespearean tragic hero (17-26) and devotes a chapter to showing it in each of the tragedies; Coriolanus is particularly appropriate since he is externally presented, is lacking in inner tragic dimension. Nevo's stages (which do not necessarily or exactly always coincide with act-division in the play) are (1) an initial predicament, when the protagonist faces an impossible choice; (2) *psychomachia*; (3) reversal of the hero's initial situation, or *peripeteia*; (4) a time of pathos, humor, and irony; and (5) the death of the hero, or *catastrophe*, which ensures the survival of human values. Although Nevo's approach avoids moral judging and emphasis on character study, she does pay attention to characters within the formal structure she has outlined, as she progresses scene by scene through the play. Nevo argues that the hero does not recognize the necessary interdependence of strength and weakness, or of integrity and mastery: Volumnia has taught him control of emotion only. In this critic's view, Coriolanus defines himself by opposition to something rather than interdependence with it

(364); without opposition within Rome, he loses identity, and then seeks to regain it by joining Aufidius and the Volscians. Nevo sees the play as ironic in that "the retardation of recognition ... entails a protagonist who shall be in error, or ignorance, or blind to himself and others for the greater part of the play" (357).

253. Poole, Adrian. *"Coriolanus."* Harvester New Critical Introductions to Shakespeare. Hemel Hempstead and NY: Harvester Wheatsheaf; Boston: Twayne, 1988.

After brief summaries of *Cor.*'s stage history (xv–xvii) and its critical reception (xvii–xx), Poole discusses the play from act 1 through act 5 in five chapters, commenting on characterization and action, and pausing to comment on other critics as he goes along. In chap. 1 (1–22), Poole discusses Menenius's fable of the belly and the members and the relations that exist between characters and between them and the state. Although in the nature of Poole's approach he discusses many different topics, he particularly focuses, in chap. 2, 23–46, on Coriolanus ; in chap. 3, 47–73, on his relations to the way Rome is presented in the play; in chap. 4, 74–95, on the effects on Coriolanus of having been "cut loose from [Roman] life, violently and absolutely" (78); and, in chap. 5, 96–121, on the confrontation with Volumnia and his accession to her wishes. Poole often uses, or discusses and rejects, other critics' views (he offers full documentation in the notes, 122–32); he provides a bibliography for further reading (133–37) and an index (138–40).

254. Rabkin, Norman. *"Coriolanus*: The Tragedy of Politics." *SQ* 17 (1966): 195–212.

Rabkin groups *Cor.* with *Ant.* because both plays place their protagonists between starkly opposing value systems. Rabkin argues that Coriolanus's primary virtue is also his primary vice, and that the play eliminates any optimistic hopes for peaceful resolution. He contends that Menenius and the patricians, Volumnia, and Coriolanus are all too limited in their response to Rome's political problems, yet the play presents no character with an outlook so sufficiently broad as to be viable. For Rabkin, although *Ant.* portrays a large world in which romantic passion exists and *Cor.* a narrow one, cold and inhuman, both show that corrupt political realities extinguish real heroism. A revised version of this article appears in Rabkin's *Shakespeare and the Common Understanding* (NY: The Free Press; London: Collier-Macmillan, 1967), chap. 3, 120–44.

255. **Rosen, William.** *Shakespeare and the Craft of Tragedy.* Cambridge: Harvard Univ. Press, 1960. Chap. 4, 161–207.

In stressing issues of dramatic technique, Rosen concentrates on how Shakespeare sets up the audience's point of view towards characters: for instance, the citizens (167–71), and the conflict inherent in "voices" (30 references in 2.2 alone) and its relation in *Cor.* to such terms as "noble," "nobility," "worth," "honor," and "fame." In *Cor.* (but not in *King Lear* or *Macbeth*) there is no rapport between audience and character, and onstage the text provides many explicit analyses and judgments about the central figure (185); the resultant dispassionate distance creates a play that, in Rosen's view, questions human worth and shows its fragility (201–07).

256. **Sanders, Wilbur.** "An Impossible Person: Caius Martius Coriolanus." In *Shakespeare's Magnanimity: Four Tragic Heroes, Their Friends, and Families*, ed. Wilbur Sanders and Howard Jacobson, chap. 5, 136–87. NY: Oxford Univ. Press, 1978.

Developing his study of *Cor.* from an interchange published in Charlotte Bronte's novel *Shirley* (1849), Sanders presents a number of detailed readings of moments in the play (at times referring to the 1623 Folio text and overruling editors' emendations, as in *Cor.* 1.1 [138]) that show Shakespeare's dramatization of "the staggering variety of ways men have found of *being* political and social" (138). Sanders discusses the contradiction of this variety chiefly in Coriolanus, Volumnia, and Aufidius; Volumnia, in this view, is less the cause of her son's death than some critics believe (151–56). For Sanders, the play poses questions and provides no answers (160): the protagonist's tragedy lies in yielding to contradictions "at the heart of things" (171), and in his "acquiescence to the voice of 'Great Nature'" (183).

257. **Simmons, J.L.** "*Antony and Cleopatra* and *Coriolanus*, Shakespeare's Heroic Tragedies: A Jacobean Adjustment." *Shakespeare Survey* 26 (1973): 95–101. Repr. Wheeler (no. 271), 111–22.

Simmons links *Cor.* and *Ant.* as aristocratic tragedies: like Cleopatra, Coriolanus is disgusted by the prospect of any close contact with social inferiors. This aristocratic bias, Simmons argues, is a departure from Shakespeare's earlier, Elizabethan, practice, and expresses the new, unsettled, world of Jacobean England (97–101). In Simmons' reading, Shakespeare attempted to unite the new diversity by presenting both popular elements and aristocratic, heroic values together. Simmons develops some aspects of this reading in no. 43, chap. 2, 18–64.

258. Velz, John W. "Cracking Strong Curbs Asunder: Roman Destiny and the Roman Hero in *Coriolanus*." *English Literary Renaissance* 13 (1983): 58–69.

Velz argues for a Virgilian influence in *Cor.* instead of the more usual Plutarchan one emphasized by many other critics, and stresses the interplay of the forces of history and the individual; the play reflects Virgil's concern with history as providential and diachronic. Like Shakespeare's other Roman plays, Velz argues, *Cor.* dramatizes a politically climactic moment in Roman history, a time of turmoil and transition in which the tragic character is anachronistic, caught between an earlier heroic-age ethos and an emerging city-state that places new demands on him. Velz compares Coriolanus to Virgil's Turnus in *The Aeneid* (Turnus also tries, without success, to move from violence to politics) and stresses the similarity between Coriolanus and his enemy Aufidius.

259. Vickers, Brian. *Shakespeare: "Coriolanus."* London: Edward Arnold, 1976.

Vickers stresses the inadequacy of both patricians and tribunes in this play which criticizes both sides. In Vickers' reading, Coriolanus is isolated but a man of integrity who is clear-sighted on Rome's problems and is sensitive to the feelings of others (38). The critic diagrams several patterns ("action: evaluation: report: adulation: advantage" [24]) and divides the play into three stages, using a variety of gauges ("pressurizer," "agent," "goal," "obstacles," and "outcome" [40]). In Vickers' interpretation, Coriolanus has integrity when he spares Rome but succumbs to a despised opportunism; the play ends with Rome in the same position it was in at the beginning of the play.

260. Waith, Eugene M. *The Herculean Hero in Marlowe, Chapman, Shakespeare, and Dryden.* NY: Columbia Univ. Press; London: Chatto and Windus, 1962. In chap. 5, 121–43. Excerpts in Phillips (no. 270), 112–14.

In the course of studying the protagonists of seven Shakespeare plays in the light of Herculean heroism (" ... the poet who associates his hero with Hercules or Achilles shows him, momentarily at least, in a pre-existing heroic form"[50] to which the typical response is admiration, "a range of responses from awe to astonishment" [53]), Waith argues that in *Cor.* the hero's character, clearly Herculean (113), is expressed largely indirectly, through the conversations of other characters and parallelisms of action. For Waith, Coriolanus rejects qualities that are inferior to his high standards. There is no irony in the play when he, exiled from Rome, leads an army against his native city, for "his first allegiance is always to his personal honour" (131); in fact, there is greatness in these actions.

However, Waith points out, the rejection of the admittedly corrupt homeland is also a rejection of nature, which the play's action condemns.

See also nos. 31, 34, 36, 43, and 46.

F. Stage History and Performance Criticism.

261. Brecht, Bertolt. "Study of the First Scene of Shakespeare's *Coriolanus.*" In *Brecht on Theatre*, ed. John Willett, 252–65. London: Methuen; NY: Hill and Wang, 1964.

In this dialogue of 1953, Brecht and his interlocutors discuss a variety of political topics that arise in the first scene of *Cor.*, including the gradual unification of the plebeians, their rejection of Menenius's fable of the belly and the members (253), and realistic dramatic conflicts that cause discomfort. Brecht points out that the play sets aside the patrician/plebeian conflict in favor of that between Roman and Volscian soldiers, and that the Romans "legalize their differences by appointing plebeian commissars (People's Tribunes)," a decision caused by the enemy attack (256, 259). Brecht suggests many details of staging to "strengthen Shakespeare's text" (258). For Brecht, the change from Coriolanus the Roman hero to Coriolanus the traitor is non-existent: "he stays the same" (264), and Brecht suggests that this interpretation should be probed for its suggestions of complexity.

262. Goldman, Michael. *Acting and Action in Shakespearean Tragedy.* Princeton: Princeton Univ. Press, 1985. Chap. 7, 140–68.

Goldman observes that the word "action," when used to describe a play's action, really refers to three different kinds of action: "the actions the characters perform; the action of the audience's mind in responding to and trying to possess the events it watches; and finally the actions by which the actors create and sustain their roles" (12). He studies all three meanings, and hence combines a literary with a theatrical approach. Although conceding that, in general, early-17th-century literary characterization does not provide the depth of psychology that the later novelistic tradition was to exploit, Goldman argues that in *Cor.* the presentation of the protagonist is an exception: Coriolanus's actions are the subject of analysis by other characters, and readers and audience are aware that these are incomplete and even erroneous. Coriolanus's inner nature remains a mystery, and his tragedy, in this reading, depends on the conflict created by a character's being radically individual and at the same time inescapably involved with others in the social and political world. Goldman stresses the importance to tragedy of the protagonist's identification of himself, typically through action: Coriolanus confronts this issue when he learns that he must interact with the world (163-68).

263. Granville-Barker, Harley. "Coriolanus." In *Prefaces to Shakespeare II*. Princeton: Princeton Univ. Press, 1947. 150-299. Excerpts repr. Phillips (no. 270), 37-42.

Contrasting Coriolanus to Antony (of *Ant*.), Granville-Barker argues that Coriolanus is without introspection and is treated by Shakespeare with detachment: a man of action and arrogant, yet with an attractive boyishness. Granville-Barker discusses the main characters in depth: Coriolanus (156-64), Volumnia (164-70; 229-33; 261-70), Aufidius (170-76), Menenius (176-83), and the tribunes (183-86). This critic makes many suggestions for performance, commenting all the while on aspects of the play's poetic language (and the dramatic effectiveness of silence, 291-92).

264. Ripley, John. *"Coriolanus" on Stage in England and America, 1609-1994*. Madison, N.J.: Fairleigh Dickinson Univ. Press; London: Associated Univ. Presses, 1998.

After a preliminary discussion of critical responses from Dryden to the present time (chap. 1, 13-33), Ripley reviews a wide variety of performances, giving details of acting and production and citing critical assessments from contemporaneous materials, from the early 17th century (chap. 2, 34-52; this discussion reviews dating and sources). Ripley covers the following historical periods: 1681-1749 (chap. 3, 54-94); 1752-1817 (chap. 4, 95-142); three chapters on the "Kemble Tradition," in England and in America (chaps. 5-7, 143-239); and, in the 20th century, the "modernist" period of 1920-38 (chap. 8, 240-69); the period of 1938-59 (the period of "a depression, the rise of fascism, World War II and its aftermath" [270], chap. 9, 270-98); and a chapter on productions influenced by psychoanalysis, 20th-century politics, and "postmodernity," a period of renewed interest in *Cor*. (chap. 10, 299-333). In an "Afterword," Ripley reviews the play's entire bleak theater history of distortion and textual maiming, and argues that *Cor*. should be accepted, and acted, as it stands printed (334-42). The critic also provides a valuable "chronological checklist" of productions, 1609-1994 (343-66). (For a study on a recent European [Continental] production, see David Daniell, *"Coriolanus" in Europe* [London: Athlone; Atlantic Highlands, N.J.: Humanities Press, 1980].)

See also nos. 253, 265, 271, and 274.

G. Adaptations.

265. Cohn, Ruby. *Modern Shakespeare Offshoots.* Princeton: Princeton Univ. Press, 1976. In chap. 1, 10-26, and in chap. 8, 364-70.

"Almost all art builds on previous art," Cohn observes, "but much modern art builds with previous art" (x); with this idea in mind, the author studies how Shakespeare plays have been points of departure for later dramatists. In chap. 1, under the heading "Adaptations and Transformations," Cohn discusses a succession of stage productions of *Cor.* from Nahum Tate's English performance of 1681, the earliest recorded (10), through John Osborne's 1973 adaptation (22-26). In particular, Cohn studies the February, 1934, Paris production of René-Louis Piachaud (11-16) and Bertolt Brecht's *Coriolan* (left unfinished at his death, but later adapted, modified, and performed successfully by the Berliner Ensemble in 1963 [16-22]); in chap. 8, Cohn studies changes that Brecht made to the Shakespeare play in order "to convert a tragedy of pride into a tragedy of illusion, since Coriolanus believes himself to be indispensable" (364). See also Brecht, no. 261.

266. Eliot, T.S. "Coriolan." In *Collected Poems 1909-62*, 125-29. NY: Harcourt, Brace Jovanovich, 1963.

"Coriolan" consists of "Triumphal March," 1931, and "Difficulties of a Statesman," 1932, two completed poems out of a projected four. In the first, Eliot portrays the triumphal return to Rome of the victorious Coriolanus and, in a montage of poetry and prose, the exuberant throngs that crowd to witness the remote hero; the second poem places Coriolanus in a social, economic, and political context, intertwined with longing references to Volumnia. (Eliot also referred to Coriolanus in *The Waste-Land*, 1922, part 5, line 417.)

H. Teaching and Collections of Essays.

267. Bloom, Harold, ed. *William Shakespeare's "Coriolanus."* Modern Critical Interpretations. NY: Chelsea House Publishers, 1988.

This useful collection reprints critical discussions, some of them annotated in the present volume.

268. Brockman, B.A., ed. *Shakespeare, "Coriolanus": A Casebook.* London: Macmillan, 1977.

Brockman's introduction (11-22) surveys earlier reception of the play (especially the critical reception, excerpts from which are collected in the volume, and some of which are also annotated in the present annotated bibliography): Part I, 23–50, covers 1765–1919, and Part II, 51–224, covers the 20th century. Brockman includes a select bibliography (225–27), notes on the contributors to Part II (229–30), and a general bibliography (231–36).

269. Charney, Maurice, ed. *Discussions of Shakespeare's Roman Plays*. Boston: Heath, 1964.

In this anthology of criticism, Charney reprints several of the articles and excerpts from books annotated in the present volume.

270. Phillips, James E., Jr., ed. *Twentieth Century Interpretations of "Coriolanus": A Collection of Critical Essays*. Englewood Cliffs, N.J.: Prentice-Hall, 1970.

In the introduction (1–14), Phillips reviews Shakespeare's career, places *Cor.* in the context of his English Histories and other Roman plays, and discusses the political setting and its pressures on the major characters. In Part One (15–99), Phillips reprints essays by earlier scholars, some of which are annotated in the present volume; in Part Two (100–14), the selection of reprinted material is more narrowly focused on "Theme and Structure" (100–01) and a number of the play's characters (101–14). Phillips concludes the volume with a chronology of important dates, notes on the editor and contributors, and a bibliography for further reading (115–20).

271. Wheeler, David. *"Coriolanus": Critical Essays*. Garland Reference Library of the Humanities: Shakespeare Criticism 11. NY: Garland Publishing, 1995.

This useful anthology is listed because it reprints a number of the essays annotated in the present volume. In his introduction (xv–xxxii), Wheeler discusses *Cor.*'s long history of unpopularity on the stage (xv–xviii), reviews a number of approaches to the play, especially political (xix–xxix) and "the formal, structural studies and 'great themes' approaches" (xxix). Wheeler concludes the volume with photographs from several productions, essays on performance criticism, and review essays, as well as reviews (369–434). The book is not indexed.

272. Wofford, Susanne L., ed. *Shakespeare's Late Tragedies: A Collection of Critical Essays*. Upper Saddle River, NJ: Prentice-Hall, 1996.

This useful collection reprints several essays annotated in the present volume.

I. Bibliographies.

273. Charney, Maurice. "*Coriolanus* and *Timon of Athens.*" In *Shakespeare: A Bibliographical Guide*, New Edition, ed. Stanley Wells, 295-304 and 312-17. Oxford: Clarendon Press, 1990.

This volume, a rewritten, updated version of the first edition (1973), aims to provide a selectively critical guide to the best in Shakespearean scholarship and criticism. Charney's discussion of *Cor.* (295-304) surveys recent editions and summarizes literary criticism from T.S. Eliot to the mid 1980s, with references listed in the bibliography (312-17).

274. Leggatt, Alexander, and Lois Norem. *"Coriolanus": An Annotated Bibliography.* NY and London: Garland, 1989.

Leggatt and Norem introduce this volume with a short history of interpretation of *Cor.*, highlighting notable trends in the period 1940-86; this discussion is keyed to such critical issues as the nature of the hero (xiv-xviii), the play's depiction of politics (xviii-xix), and its "underlying vision" (xix); they then survey source studies (xx-xxi), textual studies (xxii), editions (xxii-xxiii), adaptations and influence (xxiii-xxvi), translations (xxvi), and stage history (xxvi-xxviii). The editors arrange the bibliography into sections devoted to Criticism, whether separately-published essays or chapters in books (3-440, items 1-631); Sources and Background (441-77, items 632-86); Textual Studies (479-506, items 687-729); Editions (507-34, items 730-66); Adaptations and Influence (535-75, items 767-831); Translations (577-83, items 832-64); Bibliographies and Reference Works (585-607, items 865-921); and a final section, divided into two parts, Staging and Stage History (609-37, items 922-63) and Productions (639-701, items 964-1062). The editors arrange the entries chronologically and then alphabetically within the year. The Stage History section, which often focuses on specific productions, is especially full; and the index, 703-38, is detailed.

275. Sajdak, Bruce T., ed. *Shakespeare Index: An Annotated Bibliography of Critical Articles on the Plays 1959-83.* 2 vols. Vol. 1, Citations and Author Index. Vol. 2, Character, Scene, and Subject Indexes. Millwood, NY: Kraus International Publications, 1992.

Sajdak seeks to provide the student with a means to "quickly locate, amongst the thousands of possible sources, those few most relevant articles on specific ideas, characters, or scenes" (1.xi). He provides a statement of scope, a list of sources he consulted (xiii-xvii), and a guide on how to use the *Index* (xxi-xxii). Sajdak divides the Index into 48 chapters (arranged chronologically by date of publication), initially by research area, then by play title (arranged by period, genre, and title). For each entry, Sajdak gives full publication information and an annotation. There are indexes for authors and, beginning with vol. 2, for character (803–1033), scene (1035–1197), and subject (1199–1765), with extensive subdivisions. *Cor.* is covered in 1.251–62, items S 1–102. This *Index* does not include chapters in books unless these were published separately as articles.

See also nos. 224, 226, 253, 268, and 270.

INDEX I: AUTHORS AND EDITORS
(FOR SECTIONS II–VII)

Abbott, E.A., 106
Adelman, Janet, 176, 177, 240
Andrews, John F., 44

Bains, Yashdip S., 220
Baker, Peter, 62
Bamber, Linda, 31, 178
Barrett, Lawrence, 149
Barroll, J. Leeds, 28, 130, 164
Bartels, Emily C., 78
Barthelemy, Anthony Gerard, 78
Barton, Anne, 179, 227, 236
Barton, John, 141
Batchelor, John, 70
Bate, Jonathan, 67, 70, 74
Benjamin, Walter, 128
Bevington, David, 106, 159, 211, 240
Binz, Gustav, 108
Bitot, Michel, 151a
Bliss, Lee, 222a
Blits, Jan H., 123
Bloom, Harold, 213, 214, 267
Bonfiglio, Joe, 154a
Bonjour, Adrien, 124
Bono, Barbara J., 165
Booth, Stephen, 142
Bowers, Fredson, 71, 107. See also Index II.
Bradley, A.C., 43, 180, 241. See also Index II.
Braunmuller, A.R., 80
Brecht, Bertolt, 261
Bristol, Michael D., 242
Brockbank, [J.] Philip, 125, 223

Brockman, B.A., 268
Broude, Ronald, 83, 84
Brower, Reuben A., 85, 109, 181, 243
Brown, John Russell, 215
Bryant, J.A., Jr., 110
Buckman-de Villegas, Sabine U., 161
Bullough, Geoffrey, 52, 153
Burckhardt, Sigurd, 153
Burke, Kenneth, 244
Bush, Douglas, 50

Cabat, Joshua, 154a
Cain, Tom, 70
Cantor, Paul A., 37, 166, 228
Carducci, Jane S., 70
Cartwright, Kent, 182
Cavell, Stanley, 183, 245
Charnes, Linda, 184
Charney, Maurice, 86, 152, 153, 174, 237, 269, 273
Clarke, M[artin] L[owther], 111
Clayton, Thomas, 226
Cohen, Derek, 87
Cohn, Ruby, 143, 207, 265
Colie, Rosalie, 175
Collier, John Payne, 224
Cook, Albert, 37
Coote, Stephen, 238
Costa, C.D.N., 90
Culler, Jonathan, 206

Daiches, David, 153
Danby, John F., 185
Daniell, David, 104, 264

INDEX I: AUTHORS AND EDITORS

Danson, Lawrence, 239
Davenport, E.L., 149
Davies, H. Neville, 167
Dean, Leonard F, 153
Derrida, Jacques, 231
Dessen, Alan C., 100
Dickey, Franklin M., 186
Dollimore, Jonathan, 187, 229
Donaldson, Ian, 53, 61
Doran, Madeleine, 29
Dorsch, T. S., 104
Dowden, Edward, 152
Drakakis, John, 216
Dubrow, Heather, 59
Dubu, Jean, 151a

Edwards, Philip, 126
Eliot, T.S., 88, 266
Ellwood, Colin, 151a
Enterline, Lynn, 53a
Ettin, Andrew V., 79

Foakes, R.A., 153
Fortin, René E., 127
Franz, Wilhelm, 106
Freedman, Gerald, 100
Frye, Northrop, 153, 206
Furness, Horace Howard, Jr., 224
Fuzier, Jean, 121

Garber, Marjorie, 128
Garner, Shirley Nelson, 184
Gielgud, John, 144. See also Index II.
Girard, René, 62
Godshalk, William Leigh, 89
Goldman, Michael, 208, 262
Goodwin, Nancy, 154a
Goodwin, Sarah Webster, 62
Gordon, D.J., 246
Gramsci, Antonio, 125
Granville-Barker, Harley, 145, 153, 209, 263
Gregson, J. M., 30
Grene, Nicholas, 188
Grezgorzewska, Malgorzata, 151a

Haaker, Ann, 72
Halio, Jay L., 80, 151, 240
Handwerk, Gary, 62
Harbage, Alfred, 51, 105
Harrison, G. B., 154
Hartman, Geoffrey, 245
Hartsock, Mildred E., 127
Hawkins, Harriet, 53
Heilman, Robert B., 153
Heuer, Hermann, 42
Higgins, Lyn, 63
Highfill, Philip H., Jr., 236
Hill, R.F., 42
Holloway, John, 189
Honigmann, E.A.J., 70
Hosley, Richard, 130
Houseman, John, 146, 147. See also Index II.
Howard, Jean E., 242
Huffman, Clifford Chalmers, 83, 230
Hughes, Alan, 68
Hulse, Clark, 54
Humphreys, A. H., 106, 138
Hunter, G.K., 90

Jacobson, Howard, 256
Jagendorf, Zvi, 247
James, Heather, 74
Jenkins, Harold, 163
Johnson, S. F., 105
Jones, Emrys, 112, 129

Kahn, Coppélia, 31, 63, 240
Kaula, David, 118a
Kelley, Brian J., 154a
Kermode, Frank, 239a
Kernan, Alvin [B.], 130
King, Bruce, 248
Kirschbaum, Leo, 153
Kistner, A.L., 73
Kistner, M.K., 73
Knight, G. Wilson, 32, 131, 132, 190
Knights, L.C., 153, 249
Kolin, Philip C., 101
Koppenfels, Werner von, 54a

INDEX I: AUTHORS AND EDITORS 135

Kott, Jan, 250
Kujawinska-Courtney, Krystyna, 33
Kurland, Stuart M. 135

Lamb, Margaret, 210
Lamont, Claire, 70
Lanham, Richard A., 60
Leggatt, Alexander, 34, 130, 274
Lever, J. W., 66
Liebler, Naomi Conn, 113, 154a, 231
Lindley, Michael, 191
Lloyd, Janet, 91
Lomonico, Miachael, 154a

MacCallum, M[ungo] W., 35, 168, 232
MacDonald, Joyce Green, 55, 78
Mack, Maynard, 153
Madelaine, Richard, 211
Maguin, Jean-Marie, 151a
Mahon, John W., 163
Majors, G. W., 56
Mankiewicz, Joseph, 144, 146
Marienstras, Richard, 91
Markels, Julian, 192
Martindale, Charles, 36
Martindale, Michelle, 36
Mason, H.A., 193
Maus, Katharine Eisaman, 61
Maxwell, J.C., 42
McAlindon, T., 194
McGrail, Mary Ann, 37
McIver, Bruce, 155
Mendilow, A.A., 75
Merchant, W.M., 42
Metz, G. Harold, 92
Miles, Gary B., 38
Miles, Geoffrey, 39, 169, 233
Mills, Laurens J., 195
Miola, Robert S., 40, 74, 114, 115, 116, 170, 234
Moore, Edward M., 145
Moulton, Richard G., 152
Muir, Kenneth, 80
Munkelt, Marga, 161
Murry, John Middleton, 251

Neill, Michael, 160
Nelson, Shirley, 184
Nettles, John, 147a
Nevo, Ruth, 75, 196, 252
Newman, Jane O., 57a
Nicoll, Allardyce, 42
Nochimson, Richard L., 197
Norem, Lois, 274

O'Connor, Marion F., 242
Orgel, Stephen, 246
Osborne, John, 265

Palmer, D.J., 80, 81
Palmer, John, 133, 153
Parker, Barbara L., 117
Parker, Patricia, 245
Parker, R.B., 225
Pelling, Christopher, 37
Pendleton, Thomas A., 163
Phillips, James E., 270
Pickup, Ronald, 148
Platt, Michael, 239
Poole, Adrian, 253
Price, Hereward T., 93
Prince, F. T., 48
Prior, Moody E., 145

Quiller-Couch, Sir Arthur, 159

Rabkin, Norman, 134, 153, 254
Rackin, Phyllis, 198
Ray, Sid, 76
Redmond, James, 74
Ribner, Irving, 118
Richmond, Hugh M., 151, 153
Riemer, A.P., 199
Ripley, John, 149, 264
Roe, John, 49
Rollins, Hyder Edward, 50
Ronan, Clifford J., 41
Rose, Mark, 118a, 217
Rosen, Barbara, 153
Rosen, William, 153, 200, 255
Rosenberg, Marvin, 151

Rumbelow, Steve, 143

Sajdak, Bruce T., 102, 156, 221, 275
Sanders, Norman, 135
Sanders, Wilbur, 256
Schanzer, Ernest, 108, 110, 135a, 152, 153, 201
Schlesinger, John, 148
Schlueter, June, 77
Scholz, Susanne, 64
Schwartz, Murray M., 240
Scott, Mark W., 140
Scott, Michael, 212
Sewell, Arthur, 153
Silver, Brenda, 63
Simmons, J. L., 43, 44, 171, 257
Simonds, Peggy Muñoz, 202
Smallwood, Robert, 147a
Smith, Gordon Ross, 136
Sohmer, Steve, 108
Sommers, Alan, 94
Spencer, T.J.B., 35, 42, 152, 232
Spevack, Marvin, 106, 161, 163
Spivack, Bernard, 78
Sprengnether, Madelon, 184
Steppat, Michael, 161, 203
Stevenson, Ruth, 155
Stirling, Brents, 113, 137, 153

Taborski, B., 250
Takada, Yasunari, 37
Taymor, Julie, 100a
Teague, Frances, 118b
Thomas, Vivian, 45, 79, 138, 172, 235
Tillyard, E.M.W., 103
Traversi, Derek A., 44, 139
Tricomi, Albert H., 82, 95

Utley, Katherine, 154a

Van Doren, Mark, 153
Vaughan, Virginia Mason, 78
Vawter, Marvin L., 119
Velz, John W., 37, 47, 120, 122, 140, 147, 150, 157, 258
Vickers, Brian, 259

Waith, Eugene [M.], 42, 69, 96, 204, 260
Walch, Günther, 151
Warner, Deborah, 70, 100
Wayne, Valerie, 98
Weber, A.S., 205
Weis, R. J. A., 158, 222
Wells, Stanley, 70, 103, 108, 151a, 158, 222, 273
Wheeler, David, 239, 241, 257, 264, 271
White, R.S., 103
Wilbur, Richard, 51
Wilcher, Robert, 206
Wilders, John, 155, 162
Willbern, David, 97
Willett, John, 261
Williams, Carolyn D., 57b
Williams, George Walton, 120a, 226
Willson, Robert F., Jr., 140a
Wilson, Harold S., 152
Wilson, John Dover, 42, 68, 159. See also Index II.
Wilson, R. Rawdon, 65
Wofford, Susanne L., 218, 272
Wood, Nigel, 219
Wynne-Davies, Marion, 98

Yachnin, Paul, 173
Young, Arthur M., 58

Zeeveld, W. Gordon, 99

INDEX II: SUBJECTS
(FOR SECTIONS II–VII)

Aaron, 75, 78, 80, 85, 87, 93, 95, 97, 98, 99, 101, 103
Ab urbe condita (Livy), 57b, 227
Abbott, E.A., 106
Achilles, 243, 260
Actium, 164, 182, 193, 195, 206, 209
actors, 44, 48, 69, 77, 100, 106, 108, 132, 140a, 141, 142, 143, 144, 145, 149, 155, 182, 208, 209, 210, 224, 226, 262
admiratio, 81, 96, 204, 260
Advancement of Learning (Francis Bacon), 173
Aeneas, 30, 115, 176, 201
Aeneid, 74, 115, 165, 258
Aesop, 151
Agamemnon, 112
aggression, 240
Alarbus, 83, 91, 94
alchemy, 194, 205
allegory, 78, 205
ambiguity, 56, 105, 114, 127, 135a, 178, 185, 226, 231
amputation, 76
Amyot, Jacques, 38, 42, 109, 232
anachronism, 36, 41, 47, 236, 258
anadiplosis, 59
animals, 95, 132, 176, 177, 233
antagonist, 29, 115, 184
Antigone, 58
anti-Stoicism, 119
antithesis, 29
Antonius (Robert Garnier), 38, 106, 113, 161, 186, 201

Antony and Cleopatra, general, 28, 29, 30, 32, 33, 34, 35, 36, 37, 39, 43, 45, 46, 142, 143, 154a, 159–222, 237, 254, 257, 263
Antony and Cleopatra, act and scene:
— (1.1–3.9), 206
— (1.1–1.3), 199
— (1.1), 185, 193, 211
— (1.2–1.5), 193
— (1.2), 185
— (1.3), 185
— (1.4–3.6), 199
— (2.1–3.7), 193
— (3), 180, 196
— (3.7–5.2), 195
— (3.7–4.15), 195, 199
— (3.11–4.13), 206
— (3.12–4.14), 209
— (4), 180
— (4.14), 174, 175, 182, 200, 204, 206
— (4.15), 159, 160, 166, 174, 175, 179, 181, 182, 191, 197, 200, 210
— (5.2), 159, 160, 166, 169, 174, 175, 177, 179, 180, 181, 182, 186, 189, 190, 196, 197, 199, 200, 205, 206, 209
Antony, Mark (*Julius Caesar*), 30, 44, 104, 109, 114, 115, 117, 121, 131, 133, 134, 135, 135a, 139, 140, 140a, 141, 142, 143, 146, 148
Antony, Mark (*Antony and Cleopatra*), 37, 159–222, 228, 230, 232, 254, 263
apotheosis, 37, 123, 188, 192, 205

Appian, 28, 135a, 154
aristocracy, 118, 187
Aristotle, 162, 205, 230
art, 49
assassination, 44, 109, 110, 113, 114, 118, 118a, 128, 132, 134, 135a, 138, 140a, 153
astrology, 81, 108
audience, 33, 34, 36, 43, 70, 78, 80, 81, 91, 96, 100, 118a, 127, 138, 140, 142, 143, 145, 165, 168, 172, 173, 178, 179, 182, 188, 197, 206, 208, 209, 230, 240, 244, 255, 262
Aufidius, 29, 229, 236, 239, 241, 252, 256, 258, 263
Augustine, St., 28, 38, 164, 165
authorship, 104. See also disintegration.

BBC (British Broadcasting Corporation), 141
Bacchae, (Euripides) 110, 245
Bacchus, 205
Bacon, Francis, 173
Barrett, Lawrence, 149
belly, fable of, 222a, 224, 235, 237, 238, 242, 245, 247, 250, 253, 261
Benjamin, Walter, 128
Benson, Frank, 149
Berlin Wall, 151
Berliner Ensemble, 265
betrayal, 143
blackness *(Ant.),* 176
blood, 86, 91, 113, 132
Book of Common Prayer, 76
Booth, Edwin, 142, 149
Bowers, Fredson, 103. See also Index I.
boy actors, 209
Bradley, A.C., 32, 43, 203. See also Index I.
Brando, Marlon, 146, 148
Brecht, Bertolt, 265
Bridge-Adams, William, 149
Bronte, Charlotte, 256
Brook, Peter, 100, 210

Brutus, Lucius Junius, 53, 56, 59, 120a
Brutus, Marcus, 29, 30, 38, 39, 43, 44, 106, 109, 110, 111, 113, 118, 118a, 119, 120a, 121, 123, 124, 125, 126, 130, 131, 133, 134, 135, 135a, 136, 138, 139, 140, 141, 142, 143, 146, 147, 147a, 150, 152
Büchner, Georg, 125
burlesque, 100
Bush, Douglas, 50

Caesar, Julius, 38, 44, 47, 104–58, 207
Caesar, Octavius, see Octavius Caesar.
Caesar and Cleopatra (George Bernard Shaw), 154, 207
Calhern, Louis, 146
Callisto, 57b
Calphurnia, 141, 146
Calvin, John, 39
Camden, William, 223
cannibalism, 245
carnival, 191, 242
Casca, 44, 135a
Cassius, 28, 38, 44, 109, 110, 115, 126, 130, 131, 133, 135, 135a, 139, 140, 141, 146, 147a, 148
catastasis, 238
catastrophe, 75, 125, 165, 179, 196, 206, 238, 252
Catiline (Ben Jonson), 230
ceremony, 32, 76, 118a
chaos, 85, 90, 91, 96, 132
chapbook, *(Tit.),* 68, 69
chastity, 55, 64
Chaucer, Geoffrey, 48, 50, 52, 164
children, 89
choric characters, 137, 160
Christian IV, King, 167
Christianity, 28, 43, 44, 53, 83, 118a, 164, 183, 205, 243, 245
Church of England, 118a
Cicero, 28, 37, 38, 39, 106, 119, 135a, 154, 186, 246
cinematic techniques, 210
Cinna the Poet, 135, 140a

INDEX II: SUBJECTS

civil war (aftermath of *Lucrece*), 57
civil wars (in *Julius Caesar*), 28, 114
Civil Wars (Julius Caesar), see *Commentaries* (Julius Caesar).
civilization, 79, 84, 85, 94, 234
class struggle, 228, 250
Cleopatra, 44, 142, 143, 159–222
— blackness of, 176
Cléopatre Captive (Jodelle), 186
clown, 193, 196
Coleridge, Samuel Taylor, 133, 160, 203, 222
Collatine, 48, 57, 61, 62, 63
comedy/the comic, 62, 171, 176, 179, 206, 207, 241
comic elements (in *Ant.*), 169, 171, 176, 178, 179, 193, 197
Cominius, 226, 239
Commentaries (Julius Caesar), 35, 38, 44, 47, 154, 264
conjuring (exorcism), 118a
conspiracy, 115, 118a, 140, 140a, 151
constancy (*constantia*), 36, 39, 41, 45, 169, 233, 247
copia, 57, 59, 65
Cordelia, 185
Coriolanus, Caius Martius 30, 31, 39, 42, 46, 133, 169, 223–75
Coriolanus, general, 29, 30, 31, 32, 33, 34, 35, 36, 37, 39, 42, 43, 44, 45, 46, 65, 79, 133, 166, 169, 174, 187, 188, 223–75
Coriolanus, act and scene:
— (1), 253
— (1.1), 235, 237, 238, 242, 247, 250, 256, 261
— (1,2), 230
— (1.4–1.9), 29
— (1.4–1.10), 238
— (2), 253
— (2.1–4.2), 238
— (2.1), 29
— (2.2), 255
— (2.3), 242, 245
— (3, 4, 5), 230
— (3), 253
— (3.2), 29
— (4), 253
— (4.1), 29
— (4.3–5.6), 238
— (4.5), 229
— (5), 253
— (5.3), 29, 30, 42, 236, 241, 246
— (5.6), 236
Corioli, 29
Cornwallis, Sir William, 39
costumes, 42, 144, 147, 210
Cranach, Lucas, 49
critical approaches, 150
— close reading (including new critical and formalist), 29, 32, 33, 46, 94, 95, 124, 129, 131, 132, 139, 140, 174, 179, 190, 192, 193, 195, 197, 199, 244, 246, 249, 254, 256
— cultural, 53, 55, 58, 76, 87, 183, 191, 206, 242, 245. See also *Romanitas*.
— feminist and gender studies, 31, 55, 57a, 57b, 63, 64, 98, 177, 178, 198
— historical, 28, 35, 36, 38, 39, 40, 41, 43, 44, 47, 56, 57, 63, 83, 84, 111, 113, 115, 116, 118, 122, 123, 125, 128. See also *Romanitas*.
— intertextuality, 28–47, 49, 52, 53, 54a–58, 60, 62, 65, 67, 69, 71, 72, 74, 75, 77–79, 87, 88, 90, 92–94, 96, 110, 118b, 120, 128, 129, 135, 140a, 143, 145, 154, 160, 161, 164–66, 168–71, 176, 179, 181, 186–88, 190, 192, 194, 199, 201, 204, 205, 207, 223, 225, 228, 230, 232, 234–38, 243, 245, 254–57, 260, 263, 265, 266
— metatheatricality, 128, 140a
— mimetic, 33, 62
— new historicist and cultural materialist, 187, 216, 219, 229
— postmodern, 33, 136, 138, 150, 264
— psychoanalytic, 76, 97, 136, 157, 177, 240
— ritual, 113
— textual, see subsections A and B for

each play
— theatrical, see subsection F for *Ant.*, *JC, Tit.* and *Cor* (and also G under *Cor.*).
crocodile, 176
crowds, 137. See also plebeians.
crown, 91, 125
cruelty, see *saevitia*.
Culler, Jonathan, 206

Daiches, David, 153
Daniel, Samuel, 161, 186, 197, 199, 201, 264
Daniell, David, 264
Dante, 165
darkness, 181
Davenport, E.L., 149
De clementia, (Seneca), 120
deafness (in *JC*), 104, 125
death scenes (in *Ant.*), 165, 169, 170, 179, 181, 186, 188, 189, 197, 200, 206, 212
Derrida, Jacques, 231
destiny (of Rome), 258. See also fate.
detachment, 182, 263. See also engagement.
Deutsche Demokratische Republik, 151
Dido, 30, 176, 201
Dido, Queen of Carthage (Christopher Marlowe), 176
diegesis, 33
dignitas, 38, 41, 57. See also fame and reputation.
dilemma, 29
Dio Cassius, 28
Dionysius of Halicarnassus, 37, 58
Discorsi (Machiavelli), 227
disease, 237
disintegration, 74, 104
dismemberment, 89, 97
dissolution, 177, 188
divine right of kings, 173
Doctor Faustus (Christopher Marlowe), 91
Don John (*Much Ado About Nothing*), 78
doubling, theatrical, 68, 69, 135
doubt, 46, 176, 182
Dowden, Edward, 152
dream (Cleopatra's, of Antony in *Ant.*), 177, 181, 188, 191, 193, 205

echo, 58, 80, 201
Egypt, 31, 33, 172, 174, 178, 184, 191, 201, 206, 211
ekphrasis, 49, 51, 54, 55, 65
Elizabeth I, Queen, 28, 31, 40, 42, 54, 67, 71, 76, 81, 84, 88, 91, 103, 108, 113, 118, 118a, 151, 152, 163, 179, 230, 257
elogia, 38
emblem books, 72, 202
emblems, 55, 72
Empire (Roman), 29, 37, 166, 228
empire, fourth world, 43
engagement, 182. See also detachment.
Enobarbus, 160, 164, 168, 173, 182, 184, 193, 195, 196, 197
epistemology, 127
epitasis, 238
Erasmus, Desiderius, 39, 76, 110, 112
eroticism, 54a, 131, 190
Essex Affair, 151
Essex, Earl of, 222a
ethics, 123
ethnicity, 33
Euripides, 110, 112, 245
evil, 95
exorcism, 118a
extravagance, 186
eyewitness accounts, 211

fame, 184, 246, 255. See also *dignitas* and reputation.
family, 115, 246
fascism, 147, 151, 264
Fasti (Ovid), 48, 52, 53a, 56, 57b, 58
fate, 115. See also destiny (of Rome).
Faucit, Helen, 210
feast, 32

INDEX II: SUBJECTS 141

fertility, 113, 175, 231
Field, Richard, 49
film, 144, 146, 148, 150, 211
fire, 132
Fisher King, 113
Florus, L.A., 38, 44
folk ritual, 113
Ford, John, 91
foreshadowing, 73, 114
forest, 89, 91, 95
forgery, 118b
Fortescue, Sir John, 76
Fortinbras (*Hamlet*), 56
fortitude, 45
Fortune, 202
foul papers, 107
Franz, Wilhelm, 106
Freedman, Gerald, 100
French Revolution, 151
Freud, Sigmund, 128
friendship, 37, 45, 96, 115, 119, 123
Frye, Northrop, 153, 206

Garnier, Robert, 161, 165, 186, 197, 199, 201
Garrick, David, 210
Garson, Greer, 146
gender, 31, 33, 55, 57a, 57b. See also feminist and gender studies, under critical approaches.
genre, 31, 102, 104, 138, 150, 153, 159, 161, 164, 178, 206, 221, 231, 275
German Democratic Republic, 151
German version (of *Tit.*), 67, 71, 77
ghosts, 128, 143
Gielgud, John, 144, 146, 148. See also Index I.
Globe Theatre, 108, 138
glory, 140
God, 183
god(s), 38, 45, 110, 114, 175, 233
Goethe, Johann Wolfgang von, 203
Goldenthal, Eliot, 100a
Goths, 67, 74, 84, 91, 99
Gramsci, Antonio, 125

Greene, Robert, 93, 112, 129
guilt societies, 57b, 59

Hal, Prince 37, 39, 56, 58, 80, 133, 142, 151, 153, 217, 218, 240, 270, 272
Hall, Joseph, 39
Hamlet, 120a
Harbage, Alfred, 51, 105
Hartman, Geoffrey, 245
Hecuba, 31, 55
Hecuba (Euripides), 110
Heilman, Robert B., 153
Helen of Troy, 55, 64
Henslowe's Diary, 77
Hercules, 165, 175, 201, 204, 205, 233, 260
heroism, 37, 109, 131, 135a, 179, 181, 204, 231, 243, 254, 257, 258, 260. See also nobility.
history, 28, 31, 34, 43, 44, 46, 55, 74, 85, 111, 115, 122, 125, 128, 151, 170, 174, 179, 194, 203, 222, 258. See also time.
Hitler, Adolph, 151
holidays, 118a
Holy Grail, 113
Homer, 109
honor, 32, 38, 131, 171, 192, 200, 228, 232, 246, 255
Hopkins, Anthony, 100a
Horace, 28, 31, 176
Houseman, John, 146, 147, 150
humanism, 38, 165, 238
humor, see comedy/the comic.
Humphreys, A.H., 138
hunger, 240, 245
hunting, 91
hyperbole, 29, 174, 175

Iago, 78
iconography (Renaissance), 118a, 202. See also imagery.
ideology, 31, 140, 154a, 155, 242
illeism, 47
imagery, 32, 57, 61, 63, 80, 86, 89, 95, 96, 98, 119, 124, 132, 162, 174, 176,

181, 202, 205, 237, 248. See also tropes.
Imperium, 122
injustice, 91
intertextuality, see under critical approaches.
Io, 57b
Iphigeneia at Aulis (Euripides), 110, 112
Iras, 197
Iron Age, 74
irony, 31, 43, 44, 89, 110, 127, 139, 140, 141, 151, 180, 196, 199, 252, 260
Isis, 165, 175, 177, 191, 194

Jacobean England, 162, 211, 225, 230, 257
James I, King, 167, 173, 230
James IV (Robert Greene), 112, 129
Jodelle, Pierre, 186
Johnson, Samuel, 131
Jonson, Ben, 135, 230
Julius Caesar, general, 28, 29, 30, 32, 33, 34, 35, 37, 38, 39, 43, 44, 45, 46, 47, 79, 104-58, 160, 170, 174, 192, 201, 207, 222, 230, 232, 236, 237
Julius Caesar, act and scene:
— (1-3), 122, 129
— (1), 113, 119, 120a
— (1.1), 106, 117, 119, 123, 137
— (1.2), 115, 120a, 123, 126, 129, 131, 133, 142
— (1.3), 37, 118b
— (2.1), 107, 119, 125, 129, 132, 134, 138, 141
— (2.2), 113, 123, 134, 141
— (3), 120a, 129
— (3.1), 120, 134, 135, 140a, 143
— (3.2-5.5), 134
— (3.2), 44, 121, 122, 129, 137, 140a, 141
— (3.3), 135, 140a
— (4), 114
— (4.1), 129, 135
— (4.2), 105
— (4.3), 105, 107, 112
— (5), 114, 120a, 122, 135, 144, 146
— (5.1), 38, 129, 148
— (5.3), 143
— (5.5), 143
justice, 79, 83, 90, 103, 203
Justus Lipsius, 39

Kemble, John Philip, 149, 210, 211, 264
Kerr, Deborah, 146
kingship, see monarchy and tyranny.
Kyd, Thomas, 71

Lange, Jessica, 100a
language, 29, 61, 67, 73, 80, 81, 82, 87, 104, 109, 129, 161, 162, 174, 175, 187, 188, 192, 196, 198, 199, 203, 208, 225, 228, 231, 233, 236, 239, 247, 248, 263
Latin, Shakespeare's, 38, 42
Lavinia, 31, 81, 86, 87, 89, 95, 97, 101
law (Roman), 67, 79
Legend of Good Women (Geoffrey Chaucer), 48, 52
Lennix, Harry, 100a
Lent, 242
Lepidus, 164, 173
Letters (Cicero), 154
Life of Alexander the Great (Plutarch), 125
Ligarius, 107
Lives of the Caesars (Suetonius), 154
Livy, 35, 38, 44, 48, 50, 52, 56, 57b, 58, 62, 67, 227
Longleat manuscript, 77, 92 (see also Peacham drawing)
Lucius (*Titus*), 31, 44, 74, 75, 83, 84, 85, 91, 97, 99, 101
Lucius Junius Brutus (*Lucrece*), see Brutus, Lucius Junius.
Lucius (slave boy, *Julius Caesar*), 131
Lucrece, 31, 36, 41, 44, 48, 49, 50, 51, 52, 53, 54, 55, 56, 57, 59, 60, 61, 62,

INDEX II: SUBJECTS

63, 64, 65, 66, 230
Lucretia, 48, 49, 52, 53, 55, 58, 62, 96
Lupercalia, 113
lust, 62, 171, 186

Macbeth, 114
Machiavelli, Niccolo, 56, 71, 227
Macready, W.C., 210, 211
madness, 71, 86, 90
magnificence (as theme), 190
majestas, 41
Mankiewicz, Joseph, 144, 146, 154a
manliness, 123
Marlowe, Christopher, 54a, 91, 93, 165, 176
marriage, 63, 76, 166, 183
Mars, 56, 58, 175, 176, 212
Marx, Karl, 125, 128
Marxism, 151
masculinity, 31, 177
Mason, James, 78, 146
masque, 78
medievalism/Middle Ages, 58, 60, 114, 165, 186, 230
melodrama, 103
Menas, 173
Mendilow, A.A., 75
Menenius, 222a, 235, 237, 238, 241, 242, 244, 245, 247, 250, 253, 254, 261, 263
Mercury Theatre, 144, 150
metalepsis, 61
Metamorphoses (Ovid), 42, 52, 57b, 74, 96, 194
metamorphosis, 95, 96
metaphor, 31, 57, 61, 63, 82, 115, 164, 198, 239
metatheatricality, see critical approaches.
metonymy, 239
microcosm/macrocosm, 175
military, 59, 61, 118, 122, 150, 164, 169, 184, 229
mimesis, 33, 62
mixed state, 118, 230

mobs, 250. See also plebeians.
monarchy, 28, 62, 76, 118, 120, 250. See also tyranny.
monologues, 154a
Montaigne, Michel de, 39, 233
monument scenes (*Antony and Cleopatra*), 159
Moors, 99
moral ambiguity, 105, 114, 127
moral standards, 38, 41, 90, 114, 164, 188
mothers, 30, 31, 97, 177, 240, 241, 256
Moulton, Richard G., 152
mummers' plays, 231
Musaeus, 54a
music, 53a, 69, 92, 155, 220, 225
Mussolini, Benito, 144
mutability, 169
mutilation, 81, 95, 98
myth/mythology, 31, 36, 74, 162, 165, 170, 176, 181, 201

names/naming, 29, 57, 229, 231, 239, 246
narrativity, 33, 65
Nashe, Thomas, 92
National Theater, 148
nature, 32, 59, 75, 77, 78, 91, 94, 152, 162, 164, 165, 171, 178, 179, 180, 190, 192, 194, 198, 203, 204, 209, 220, 225, 240, 241, 247, 249, 253, 256, 260, 262, 274
Nietzsche, Friedrich, 128
night weasels, 49
Nile river, 174, 191
nobility, 41, 181, 189, 255. See also heroism.
North, Sir Thomas, 35, 37, 38, 39, 42, 104, 106, 109, 116, 153, 160, 223, 224, 232, 245. See also Plutarch.

Octavia, 164, 178, 185, 194
Octavius Caesar, 37, 38, 56, 122, 129, 135, 139, 140, 164, 172, 173, 177, 182, 184, 185, 191, 194, 204, 209

Oedipus/Oedipal complex, 97, 177
Offices (Cicero), 38
oligarchy, 118, 151
Olivier, Laurence, 100
opposites (combining of), 185
opposites, see paradox and *syneciosis*.
orality, 78, 97
oratory, 30, 44, 45, 47, 68, 94, 114, 117, 121, 122, 137, 140, 141, 166, 203, 210, 211, 225, 236, 247, 249
order, 34, 46, 57, 61, 79, 83, 84, 91, 94, 99, 103, 132, 194, 237, 265
Orosius, 28
Orpheus, 53a
Osborne, John, 265
Osiris, 165, 194
Ovid, 28, 31, 35, 36, 42, 44, 48, 50, 52, 53a, 54a, 56, 57a, 57b, 58, 60, 65, 67, 74, 82, 85, 86, 96, 103, 176, 194
oxymoron, 59

Painter, William, 48, 50, 52, 54
paintings, 49, 53
Palace of Pleasure (William Painter), 48
paradox, 29, 59, 125, 165, 176, 183, 212, 246
parody, 85, 103, 182
patriarchy, 31, 63, 98
Paul, St., 47
Paulus Marsus, 56, 58
Peacham drawing, 67, 68, 69, 77, 92 (See also Longleat manuscript)
Peele, George, 93
Pentheus, 110
performance, 31, 68, 69, 86, 100, 101, 108, 142, 149, 159, 160, 161, 162, 202, 211, 212, 248, 263, 264, 265, 271
peripeteia, 196, 252
Petrarchism, 53a
pharmakon, 231
Philippic II (Cicero), 154
Philo, 31, 83, 93, 96, 118, 134, 173
Philomela, 31, 96, 57a, 57b
philosophy, 36, 38, 134

Piachaud, René-Louis, 265
pietas, 115
pit, 79, 81, 97, 98, 144, 186, 188, 234
Plato, 33, 39, 117, 164
Platt, Michael, 239
Platter, Thomas, 108
play-within-play, see metatheatricality under critical approaches.
pleasure, living for, 186
plebeians, 30, 135, 137, 229, 232, 261
Plutarch, 28, 30, 33, 35, 37, 38, 39, 42, 44, 45, 46, 104, 105, 106, 109, 113, 115, 116, 117, 118b, 122, 135a, 137, 138, 139, 154, 154a, 160, 161, 164, 165, 168, 176, 194, 197, 199, 222a, 223, 224, 227, 232, 235, 258. See also North.
Polybius, 230
Pompeius Magnus, 38, 120a, 140
Ponet, John, 76
portents, 118a, 118b
Portia, 107, 130, 154a
predication, 59
primogeniture, 98
Prior, Moody E., 145
private, vs. public, life, 147a
problem plays, 201
promptbooks, 107, 211, 226
prosopopoeia, 61
protagonist, 75, 106, 110, 164, 166, 168, 173, 174, 175, 182, 187, 189, 196, 198, 204, 206, 208, 227, 240, 252, 254, 256, 260, 262
providence, 229
psychoanalysis, 125, 264
psychomachia, 252
puns, 41, 62, 90, 105, 119, 132
Puritans, 118a

Quarles, John, 50
Quiller-Couch, Sir Arthur, 159

race, 28, 78
Ralegh, Sir Walter, 222a
rape, 48, 49, 53, 53a, 54, 56, 57, 57a,

57b, 59, 60, 61, 62, 63, 64, 76, 86, 87, 95, 97, 247
Rape of Lucrece, The, general, 36, 41, 48–66, 230
Rape of Lucrece, The, lines:
— Argument, 49
— ll. 15–42, 62
— ll. 183–280, 52
— l. 307, 49
— ll. 365–686, 54a
— ll. 428–76, 64
— ll. 615–21, 62
— l. 640, 61
— l. 730, 59
— ll. 764–1036, 53, 61
— l. 816, 61
— l, 979, 57a
— ll. 1170–76, 61, 64
— ll. 1214–95, 57
— ll. 1366–1568, 51, 54, 55, 65
— ll. 1688–91, 56
— l. 1721, 49
— ll. 1740–41, 64
— ll. 1807–55, 56
rapere (raptus), 63
Ravenscroft, Edward, 100
reception, critical, 86, 92, 101, 150, 159, 203, 253, 268
Redmond, James, 74
regicide, see tyrannicide.
Remaines (William Camden), 223
Republic (Roman), 37, 118, 123, 166, 227, 228
Republic (Plato), 37, 117, 118, 123, 133, 166, 227, 228
republicanism, 140, 166
reputation, 38, 200. See also *dignitas* and fame.
revenge, 31, 57a, 67, 71, 83, 85, 91, 94, 97, 99, 103, 134, 140b, 207
revision, Shakespeare's, 92, 107
rhetoric, 29, 30, 33, 36, 42, 44, 48, 49, 53, 59, 60, 61, 62, 65, 73, 75, 82, 121, 122, 175, 198, 238, 239, 250
ritual, 113, 118a, 156, 166, 190, 209, 231, 247
Romanitas, 28, 29, 31, 35–47, 59, 63, 115, 138, 139
Rome, 28, 29, 31, 33, 36, 40, 41, 42, 43, 44, 46, 47, 57, 74, 75, 79, 81, 85, 89, 91, 94, 97, 98, 99, 101, 103, 113, 115, 122, 128, 166, 169, 170, 172, 174, 178, 184, 186, 188, 191, 195, 201, 225, 227, 228, 230, 231, 232, 233, 234, 235, 236, 239, 240, 245, 246, 247, 249, 250, 252, 253, 254, 259, 260, 266
Romulus, 113
Rose Theater, 108
Royal Shakespeare Company, 100, 141, 210
Rumbelow, Steve, 143

sacrifice, 83, 91, 110, 113, 189, 202, 244, 245
saevitia, 41
St. George plays, 231
Sallust, 38, 44
Saturninus, 81, 91
scene division, 105
scenery, 210
scenic form, 129
Schlegel, A.W., 203
Schlesinger, John, 148
Schücking, Levin Ludwig, 203
Schwartz, Murray M., 240
Scofield, Paul, 146
Scott, Mark W., 140
Seleucus, 173
Seneca, 35, 36, 39, 44, 73, 82, 88, 90, 120, 165, 246
serpents, 174, 176
Sewell, Arthur, 153
sexuality, 31, 97, 98, 175, 189, 202, 240. See also rape.
Shakespeare, William (works)
— *Cymbeline*, 39, 40, 41, 43, 44
— *Hamlet*, 43, 65, 71, 120a, 128, 130, 140a, 145, 177, 192, 240
— *Henry IV, Part 1*, 65, 112, 157; (2.4),

62; (3.2), 62
— *Henry V*, 34, 70, 112, 128, 129, 133, 138, 145, 192
— *Henry VI, Part 2*, 112
— *Henry VI, Part 3*, 34, 70, 129
— *King Lear*, 43, 75, 86, 90, 118b, 145, 185, 192, 255
— *A Lover's Complaint*, 49
— *Macbeth*, 43, 91, 132, 140a, 145, 188, 190, 255
— *Measure for Measure*, 131, 145, 201
— *A Midsummer Night's Dream*, 65
— *Much Ado About Nothing*, 171
— *Othello*, 43, 78, 91, 129, 145; (3.4), 129
— *The Passionate Pilgrim*, 49
— *The Phoenix and the Turtle*, 49, 66
— *Richard II*, 34, 78, 112, 114, 133, 157, 192
— *Richard III*, 34, 78, 112, 114, 133, 140a
— *Romeo and Juliet*, 90, 130
— *The Tempest*, 91, 177, 192, 240
— *Troilus and Cressida*, 130
— *Venus and Adonis*, 36, 48, 49, 50, 51, 52, 60, 66
Shaw, George Bernard, 143, 154, 207
sickness, 119, 132
Sidney, Sir Philip, 118b, 171, 185, 186
Sidonius, 186
silence, 53a, 55, 57b, 59, 164, 225, 229, 236, 251, 263. See also speechlessness.
Skeat, W.W., 104
skepticism, 162, 183, 233
sleep, 124
Smith, Sir Thomas, 76
Sohmer, Steve, 108
soliloquy, 125, 134, 138, 141
Spanish Tragedy (Thomas Kyd), 71, 73
speech headings, 226
speechlessness, 59. See also silence.
Spenser, Edmund, 165, 171
staging, issues of, 100, 104, 105, 144, 157, 159, 160, 161, 170, 202, 210,

225, 237, 261, 274
statuary, 38, 118a
statue art, 154a
Stoicism, 38, 39, 41, 88, 109, 119, 121, 131, 169, 205, 233
Strato, 147a
structure, 72, 73, 75, 90, 94, 106, 112, 124, 129, 134, 140, 146, 150, 151, 153, 155, 159, 162, 176, 196, 198, 200, 203, 252, 270
stychomythia, 73
style, see rhetoric.
subplot, 140
subtext, 116, 123, 139
Suetonius, 28, 135a, 154
suicide, 31, 41, 49, 53, 57b, 61, 63, 124, 160, 164, 168, 169, 182, 188, 197, 204
superbia, 41
supernatural, 124
superstition, 124
symbolism, 32, 47, 59, 63, 64, 79, 81, 87, 94, 97, 176, 192, 205
synecdoche, 59, 64, 239
syneciosis, 59

Tacitus, 38, 44, 176
Tamora, 31, 75, 78, 83, 85, 86, 87, 95, 97, 98, 99, 101
Tarquin, 50, 54, 57, 59, 60, 61, 62, 63, 64
Tarquin Banished (John Quarles), 50
Tarquinius (Livy's), 62
Tate, Nahum, 265
television, 220
theatrum mundi, 182
Thyestes (Seneca), 90
Tieck, Ludwig, 203
Tillyard, E.M.W., 103
time, 179, 179, 194. See also history.
'Tis Pity She's A Whore (John Ford), 91
Titian, 49
tittus & vespacia (anonymous), 77
Titus, 31, 67, 73, 74, 75, 83, 85, 86, 89, 90, 91, 93, 94, 99, 100

Titus Andronicus, general, 36, 39, 42, 44, 67–103, 230
Titus Andronicus, act and scene:
— (1), 72
— (2.3), 95
— (3.2), 67
— (4.3), 69
— (5), 90, 93
— (5.2), 78
— (5.3), 100
tragicomedy, 165, 169
Tree, Beerbohm, 149, 210, 211
tribunes, 230, 232, 238, 240, 259, 263
tropes, 48, 49, 61
Troy, 36, 49, 51, 54, 55, 57, 65
tyrannicide, 114
tyranny, 57, 73, 114, 117, 118, 120. See also monarchy.

Unfortunate Traveller (Thomas Nashe), 92
unities, 72, 122, 162, 220
usurpation, 239

valley, 98
vengeance, see revenge.
Venus, 36, 48, 49, 50, 51, 52, 60, 66, 165, 175, 176, 191, 212

Vergil (see Virgil)
vestments, 118a
Vice figure, 78
Virgil, 28, 31, 35, 36, 40, 44, 55, 57, 74, 115, 120, 165, 176, 258
Virgilia, 115, 251
virginity, 63
virtus, 31, 44, 187, 243
Volscians, 29, 236, 252, 261
Volumnia, 29, 31, 42, 222a, 232, 236, 238, 240, 252, 253, 254, 256, 263, 266

Warner, Deborah, 70, 100
water (includes wave, tide, storm, sea), 140, 191. See also Nile river.
weeping, 132
Welles, Orson, 144, 146, 147, 150, 154a
will (volition), 53a
Wilson, John Dover, 163. See also Index I.
wombs, 97, 98
wonder, see *admiratio*.
World War II, 146, 264